D1547594

The Status Quo Crisis

The Status Quo Crisis

Global Financial Governance After the 2008 Financial Meltdown

ERIC HELLEINER

OXFORD
UNIVERSITY PRESS

Oxford University Press is a department of the University of Oxford.
It furthers the University's objective of excellence in research, scholarship,
and education by publishing worldwide.

Oxford   New York
Auckland   Cape Town   Dar es Salaam   Hong Kong   Karachi
Kuala Lumpur   Madrid   Melbourne   Mexico City   Nairobi
New Delhi   Shanghai   Taipei   Toronto

With offices in
Argentina   Austria   Brazil   Chile   Czech Republic   France   Greece
Guatemala   Hungary   Italy   Japan   Poland   Portugal   Singapore
South Korea   Switzerland   Thailand   Turkey   Ukraine   Vietnam

Oxford is a registered trademark of Oxford University Press
in the UK and certain other countries.

Published in the United States of America by
Oxford University Press
198 Madison Avenue, New York, NY 10016

Library of Congress Cataloging-in-Publication Data
Helleiner, Eric, 1963-
The status quo crisis : global financial governance after the 2008 financial
meltdown / Eric Helleiner.
    pages cm
Includes bibliographical references and index.
ISBN 978-0-19-997363-7 (alk. paper)
1. International finance—Government policy.   2. Economic policy—International
cooperation.   3. Global Financial Crisis, 2008-2009.   I. Title.
HG3881.H4183 2014
332'.042—dc23
2013048334

9 8 7 6 5 4 3 2 1
Printed in the United States of America
on acid-free paper

CONTENTS

The book has emerged from my experience participating in a large number of public, academic, and policy meetings concerned with international financial reform during and since the 2008 global financial crisis. Like many others in these meetings, I initially anticipated that global financial governance would be transformed in very significant ways in the immediate wake of this massive crisis. Indeed, some of my colleagues will recall that I was often quite a vocal proponent of this perspective in 2008–2009. Five years after the height of the crisis, I have come to a rather different view. The crisis has turned out to be much more of a status quo event – at least so far—than a transformative one. This book explains how and why the widespread expectations of change did not pan out during the first half decade after the meltdown. I hope it serves as a useful record of this period as well as a helpful analysis of the politics of global finance in the contemporary era.

It is impossible for me to mention everyone who helped shaped my thinking for this book, but I am very grateful to all those asked helpful questions and commented on various presentations I made on these issues at the following locations in the last few years: American University, Brookings Institution, Centre for International Governance Innovation, Council on Foreign Relations, Columbia University, Cornell University, Hanse-Wissenschaftskolleg, Harvard University, the Hong Kong Monetary Authority, Kyung Hee University, London School of

Economics, Montego Bay, New Delhi, Northwestern University, Oxford University, Princeton University, Rockefeller Foundation Bellagio Center, Royal Institute of International Affairs, Russell Sage Foundation, Shanghai Institute for International Studies, Southern Alberta Council on Public Affairs, St. Thomas University, University of Lethbridge, University of Oslo, University of Ottawa, University of Virginia, University of Western Ontario, and meetings of the American Political Science Association, Canadian Political Science Association, the International Studies Association, and Society for the Advancement of Socio-Economics.

For their insights and support, I also thank many colleagues at the University of Waterloo, the Balsillie School of International Affairs, the Centre for International Governance Innovation, the New Rules for Global Finance, the Warwick Commission on International Financial Reform, and the High Level Panel High on the Governance of the Financial Stability Board. I have also learned an enormous amount from a number of people with whom I have co-authored publications since the outbreak of the crisis, including Andy Cooper, Greg Chin, Stephanie Griffith-Jones, Jonathan Kirshner, Troy Lundblad, Anton Malkin, Bessma Momani, Stefano Pagliari, Tony Porter, Paola Subacchi, Jason Thistlethwaite, Ngaire Woods, and Hubert Zimmermann. I am also indebted to the many students who have offered fascinating perspectives on the global financial crisis in courses I have taught since 2008 as well as to Anastasia Ufimtseva for her very helpful research assistance. Many thanks, too, to the Trudeau Foundation and the Social Sciences Research Council of Canada for their generous support.

I am very grateful to Dave McBride for his insights, interest, and enthusiasm for this project. Many thanks as well to a number of people who commented directly on different parts of this book during its preparation in very useful ways: two anonymous reviewers, Diego Sanchez Anchochea, Cyrus Ardalan, Andrew Baker, Paul Blustein, Phil Cerny, Kevin Gallagher, Macer Gifford, Bill Grimes, Thomas Hale, Brian Hanson, Gerry Helleiner, Randy Henning, Nicolas Jabko, Emily Jones, Paul Langley, Walter Mattli, Kate McNamara, Steve Nelson, Stefano Pagliari, Rahul Prabhakar, Herman Schwartz, Jack Seddon, Hendrik

Spruyt, Taylor St. John, Geoffrey Underhill, Jakob Vestergaard, Max Watson, Ngaire Woods, and Kevin Young. Of course, none of these individuals is responsible for the contents of this book.

Finally, this book could not have been written without the inspiration of some very special people. Zoe, Nels, and Jennifer are three of them. They have heard more about global financial governance than they probably ever wanted to in the last few years. Thanks to each of them for their patience about this and much else. And thanks particularly to Peter to whom this book is dedicated for being both a constant source of inspiration and such a helpful and supportive companion walking alongside me on this and many other journeys in our lives.

Waterloo, January 2014

AIG	American International Group
ASEAN	Association of South-East Asian Nations
BCBS	Basel Committee on Banking Supervision
BIS	Bank for International Settlements
BRIC	Brazil, Russia, India, China
BRICS	Brazil, Russia, India, China, South Africa
CCP	central counterparty
CDS	credit default swap
CGFS	Committee on the Global Financial System
CMI	Chiang Mai Initiative
CMIM	Chiang Mai Initiative Multilateralization
CPSS	Committee on Payment and Settlement Systems
ECB	European Central Bank
EU	European Union
FASB	Financial Accounting Standards Board
FCL	Flexible Credit Line
FDIC	Federal Deposit Insurance Corporation
FSAP	Financial Sector Assessment Program
FSB	Financial Stability Board
FSF	Financial Stability Forum
FTT	financial transaction tax
FVA	fair value accounting

GATT	General Agreement on Tariffs and Trade
GDP	gross domestic product
GSM	global stabilization mechanism
IAIS	International Association of Insurance Supervisors
IASB	International Accounting Standards Board
IFRS	International Financial Reporting Standards
IMF	International Monetary Fund
IOSCO	International Organization of Securities Commissions
LDC	less developed country
NCJ	non-cooperating jurisdiction
OECD	Organization for Economic Cooperation and Development
OFC	offshore financial center
OTC	over-the-counter
PCL	Precautionary Credit Line
RMB	renminbi
ROSC	Reports on the Observance of Standards and Codes
SBA	Stand-By Arrangement
SCSI	Standing Committee on Standards Implementation
SDR	Special Drawing Rights
SIFI	systemically important financial institution
SNB	Swiss National Bank
SSB	standard setting body
SWF	sovereign wealth fund
TARP	Troubled Asset Relief Program
UN	United Nations
WTO	World Trade Organization

The Status Quo Crisis

Introduction and Overview

The financial crisis of 2008 was the worst global financial meltdown experienced since the early 1930s. Major financial institutions collapsed or were nationalized, and many others stayed afloat only because of extensive public support. Global industrial production, world trade, and the value of world equity markets all fell more rapidly in the first ten months after April 2008 than they had during the same period after the start of the Great Depression.[1] Although the impact of the crisis was felt differently across the world, all regions were affected by it in some way.

Because of the severity of the crisis, many analysts immediately predicted that it would be very transformative for global financial governance. Four developments in 2008–09 reinforced these expectations. The first was the decision in November 2008 by the heads of state of the world's most important economies to create a new body—the G20 leaders' forum—to help manage the crisis. The future of the dollar's role as the world's key currency also quickly became a topic of widespread debate in public policy circles. In addition, the G20 leaders committed quickly to an extensive agenda for international regulatory reforms, reinforcing the widespread view that the crisis would provoke a major backlash against the market-friendly nature of pre-crisis international financial standards. Finally, a new international institution was created in April 2009—the Financial Stability Board (FSB)—that top policymakers described as a novel "fourth pillar" of the global economic architecture, alongside the International Monetary Fund, World Bank, and World Trade Organization.

From the vantage point of five years after the crisis, this book argues that none of these developments looks as significant as it initially appeared. The G20's contribution to the financial management of the crisis ended up being much less significant than advertised. The US dollar remained unchallenged as the world's dominant international currency. The market-friendly character of international financial standards was not overturned in a significant way. And the FSB's capacity to act as a kind of fourth pillar of global economic governance turned out to be very limited.

In these respects, the crisis of 2008 has been—at least so far—more of a status quo event than a transformative one. The crisis may, of course, have unleashed developments that could generate important change in the spheres of global financial governance over the medium to long term, a possibility that is explored in the final chapter of the book. The main focus of the book, however, is on what was witnessed across these four issue areas in the first half decade since the peak of the crisis in the fall of 2008.[2] From this vantage point, the crisis was a strangely conservative event.

Why were the expectations of transformation in global financial governance not borne out? The book attributes this outcome largely to a specific configuration of power and politics among and within influential states. Particularly important were the structural power and active policy choices of the country at the center of the crisis: the United States. In many key instances, status quo outcomes also reflected the unexpected weakness of Europe and conservatism of governments in China and other large emerging market countries. This explanation of the status quo nature of the crisis calls attention to the enduring state-centric foundations of global financial governance in contrast to analyses that focus more on the growing significance of international institutions or of transnational elites and ideologies. If global financial governance is to be transformed in more substantial ways in the coming years, the argument suggests that power and politics among and within these key states will play the central role.

THE CRISIS

The sequence of events involved in the unfolding of the 2008 global financial crisis is by now very well known and can be recounted quickly. The first signs appeared when US real estate prices began to decline in 2006 and defaults on US subprime mortgages started increasing. By the summer of 2007, financial institutions that had invested heavily in securities linked to those mortgages—particularly in the United States and Europe—faced huge losses. As concerns grew about the extent of the exposure of various financial firms, some international financial markets began to freeze up in August 2007. This phenomenon only compounded the difficulties many financial institutions faced, particularly those that were highly leveraged and dependent on short-term funding. Confidence was eroded further in September 2007 when one such institution in Britain—Northern Rock—experienced the first serious bank run in that country since the mid-19th century.

The crisis then intensified in March 2008 when the large US investment bank Bear Stearns ran into deep trouble and was rescued only by a takeover by J.P. Morgan Chase, assisted by the Federal Reserve Bank of New York. The most acute phase of the crisis then came in September 2008. Early in the month, the US government effectively nationalized the giant US mortgage lending institutions Fannie Mae and Freddie Mac by placing them under a public "conservatorship." In mid-September, the US investment bank Lehman Brothers collapsed, triggering massive panic in global financial markets because of its size and the extent of its connections with other financial institutions. Fear among investors only intensified when it became clear that the American International Group (AIG)—the world's largest insurance company—was on the verge of bankruptcy as well. It was quickly rescued by a massive initial $85 billion bailout from the US government.

This combination of events generated severe downward pressure on asset values in major world financial markets in the fall of 2008. As financial institutions struggled to cope with their losses and reduce their exposure to the financial instability, enormous deleveraging took place, generating a vicious downward spiral of selling, further price declines, and more deleveraging. Many financial institutions did not survive, while others were saved only with extensive public support.

Although the 2008 crisis was centered in US and European markets, it had worldwide repercussions. Indeed, economic historians show that the 2008 meltdown was the first truly global-scale financial crisis of the post-1945 period because it affected all regions and major financial centers.[3] Its impact was also felt well outside of the financial sector. International trade and financial flows declined rapidly as the crisis intensified, and by the fall of 2008, the entire world economy had entered a severe recession.

Given its scale, it is not surprising that many anticipated that the crisis would quickly usher in major transformations in global financial governance. By November 2008, prominent figures such as Nobel Prize winning economist Joseph Stiglitz were arguing that that it was a "Bretton Woods moment."[4] The phrase invoked the 1944 conference at Bretton Woods, New Hampshire where an entirely new international financial order was created for the postwar world. This historical precedent was even invoked by leading politicians such as French President Nicolas Sarkozy who argued in September 2008 that "we have to redesign the entire financial and monetary system, as was done in Bretton Woods."[5] As few weeks later in mid-October, British Prime Minister Gordon Brown also called for "very large and very radical changes" that would be a "new Bretton Woods."[6]

This book details how and why these expectations of major transformation in global financial governance did not pan out. It is not the first work to call attention to the unusually conservative nature of the political response to the crisis. Some have remarked on this phenomenon within specific country contexts. Others have noted how global economic governance as a whole seems remarkably unchanged by the crisis experience.[7] This book provides the first integrative analysis of this phenomenon across four core aspects of the sector of the global economic governance—that of finance—where analysts expected particularly significant change.

DID THE G20 SAVE THE DAY?

The first set of arguments in the book concerns the significance of the G20 as a financial crisis manager. Immediately after its creation, the G20 leaders' forum was seen as a major institutional innovation in global financial governance that would help manage the financial crisis. Unlike the G7, the G20 included all the large emerging market countries, many of which could make an important contribution to addressing the financial turmoil. The G20 had already met regularly since 1999 as a grouping of finance ministry and central bank officials. By creating a G20 leaders' forum, heads of state of the most important economies seemed to be signaling the seriousness of their intention to develop cooperative solutions to the crisis.

The expectations for the G20's crisis management role were only reinforced by the results of its first two summits in November 2008 and April 2009. At both meetings, the G20 leaders signaled their determination to fight the crisis collectively through what appeared to be bold initiatives. In the financial realm, they committed to coordinate national macroeconomic stimulus programs and even backed an ambitious $1.1 trillion support program for the world economy, the centerpiece of which was a massive increase in the lending capacity of the International Monetary Fund (IMF). When the crisis began to subside in the summer of 2009, the G20 leaders' forum was widely heralded—including by the leaders themselves—as an innovative institution that had helped prevent a repetition of the 1930s dilemma. The host of the April 2009 summit, Gordon Brown, made the case as follows a year later: "Starting in April the world started to move forward again. That is why the years 1929–32 are known forever as the Great Depression and the years 2008–9 will be known as the Great Recession. The G20 had averted a second global depression."[8]

Chapter 2 argues that this narrative seriously overstates the significance of the G20's creation for the financial dimensions of the management of the crisis. Though there is little doubt that the expansionary monetary and fiscal policies of G20 countries helped avert a second Great Depression, the role of the G20 leaders' forum in coordinating these policies is questionable. Governments were responding more to domestic political pressures in the context of a common global economic shock than to the G20 summits. The economic significance of the headline-grabbing $1.1 trillion support program announced at the London summit should also not be exaggerated. Particularly important was the fact that many poorer countries were reluctant in 2008–09 to borrow from the international institution—the IMF—whose resources had been so dramatically boosted by the G20. Those countries had become extremely wary of the Fund because of its role in the East Asian financial crisis of 1997–98, a wariness that had encouraged them to build up foreign exchange reserves before the 2008 crisis in ways that helped buffer them from the shock without IMF assistance.

Even more striking was the fact that the G20 leaders' forum was completely uninvolved in organizing the most important cooperative dimension of the financial management of the crisis: large-scale lending by the US Federal Reserve to foreign central banks. The Fed's loans came in the form of a series of ad hoc bilateral swaps created between December 2007 and October 2008, all in advance of the first G20 leaders' meeting. Foreign drawing on these Fed swap lines was very large, peaking at almost $600 billion in late 2008—a figure far higher than IMF lending during the crisis. In addition to supporting the balance of payments position of some countries, the Fed's loans were critically important in enabling many foreign central banks to provide much-needed dollar liquidity to troubled firms and markets in their respective jurisdictions. With its extensive swap program, the Fed acted as a crucial international lender-of-last-resort during the crisis. To some extent, this role was also played by the Fed through the unilateral provision of dollar liquidity directly to distressed foreign financial institutions, as well as the US Treasury whose assistance to troubled domestic institutions also supported the foreign counterparties of those firms.

The fact that the United States acted as a key international lender-of-last-resort in the crisis signaled a continuity in global financial governance rather than change. During previous post–World War II international financial crisis, US authorities had often played this critical role. During the 2008 crisis (as in the past), they had a unique capacity to produce unlimited sums of dollars, the currency that many foreigners needed because of the greenback's dominant role in the global financial system. As in the past, the enduring centrality of the United States in global finance also helped motivate its authorities to act as international lender-of-last-resort: internationally oriented US financial firms, US financial markets, and the dollar were all vulnerable to financial instability abroad. The financial dimensions of the successful cooperative management of the crisis thus had much more to do with this ongoing US ability and willingness to act as international-lender-of-last-resort than with the establishment of the new G20 leaders' forum.

When the G20 subsequently explored initiatives to reform global financial governance to prevent future crises, it continued to refrain from taking a leadership role in this area. After the Fed swaps expired in early 2010, the G20 leaders considered proposals to expand and institutionalize a new swap regime, but ultimately rejected them. US officials were particularly concerned about the burdens and risks that this initiative might generate for the Fed. They were also reluctant to back IMF reforms that might allow that institution to assume a greater role in this field in the future. The consequence was that, five years after the financial meltdown, the crisis-management dimensions of global financial governance remained heavily dependent on ad hoc US international lender-of-last-resort activities, just as they had throughout the postwar era. Rather than demonstrating the effectiveness of a new global financial crisis manager, the crisis and its aftermath highlighted the importance of the old.

WAS THE DOLLAR'S GLOBAL ROLE UNDERMINED?

The crisis also did little to change the dollar's dominant role as the world's key currency. When the crisis first broke out, there were widespread predictions that this role would be seriously challenged by a major collapse in the value of the dollar. As an editorial in *The Economist* put it in December 2007, "a new fear now stalks the markets: that the dollar's slide could spin out of control."[9] These fears were understandable. Not only was the United States at the center of the crisis, but it had also become very dependent on foreign capital to fund large current account deficits at the time. For the first time in the postwar period, the dollar also faced a serious rival in international currency use, the euro, which had been created in 1999 and whose international role was expanding at the time the crisis began. In these circumstances, the United States looked extremely vulnerable to a serious currency crisis, a development that seemed very likely to undermine the dollar's international standing.

But no dollar crisis unfolded. Indeed, as noted in Chapter 3, the dollar's value appreciated as the global financial crisis intensified in the summer of 2008. What explains this result? One explanation is that there was strong international private demand for the US currency as the crisis intensified. Some of this demand reflected the fact that foreign financial institutions needed dollars to cover their deteriorating positions in dollar-dominated global financial markets. As the global crisis intensified, investors also perceived the dollar to be a safe haven currency because it was backed by the world's dominant power and the unique liquidity and depth of the US Treasury bill market. The dollar also benefited from eroding investor confidence in its main competitor, the euro, in the face of the uncoordinated manner by which national authorities in the Eurozone responded to distressed financial institutions at the time.

The dollar also benefitted from the support of a number of foreign governments—particularly China—that did not dump their large reserve holdings of the US currency during the crisis. This foreign official support emerged more from the unilateral decisions of these governments than from any explicit negotiations with US officials. Many governments with large reserves saw dollar holdings—particularly US Treasury bills—as a relatively more attractive asset in the crisis for the same reasons that private investors did. The crisis also reinforced, rather than undermined, some of the broader political reasons for why they had held large dollar reserves before it began. One was that reserves served as a form of "self-insurance" to protect their country against external instability—a goal that became even more significant in the crisis. In export-oriented economies, dollar reserves also helped to support their major export market and to keep their exchange rate competitive during the crisis. The risk of a dollar crisis also highlighted starkly to Chinese authorities the extent to which they now had a very large financial stake in the dollar's stability, given the enormous reserves they had already accumulated. In countries that were close geopolitical allies of the United States, support for the dollar may also have been linked to broader strategic concerns.

Rather than undermining the dollar's global role, the crisis thus provided new insights about the sources of its dominance. The decisions of private investors and foreign governments to support the dollar were shaped by the euro's governance weaknesses and broader "structural power" of the United States in the global political economy stemming from the its financial markets, centrality in world trade, geopolitical dominance, and the prominence global financial role of the US dollar itself during the pre-crisis years.[10] The dollar also benefitted from the strength of the commitments among many emerging market countries—particularly China—to self-insurance and export-oriented development strategies. Foreign support was reinforced by US policy choices such as the maintenance of open markets and decisions to bail out troubled domestic financial firms in which foreigners had heavy stakes.

In the wake of the crisis, the dollar quickly faced new challenges, as many foreign governments expressed frustrations about the dollar's global dominance and pressed for international monetary reform. One initiative was to bolster the international role of a supranational reserve asset that had first been created in the late 1960s: the IMF's Special Drawing Rights (SDRs). While the G20 leaders agreed at their second summit to the first new issue of SDRs in three decades, the SDR posed little challenge to the dollar's global role in the absence of more substantial efforts to strengthen its significance. This latter goal did have supporters in China, France, and some other countries, but it encountered a number of opponents, notably the US government, whose voting share within the IMF gave it the power to veto reforms of this kind. The reluctance of the United States to embrace major reform reflected a number of factors, including its dependence on foreign capital and the fact that various US private and public interests benefitted from the dollar's international role and the pre-crisis growth model with which it was associated.

Other foreign critics of the dollar's international role after the crisis urged the internationalization of their own countries' currencies in order to create a more multipolar currency order. Many Europeans hoped that the euro could serve as one such pole. But the European currency's ability to challenge the dollar was constrained by the outbreak of European debt crises after early 2010. These crises revealed serious weaknesses in the currency's governance and even called into question the euro's survival. Because of these troubles, the euro's international role was undermined, rather than strengthened, in the wake of the crisis.

From 2009 onward, the Chinese government expressed heightened interest in backing the greater internationalization of its currency, the renminbi (RMB), through various initiatives. The RMB's international role had previously been negligible and these initiatives encouraged some growth. But its international use remained extremely limited in comparison to that of the dollar because the Chinese government refused to embrace more far-reaching reforms that would make the RMB fully convertible and enhance the attractiveness of Chinese financial markets to foreigners. These kinds of reforms were resisted largely because they would undermine the government's tight control over finance that was at the core of the Chinese investment-led, export-oriented development model.

Some other emerging countries initially expressed support for the internationalization of their currencies, but their initiatives were even more cautious and had little significance for the dollar's international role. The result was that the dollar's status as the world's dominant currency emerged remarkably unscathed not just from the crisis experience but also from post-crisis challenges. Five years after the crisis, its international role was almost identical to what it had been just before the financial upheaval had begun. Despite widespread dissatisfaction with the dollar's international role, it was clear that the task of dislodging the greenback from its preeminent global position faced difficult political obstacles.

WAS THE MARKET-FRIENDLY NATURE OF INTERNATIONAL FINANCIAL STANDARDS OVERTURNED?

The third aspect of global financial governance explored in this book is the content of international financial standards. Throughout 2008, there were widespread expectations that the crisis would provoke a major backlash against the market-friendly nature of international financial standards that had been developed since the 1990s. Expectations were raised further by the final communiqué from the first G20 leaders' summit in November 2008 which outlined a detailed agenda for international regulatory reforms. Working closely with international standard setting bodies and other international institutions, the G20 subsequently endorsed many reforms to existing international financial standards as well as the development of a number of new standards.

Chapter 4 shows that despite the various international regulatory reforms, the market-friendly nature of pre-crisis international financial standards was not overturned in a significant way. To be sure, some existing regulations—such as the Basel framework for bank regulation—have been tightened. Public oversight was also extended to sectors where private international financial standards or voluntary rules had dominated before the crisis, such as accounting, hedge funds, credit rating agencies, and over-the-counter (OTC) derivatives. In addition, G20 financial officials endorsed the use of restrictions on cross-border financial transactions in late 2011, a move echoed by the IMF in a formal statement in late 2012. But these changes were less significant than they appeared.

In the case of bank regulation, the new minimum capital requirements and leverage ratio endorsed by 2010 Basel III agreement were still set at quite low levels. The agreement also continued the pre-crisis practice of allowing large banks to rely on their own internal models when determining minimum levels of capital. In addition, the implementation of some of the most innovative features of Basel III—such as the endorsement of counter-cyclical buffers and extra capital charges for systemically significant financial institutions—was deliberately left up to the discretion of national authorities.

The importance of the extension of public oversight to new sectors is also easily overstated. In the case of accounting, a new public "monitoring board" for the private International Accounting Standards Board (IASB) quickly clarified that it did not intend to infringe at all upon the IASB's independence. The G20 also did little to challenge market-oriented "fair value" accounting even in the face of widespread criticism of this practice during the crisis. In the cases of credit rating agencies, hedge funds, and OTC derivatives, new international financial standards focused primarily on enhancing transparency rather than constraining private sector activity. The G20 and IMF statements on capital account restrictions were also very cautious and they simply reiterated the right of all countries to use capital controls under the existing international financial rules of the IMF's Articles of Agreement.

Five years after the crisis, the content of post-crisis international financial regulatory reforms thus looked remarkably tame in comparison to the predictions made in 2008. Rather than overturning the market-friendly nature of pre-crisis international financial standards, the G20 leaders tweaked its content. To account for this outcome, it is useful to recall the assumptions underlying the predictions made at the height of the crisis.

One such assumption was that the crisis would weaken the influence in international regulatory politics of the leading financial powers—the United States and Britain—that had been among the strongest proponents of market-friendly standards before the crisis. But challenges to Anglo-American leadership turned out to be less significant than anticipated. Although officials from China and emerging market countries were admitted for the first time into the inner club of international standard-setting, they played a low-key role in the international regulatory debates after the crisis. Continental European officials initially pressed for tighter international standards in many areas, but quickly found themselves constrained by the Eurozone crisis and by the difficulties of securing EU-wide agreement, particularly when faced with British opposition.

In the end, the content of international regulatory reforms was shaped heavily by US priorities, as it had often been in the past. US influence stemmed from the global importance of its financial markets as well as the fact that US officials were "first-movers" in initiating domestic reforms which often then acted as focal points for international standards. US interest in international regulatory reform was shaped directly by those domestic reforms: internationally coordinated regulatory tightening would help minimize competitive disadvantages for US markets and firms that could result from unilateral US reforms. But the limitations of subsequent US domestic regulatory initiatives then set limits on what the US was willing to endorse at the international level. The weak nature of the challenge to pre-crisis market-friendly international financial standards often simply reflected this constraint imposed by the US domestic context.

A second assumption was that the crisis would weaken the political influence of private financial interests that had often promoted market-friendly regulation before 2008. In fact, however, those interests remained powerful in many contexts, particularly in the United States, where the generosity and success of the government's rescue operations ensured that many private interests rebounded from the crisis quickly and retained enormous influence in post-crisis regulatory debates. Those interests watered down many US domestic regulatory reforms, a result that helped to explain the weak content of a number of international regulatory initiatives.

One final assumption was that the credibility of market-friendly or "neoliberal" thinking in finance would be severely undermined by the crisis. Many of the post-crisis reforms were indeed driven by a newly influential "macroprudential" philosophy that highlighted how previous thinking had downplayed the prevalence of systemic risk in financial markets. But macroprudential thinking had somewhat ambiguous policy implications. Although it could justify anti-market regulation, many officials—particularly in the US—embraced a more minimalist version of macroprudential ideas that supported enhanced public oversight without actually constraining private financial activity in significant ways. This limitation provided a further explanation for why the market-friendly nature of international financial standards was not significantly overturned.

WAS A FOURTH PILLAR OF GLOBAL ECONOMIC ARCHITECTURE CREATED?

The fourth and final issue explored in the book is the significance of the creation of the FSB by the G20 leaders in April 2009. The FSB was the only new international institution—aside from the G20 leaders' forum itself—to emerge from the crisis and it was touted as a very important innovation in strengthening the governance of international financial standards. In a widely quoted comment, US Treasury Secretary Tim Geithner described the FSB just after its creation as a new "fourth pillar" of global economic architecture that would help to ensure that post-crisis international financial regulatory reforms were implemented in a harmonized fashion.

If it could perform this role effectively, the FSB would indeed have been an important innovation. International financial standards had long been developed by international standard setting bodies with little power and few staff. In contrast to international trade rules, these standards were "soft law" with which compliance was entirely voluntary. Not surprisingly, implementation of international financial standards by national authorities had often been inconsistent in the pre-crisis period. The FSB was promoted as a body that could address this weakness in the international financial standards regime.

Chapter 5 demonstrates, however, that the FSB's creation was much less significant than Geithner suggested. Rather than being an entirely new institution, the FSB was simply a reformed version of an ineffectual body that the G7 had created a decade earlier: the Financial Stability Forum (FSF). The latter's membership had initially included the G7 countries, international standard setting bodies, and various international financial institutions, and it had attempted to encourage implementation of international financial standards. But it had been given no charter, no formal power of any kind, and only a tiny staff. Indeed, the FSF had represented a kind of pinnacle of the loose, soft-law, network-based governance that characterized the international financial standards regime before the 2008 crisis.

When the FSB was created, it was given a formal charter, more staff, more specific mandates than the FSF, and a wider country membership that included all G20 countries. But the FSB inherited the basic weaknesses of its predecessor: it had no formal power. Although the FSB's charter committed member countries to implement international standards, the commitment had little formal meaning because membership in the body created no legal obligations of any kind. The FSB's capacity to foster implementation was restricted entirely to "soft" mechanisms such as peer review, transparency, and monitoring.

In 2010, FSB members did announce an initiative that initially appeared to signal a more serious effort to encourage implementation by threatening sanctions against noncomplying jurisdictions. But the limitations of the initiative quickly became clear. Sanctions could be applied only with the consensus of all FSB members, thereby ensuring that no member would be targeted because each could exercise a veto. Even for nonmembers, the initiative focused only on some very basic pre-crisis principles relating to international cooperation and information exchange rather than the post-crisis international regulatory reforms. Efforts to encourage compliance with the latter continued to focus entirely on voluntary mechanisms for both FSB members and nonmembers.

The establishment of the FSB thus did little to alter the soft-law character of the international financial standards regime. Despite the rhetoric touting a new fourth pillar of global economic architecture, the FSB remained—like the FSF—a remarkably toothless organization. The FSB's weakness was particularly problematic because of the political obstacles standing in the way of the implementation post-crisis international financial regulatory reforms. Some of these obstacles were familiar from the pre-crisis period such as private sector lobbying and competitive deregulation pressures. New challenges also emerged in the wake of the crisis, particularly in the context of the heightened domestic political salience of financial regulatory issues. In this new political environment, it was not surprising that the implementation of post-crisis international financial reforms was often slow and uneven.

The failure of the G20 to create a stronger international institution to address these challenges largely reflected widespread resistance to the idea of accepting infringements on sovereignty in the realm of financial regulatory policymaking. While some French and British policymakers pushed ambitious plans for a strong global institution in the regulatory arena, many others were much more wary, including US authorities who had long been reluctant to accept international constraints on their policy autonomy in this sphere. Concerns about delegating regulatory authority to an international body were only reinforced by the failures of cooperation during the crisis to resolve failing institutions or share the burden of bailouts. If the costs of distressed financial institutions were going to fall on host countries (as they had during the crisis), national authorities had good reason for wanting to keep regulatory powers in their own hands.

Since the FSB's creation, the disappointing results of G20 and FSB efforts to negotiate cooperative arrangements for cross-border resolution and burden sharing only reinforced these sentiments. Indeed, authorities in the US and elsewhere began to undertake unilateral initiatives to reduce their reliance on foreign regulators because of distrust about the prospects for cooperation. These initiatives included policies such as greater host country regulation for banks and the encouragement of local clearing mechanisms for OTC derivatives. These unilateral policies may ultimately generate greater financial market and regulatory fragmentation along national lines, a very different legacy of the crisis than Geithner had hoped for at the time of the FSB's creation. These post-crisis initiatives signaled that nation-states—rather than the FSB—remained the key pillars of global economic governance in the financial regulatory realm.

EXPLAINING THE STATUS QUO OUTCOMES

Across these four cases, many analysts and policymakers held high expectations that the crisis would generate a number of major changes in global financial governance. Five years after the crisis, these expectations had not been met. What accounts for absence of a significant transformation of global financial governance in the wake of the worst global financial crisis since the early 1930s? Although each case had its own dynamics, there were some common themes across the four issues areas that can be briefly summarized.

The first was the structural power of the country at the center of the crisis: the United States. In a number of instances, the absence of significant change reflected the fact that private actors and other states responded to the crisis in a global financial environment shaped by factors such as the dollar's global role, the relative attractiveness of US financial markets, the US role as an export market, US geopolitical strength, and US influence in institutions such as the IMF. In the early 1980s, Susan Strange noted that the US was "still an extraordinary power" in this structural sense in international financial affairs. The crisis and post-crisis period revealed starkly that it retained this position of unparalleled structural power three decades later.[11] This power helped—often with little direct agency by US officials—to inhibit major transformation of global financial governance in this period.

But US officials also made active policy choices that shaped outcomes in important ways. Some of these choices involved initiatives whereby the US government helped to preserve the status quo by performing classic global economic leadership functions such as lender-of-last-resort activities and the maintenance of open markets. In other cases, they blocked, or diluted the ambition of, post-crisis reforms, such as those relating to the IMF governance, the creation of a multilateral swap regime, SDR reform, as well as the strengthening of international regulation and the FSB's role. These various choices reflected a number of factors, including the country's dependence on foreign capital, the enduring influence of domestic groups that favored the status quo, as well as policymakers' commitments to policy autonomy, domestic financial stability, neoliberal ideas, the country's pre-crisis growth model, and the international competitiveness of US financial markets and institutions. For all these reasons, US policymakers acted as a particularly significant conservative force during and in the wake of the crisis.

The power and agency of some other leading states was also significant in explaining the limited post-crisis change in global financial governance. A number of the outcomes reflected the unexpected weakness of Europe. At the start of the crisis, European policymakers were often among the most enthusiastic in calling for more radical change in global financial governance. This ambition—and the European capacity to realize it—quickly faded in the context of the serious problems in the Eurozone and difficulties of coordinating Europe-wide positions on international reforms.

The choices of policymakers from some emerging market countries, particularly China, were also important. They contributed to status quo outcomes through their enduring preferences for self-insurance and export-oriented growth strategies as well as through their caution about internationalizing local currencies or challenging the content of international regulatory reforms. The conservatism of these policymakers across these various areas reflected the influence of entrenched policy frameworks and domestic interests as well as their risk aversion in the context of domestic political and economic challenges.[12]

These factors help to explain the status quo results across the four cases, but it is worth noting that the respective outcomes also reinforced each other in important ways. For example, if the dollar had experienced a serious crisis in 2008 or if the Fed had not acted as international lender-of-last-resort, the crisis would have been much worse—a development that might have generated much greater political pressures for more radical regulatory responses. There was also a strong complementarity between state priorities and powerful domestic interests in the United States and China favoring the continuation of pre-crisis growth models. If the domestic political context in either country had changed more significantly, reactions might have been triggered in the other with results that generated more dramatic changes in global financial governance.

These explanations of the status quo outcomes are rather state-centric ones that focus on power and politics among and within influential states. What about alternative perspectives? A number of analysts have attributed the lack of significant change in global economic governance primarily to the interests of powerful transnational elites, particularly financial interests, with strong stakes in the pre-crisis finance-led global capitalist economy.[13] That line of argument is also sometimes closely related to analyses that point to the enduring transnational dominance of neoliberal ideas in policymaking circles and even everyday life.[14]

This book confirms that financial interests and neoliberal ideology influenced state choices in a number of instances (particularly in the US and European contexts, but much less so in emerging market countries). But it argues that they were not the only factors that mattered, particularly vis-à-vis important developments such as the absence of a dollar crisis. This analysis also places considerable emphasis on political contingency and agency in contrast to the more structuralist orientation of many of those kinds of analyses. To the extent that structures helped determine outcomes, the book also suggests that US structural power was often more important than transnational elite dominance or neoliberal hegemony in influencing the course of events.[15]

From a more institutionalist standpoint, some scholars have argued that the strength of the contemporary international institutional landscape helped to foster cooperation and prevent a collapse of the global economy similar to that of the early 1930s. International economic institutions are seen to have been significant in providing focal points for coordination, rules that constrained behavior and reduced uncertainty, and expertise that helped to promote shared understandings.[16] The analysis in this book differs by highlighting the relative weaknesses and lack of influence of key international bodies such as the G20, IMF, and FSB in global financial governance. Indeed, this book even downplays the significance of international cooperation more generally in explaining key developments that helped to prevent a global economic collapse, such as the macroeconomic stimulus programs of 2008–09 and the absence of a dollar crisis. Where cooperation was key to explaining outcomes—as in the case of the Fed swaps—it often took a bilateral and ad hoc form rather than a multilateral institutionalized one.

Other scholars have invoked a different kind of institutionalist explanation to explain another aspect of the status quo outcome: the limited nature of global institutional reform. Drawing on the insights of "historical institutionalist" scholarship, they note that path dependency often characterizes global economic governance because of the large start-up costs and coordination difficulties associated with the creation of new international institutions, and because of resistance from those who benefit from their role in existing ones. In this context and given the need for quick action, policymakers turned to existing institutions such as the IMF and created institutions such as the G20 and FSB that built directly on the preexisting bodies (the G20 finance grouping and the FSF).[17] This historical institutionalist analysis offers some useful insights for understanding the incremental nature of these reforms, but it does not provide a comprehensive explanation for them or other outcomes examined in this book.

In sum, this book argues the status quo outcome had a number of causes, of which the power and agency of dominant states, especially the United States, were particularly important. Their importance provides a useful lesson for analytical understandings of the political economy of global finance. In the years leading up to the crisis, there was much scholarly analysis of the growing significance of transnational non-state actors, private regimes, and international institutions in global financial governance. Post-2008 developments highlight more than ever the fact that global financial governance continues to rest on very state-centric foundations.

WHAT NEXT?

What is in store for the future of global financial governance? This book is concerned with the consequences of the massive 2008 crisis for global financial governance and focuses on what happened in the immediate first half decade after the crisis. Although the book suggests that the crisis has been a status quo event to date, the crisis could certainly have more transformative effects over the longer term. The final chapter explores in a more speculative manner four scenarios of how the crisis might influence the evolution of global financial governance in the coming years.

Under the first scenario, the longer term legacy of the crisis would involve a strengthening of liberal multilateral features of global financial governance. As we have seen, the crisis generated new multilateral institutions such as the G20 leaders' forum and the FSB, as well as reforms to the IMF. This book highlights the limitations of these institutional innovations in the realms of crisis management (in the cases of the G20 and IMF), international currency issuance (the IMF's SDR), and the international regulatory regime (the FSB). But over time and with the support of cooperation among the major powers, these limitations may be overcome in ways that allow these international bodies to play a more central role in global financial governance. In that event, the crisis might be seen in future years as an important event that laid the groundwork for a strengthened liberal multilateral global financial order.

The second scenario anticipates an opposite outcome in which global financial governance was characterized by growing fragmentation and conflict between the major powers. Under this scenario, international financial crises would be increasingly addressed by governments through competing regional, bilateral, and unilateral mechanisms. Currency rivalries between the dollar and emerging challengers such as the euro and RMB would intensify. Global regulatory cooperation would break down as countries and regions introduced various unilateral controls to insulate themselves from instability abroad and to defend their regulatory autonomy, particularly to tighten controls over financial markets. The crisis of 2008 already encouraged some of these tendencies, which could easily intensify in the coming years if cooperation between the major powers were to break down.

A third scenario of "cooperative decentralization" sits between the first and second.[18] In this future world, multilateralism would remain an important feature of global financial governance but it would serve a more decentralized order. Crisis management would be increasingly handled through regional, bilateral, and national mechanisms but with the IMF and G20 supplementing and/or supporting these mechanisms in a number of ways. A more multipolar currency order would emerge but one characterized more by cooperation between the world's major currency zones than by conflict and rivalry. In the regulatory realm, national and regional authorities would carve out greater policy space through initiatives that created a more fragmented global financial system but in a cooperative manner that was supported and overseen by the FSB and IMF. In each of these contexts, this scenario would reconcile divergent legacies of the 2008 crisis in ways that would require cooperation between the major powers but of a much less ambitious kind than the first scenario.

A final scenario is one that would build on the initial post-crisis experience examined in this book: enduring status quo. International crisis management would remain heavily dependent on ad hoc US international lender-of-last-resort activities. The dollar would endure as the world's dominant currency. International financial standards would continue to be developed and refined with largely market-friendly content. The FSB would survive as a weak and fragile body trying, with uneven success, to encourage implementation of those standards through voluntary mechanisms. It may seem unlikely that this kind of status quo could persist over the longer term, but the experience of the crisis of 2008 highlights how plausible this scenario may be, particularly if there are no major shifts in the power and interests of dominant states in the coming years.

OBJECTIVES AND OBJECTIONS

Before launching into the detailed arguments, some final points need to be made to anticipate possible objections to the central thesis. To begin with, this book does not attempt to provide a comprehensive overview of the post-crisis trends in global financial governance. The focus is on the four aspects of global financial governance for which expectations of change were particularly high: the G20's crisis management role, the dollar's global standing, the reform of international financial standards, and the FSB's creation. In each of these areas, analysts and policymakers predicted that the crisis would encourage major transformation. The goal of the book is to explore how and why these predictions fell short of expectations.

The choice of the four issue areas might raise questions about whether the label of "status quo crisis" is entirely deserved. Would the study of other aspects of global financial governance generate a different conclusion? There have indeed been other changes in global financial governance since the crisis, such as various reforms to IMF governance, initiatives to curtail offshore tax havens, and the creation of new mechanisms for macroeconomic coordination through the G20. But the initial expectations for change in these and other areas were generally much lower, and their limited results to date have been in line with these expectations. This book focuses on "harder" cases for the status quo thesis in which prominent predictions of significant transformation were made but did not pan out.[19]

The argument that we have lived through a status quo crisis might also generate the objection that it is too rushed a judgment. As historical institutionalists highlight, major transformations in global financial governance often need more time to manifest themselves. As noted earlier, the concluding chapter does acknowledge that the 2008 crisis may have a more transformative impact with the greater passage of time. But it is also worth noting that the global financial meltdown of the early 1930s highlighted how significant change in global financial governance can also happen quickly. Five years after the beginning of the US stock market crash of 1929, the international gold standard had collapsed, rival currency blocs had emerged, and the liberal pattern of financial relations that had characterized the pre-crisis period had unraveled. By comparison, the immediate legacy of the 2008 crisis has been tame.

It is also important to clarify that the focus of this book is on *global* financial governance rather than financial governance at the national or regional level. The idea that we have lived through a status quo crisis in financial governance makes little sense for residents of a country such as Iceland. Those who live in the Eurozone have also witnessed major changes in the governance within their regional currency area. The goal of this book, however, is to show that major transformations in financial governance at the global level in the four areas discussed have been less apparent.

One final possible objection to the status quo thesis needs to be mentioned. Some might argue that the bar for measuring significant change in global financial governance has been set at too high a level. In this book, the standards against which changes are evaluated are a number of predictions that were made in 2008–09. But were the predictions unrealistic from the start? With hindsight, it is tempting to conclude that they were. But it is important to recognize that they were put forward in a serious way at the time. The fact that change has been so limited in comparison to these expectations is noteworthy and deserves to be analyzed. The task is particularly important if George Santayana is right that those who cannot remember the past are condemned to repeat it. This is not a crisis that most of the world's population are likely to wish to repeat.

Did the G20 Save the Day?

All analyses of the significance of the financial crisis for global financial governance highlight the birth of the new G20 leaders' forum. Its creation was an initiative of the US government, which announced on October 22, 2008 that it would host a summit of the leaders of the G20 in Washington on November 14–15. The G20 was not in fact an entirely new feature of global financial governance. Financial and central bank officials of this grouping had been meeting since 1999. But that organization had failed to carve out much of an influence independent of the G7 countries that had dominated global financial decision making since the mid-1970s. This dynamic changed rapidly after Bush's announcement, with the G20 leaders' forum quickly displacing the G7 from its central role in global financial governance.[1]

Subsequent chapters of this book address the effectiveness of the G20 vis-à-vis various post-crisis reforms. This chapter focuses on the activity for which the G20 leaders' forum quickly became most famous: its global crisis management role. One of the central rationales for creating the G20 leaders' forum was that its composition would be well suited to manage the financial crisis. Taken together, the members of the G20 represented two-thirds of the world's population, 80% of world trade, and 90% of the world's GNP. In contrast to the G7, the G20 also included leaders from important emerging economic powers such as China whose cooperation was critical for successful crisis management. Indeed, the G20 was seen as a key forum for bringing together during the crisis established powers such as the United States and Europe and the emerging powers such as China, India, and Brazil.

The detailed nature of the final communiqué of the first summit raised expectations that the G20 leaders' forum would indeed ensure that financial crisis was managed in a more cooperative and successful fashion than during the early 1930s experience. Those expectations were reinforced when the second G20 leaders' summit, held in London on April 2 2009, announced an ambitious agenda to address the crisis and restore global growth. By the time of their third summit in Pittsburgh in September 2009, the G20 leaders declared that this agenda had successfully stemmed the crisis and that global economic recovery was underway. As they put, "it [the agenda] worked. Our forceful response helped stop the dangerous, sharp decline in global activity and stabilize financial markets."[2]

It is not just G20 leaders themselves who trumpeted the G20's role in saving the world from another Great Depression. Many scholars and analysts have also applauded its decisive leadership role in managing the crisis.[3] Even when the G20's reputation for effective action became increasingly tarnished at subsequent summits, its image as a successful crisis manager survived largely intact. As French President Nicolas Sarkozy put it in August 2010, "[the G20] enabled the main economic powers to successfully weather the most severe crisis since the 1930s."[4] These sentiments were echoed a few months later by the head of the European Commission, José Manuel Barroso, who suggested that the G20 had "prevented the boat from sinking."[5]

How well deserved is the G20's reputation for successfully managing the financial crisis? In this chapter, I argue that the contribution of the G20 leaders' forum to the financial dimensions of the management of the crisis has been overstated. The first section explores the significance of two roles that the G20 is most commonly said to have performed in this area: marshalling macroeconomic stimulus programs and generating at the London summit a headline-grabbing $1.1 trillion support program for the world economy. I show that in both cases, these activities were less important than advertised.

The second section highlights how the G20 was irrelevant to the most important cooperative dimension of the management of the crisis: the international provision of massive sums of dollar liquidity to help foreign firms and markets in distress by the US Federal Reserve. The Fed provided these funds through a number of ad hoc bilateral swaps agreements with foreign central banks, all of which were put in place before the first G20 leaders' summit. The Fed's capacity and willingness to play this leadership role stemmed from the central position of the United States within global finance. It was this enduring core feature of global financial governance—more than the novel creation of the G20—that was critical to the international management of the crisis. It also remains central to management of future crises because of limitations in the G20's post-crisis agenda for international financial reform as it relates to international lender of last resort activities.

WHAT DID THE G20 ACTUALLY DO?

What is the G20 credited with doing at its first two summits to prevent a Great Depression? Some cite the G20 leaders' actions in the trade sphere. At their first summit, the G20 leaders committed to refrain from new trade protectionist measures for twelve months and to conclude the Doha Round of trade negotiations. At the London summit, they extended their pledge to refrain from new protectionist measures until the end of 2010 and reiterated their promise to conclude the Doha Round. These commitments are said to have helped prevent the kinds of protectionist measures that accompanied and contributed to the Great Depression.[6] The G20 leaders themselves invoked historical precedent, noting at the London summit that "we will not repeat the historic mistakes of protectionism of previous eras."[7]

Because this book is concerned with global financial governance, the significance of the G20's actions in the trade sphere is not evaluated. It is worth noting, however, that the G20 governments made little progress in advancing the Doha Round negotiations in this period and that almost

all G20 members (seventeen of them) had broken their promise not introduce new restrictive trade measures within six months.[8] A strong case
can be made that the absence of more serious protectionism had much
less to do with G20 pronouncements than with changing business preferences in the context of the internationalization of production as well as
the hard commitments and enforcement mechanisms of the World Trade
Organization (WTO) and various preferential trade agreements at the
regional and bilateral levels.[9]

Marshaling National Macroeconomic Stimulus Programs?

In the financial area, the G20 leaders' forum is often credited with mobi-
lizing national macroeconomic stimulus programs.[10] To deal with "deteriorating economic conditions worldwide," the G20 leaders agreed at their
first summit that "a broader policy response is needed, based on closer
macroeconomic cooperation." They endorsed both "the importance of
monetary policy support, as deemed appropriate to domestic conditions"
as well as the use of "fiscal measures to stimulate domestic demand to
rapid effect, as appropriate, while maintaining a policy framework con-
ducive to fiscal sustainability."[11] At the London summit in April 2009, the
G20 leaders reinforced the message, noting that "our central banks have
pledged to maintain expansionary policies for as long as needed" and that
"we are committed to deliver the scale of sustained fiscal effort necessary
to restore growth." Regarding the latter, they noted: "we are undertak-
ing an unprecedented and concerted fiscal expansion, which will save or
create millions of jobs which would otherwise have been destroyed, and
that will, by the end of next year, amount to $5 trillion."[12] By the time of
the Pittsburgh summit in September 2009, the G20 leaders congratulated
themselves for the "largest and most coordinated fiscal and monetary
stimulus ever undertaken" to restore growth.[13]

There is no question that many G20 countries introduced very substantial monetary and fiscal stimulus programs in 2008–09. This activism
contrasted dramatically with the 1930s experience. In that pre-Keynesian

era, there was more limited understanding of the role of counter-cyclical public spending and many governments responded to the economic downturn with fiscal austerity programs. Contractionary monetary policies also contributed to, and exacerbated, the Great Depression. The response to the 2008 crisis was very different, and the expansionary fiscal and monetary policies are widely seen to have helped prevent a repetition of the 1930s experience.[14]

As in the trade case, however, it is important not to overstate the significance of the G20 in generating these stimulus policies. The key national initiatives to ease monetary policy began as far back as the fall of 2007, when leading central banks started to lower interest rates dramatically. There was some coordination of rate cuts among them, most notably in the joint announcement on October 8, 2008 by the Fed, European Central Bank (ECB), the Bank of England, the Sweish Riksbank, the Bank of Canada, and the Swiss National Bank. But this coordination took place before the G20 leaders' forum held its first summit.[15] By the time of the inaugural G20 leaders meeting in mid-November, the prospects for further coordinated interest rates had diminished as nominal interest rates in countries such as the United States and Britain were approaching zero. In this context, central bankers in the United States and Europe began to consider more unconventional quantitative easing involving the purchase of longer-term securities to drive down long term interest rates. These programs were introduced unilaterally, however, and they were soon the source of much contention within the G20, as developing—or "Southern"—countries complained about their impact on capital flows and exchange rates.

The G20's role in triggering or coordinating fiscal stimulus programs is also questionable. To begin with, a considerable portion of the fiscal stimulus in this period came from automatic stabilizers rather than discretionary spending decisions.[16] By the fall of 2008 and winter of 2009, politicians across the world were also facing strong domestic pressures for policy action in the face of the economic shock. Even in the absence of the G20, it is very likely that many countries would have introduced new government spending programs. As Rajan puts it, "the G-20 leaders were pushing on an open door when they called for coordinated stimulus."[17]

It is certainly possible that the initial G20 statement at the Washington summit helped to address policymakers' fears that unilateral policies might be ineffective. For example, Britain's Chancellor of the Exchequer Alistair Darling reports in his memoirs that British officials hoped a coordinated stimulus via the G20 would strengthen their national efforts. But his discussion also implies that, because of the severity of domestic economic troubles, Britain's November 2008 stimulus program was going to proceed regardless of the specific outcome of the first G20 summit.[18] Indeed, Robert Wade argues that "almost all the [fiscal stimulus] programs announced after the [Washington] summit—as evidence of G20 cooperation—had already been decided on before the summit."[19]

The domestic imperative was particularly apparent in large countries such as the United States and China, whose stimulus programs were the most significant for the world economy as a whole. As Kahler puts, "even in the absence of a coordinated policy response...the United States and Chinese governments were likely to implement programs very similar to those that were mandated."[20] Indeed, it is noteworthy that China's massive RMB 4 trillion (approximately US$586 billion) stimulus was announced just five days *before* the first G20 summit. At the time, the country had begun to feel the full impact of the crisis, with 670,000 factories forced into bankruptcy in the third quarter of the year.[21]

The tentative nature of the Washington summit statement also undermines the claim that it helped to calm fears about unilateral action. Would policymakers really have been reassured by wording that only called for stimulus "as appropriate"? It was no secret at the time that policymakers in countries such as Germany were deeply resistant to a large fiscal stimulus and that they might not go along with the enthusiasm of others in countries such as the United States and Britain. Despite this uncertainty, many countries plowed ahead. The statements of the London summit were more definitive in endorsing stimulus programs, but most key programs had already been introduced or announced by then.

Some have suggested that the G20 statements helped legitimate Keynesian-style policies and/or generated peer pressures that prompted more conservative policymakers to embrace expansionary fiscal policies that they would normally disapproved of. For example, Drezner attributes the German stimulus in 2009 to this factor: "Even reluctant contributors like Germany—whose finance minister blasted the 'crass Keynesianism' of these policies in December 2008—eventually bowed to pressure from economists and G20 peers."[22] But detailed analyses of the German stimulus programs make no mention of the role of the G20, highlighting instead the explanatory role of domestic ideas or electoral and interest group politics.[23] Studies of other countries' experiences also highlight the primacy of domestic political factors in explaining fiscal policy choices in this period.[24] In a detailed comparative analyses of thirty-four OECD and European Union country experiences in 2008–09, Armingeon also concludes that "coordination between countries was very limited" and that "even in economically densely integrated societies, fiscal policy is still mainly framed by the domestic political actors."[25]

The Trillion Dollar Rescue Plan?

More dramatic than their endorsement of national macroeconomic stimulus plans was the G20 leaders' announcement at the London summit of an enormous "$1.1 trillion programme of support to restore credit, growth and jobs in the world economy."[26] The host of the G20 meeting, British Prime Minister Gordon Brown, himself later described this initiative as a "$1 trillion rescue plan for the world's economy" that "was the biggest economic support program ever agreed on." He continued: "It was simple: the G20 had delivered, with a sum approaching the total yearly output of countries like Britain, France and Italy."[27]

To reach the $1.1 trillion figure, the G20 leaders made the following promises. First, they committed to at least $100 billion in additional lending to low-income countries by the multilateral development banks. Second, they promised to make available at least $250 billion to support trade finance over two years from multilateral development banks and their national export credit and investment agencies. Third, they supported a new $250 billion allocation of Special Drawing Rights among

International Monetary Fund (IMF) members. Finally, the largest portion of the money was made up of a promise to increase the funds available to the IMF by $500 billion.

These large numbers may have had some shock value in boosting market confidence. But the details of the plan immediately raised questions about whether its significance was being oversold. Critics argued that the commitment relating to trade finance "was mostly the sum of existing export aid, not new support."[28] The new $250 allocation of SDRs was also less important than it sounded. As noted in Chapter 3, SDRs boost countries' official reserves, but their usefulness for addressing balance of payments crises is limited by some design features. Moreover, in the context of the crisis, SDRs were potentially most helpful for Southern countries that might suffer balance of payments crises, but only approximately $100 billion of the new allocation went to these countries. For systemically important Southern countries, the money involved was not very significant. For example, the new SDR allocation provided an extra $3.4 billion to South Korea, a sum that paled in comparison to the $30 billion swap line that Korean authorities had received from the United States the previous fall (see next section).[29] Most important was the fact the new SDR allocation did not actually take place until August. When the G20 leaders claimed the next month at their Pittsburgh summit that their London action plan had worked, it was certainly legitimate to question whether the SDR allocation had contributed much to that outcome.

What about the role of the main element of the London rescue plan: the expansion by $500 billion of resources available to the IMF? It was certainly true that this initiative was potentially a quite significant one. During the half decade leading up to the crisis, the IMF had been increasingly marginalized in global financial governance. Top officials in the Bush administration had been very critical of its large-scale lending to Southern countries affected by the 1997–98 international financial crisis. They had seen these loans as contributing to "moral hazard" problems in the markets by rewarding investors for their poor investment choices and they had little enthusiasm for giving the Fund new resources. Indeed, some Bush administration officials had even speculated about the Fund's abolition before coming into office.[30]

Even more problematic for the Fund was the fact that its reputation among potential borrowers had suffered tremendously as a result of its lending programs during the 1997–98 East Asian crisis. The conditionality attached to its loans was widely criticized for having exacerbated the economic troubles of borrowing countries and for being overly intrusive and excessively influenced by US policy goals. In the wake of that experience, policymakers in many developing —or "Southern" — countries considered it too much of a political liability to borrow from the Fund.

Indeed, many Southern governments—particularly in East Asia and Latin America—began to build up large foreign exchange reserves, at least partly to protect themselves from future balance of payments shocks in ways that would allow them to avoid having to depend on Fund assistance in the future. They did this by pursuing what Rajan calls a kind of "supercharged export-led growth strategy" to earn foreign exchange after 1997–98.[31] Between January 1999 and July 2008, the scale of the increase in the world's official reserves was enormous: reserves rose from $1.615 trillion to 7.534 trillion.[32] As demand for its services collapsed, the IMF was left—in the words of the governor of the Bank of England, Mervyn King—to "slip into obscurity."[33] Indeed, by 2007, the Fund's loan portfolio had fallen to a very low level of just $10 billion (most of which was owed by just two countries: Turkey and Pakistan).[34]

For the first year of the crisis—from August 2007 to August 2008— the IMF remained on the sidelines. But as the crisis intensified in the fall of 2008, a number of countries began to request IMF loans to cover severe balance of payments problems caused by rapid capital outflows and the collapse of exports and commodity prices. Particularly vulnerable were many East European countries that had been dependent on capital inflows and that had extensive foreign currency borrowing. Just days before the first G20 summit, the IMF announced two major loan packages for Hungary ($16.5 billion) and Ukraine ($17.2 billion), and it was clear that more were soon to follow.

At their first Washington summit, the G20 leaders appeared to give their blessing to these loans, stressing the IMF's "important role in crisis response" and their commitment to "help emerging and developing economies gain access to finance in current difficult financial conditions." They also committed that they would "review the adequacy of the resources of the IMF, the World Bank Group, and other multilateral development banks and stand ready to increase them where necessary."[35] At the London summit, they then increased the IMF's resources from $250 to $750 billion. At the same time, they welcomed an IMF decision taken a week earlier to create a new Flexible Credit Line (FCL) that provided preapproved countries with strong fundamentals access to conditionality-free funds. They also supported the IMF's decision at the time to streamline loan conditionality and increase the flexibility of its traditional Stand-By Arrangements (SBAs). In addition, the G20 called on the IMF to increase its concessional lending to low-income countries.

The Limited Demand for IMF Loans

The increase in funding for the IMF appeared dramatic, but its material significance was greatly diminished by the fact that demand for IMF loans was limited in the months following the London summit. There was, for example, very little interest in the IMF's new FCL. Three countries signed up immediately—Colombia ($10.9 billion), Mexico ($49.5 billion), and Poland ($20.5 billion)—but no other country followed their lead (and none of these three drew funds). Similarly, between the London and Pittsburgh summits, only five SBAs were established, and no more would be set up until late 2009 when the Eurozone crisis began. These five lending programs involved Bosnia and Herzegovina, Costa Rica, Guatemala, Romania, and Sri Lanka, and they totaled only approximately $24 billion (and less than one-third of this total had actually been drawn upon by early August and almost all by Romania, whose initial package had made up almost $18 billion of the $24 billion total).[36] The Fund also expanded concessional lending to some other countries but sums involved were even smaller; in 2009 as a whole, for example, total concessional lending totaled $3.8 billion.

Did the IMF's augmented resources at least help to fund crisis-related lending that had expanded during the lead-up to the London summit? Not really. From September 2008 until the London summit, the Fund approved twelve SBAs, but they totaled just under $61 billion in commitments (of which only $36 billion had been drawn by early August 2009). The largest loans by far had gone to just three countries—Hungary, Pakistan, and Ukraine—which made up about three-quarters of the commitments. The other much smaller SBAs involved Armenia, Belarus, El Salvador, Georgia, Iceland, Latvia, Mongolia, Serbia, and Seychelles.[37]

What is striking about these numbers is that the new IMF's crisis-related commitments were smaller than the $250 billion sum that the Fund already had on hand before the London summit's dramatic announcements. Adding together the FCL and SBA lending commitments made between September 2008 and August 2009, we reach a total of just under $167 billion (of which about $43 billion was drawn by the end of this period). Concessional lending adds only marginally more.[38] Even if countries had drawn on all these funds, the IMF could easily have covered the sums without the G20's London summit initiative. In other words, although it attracted headlines, the G20 initiative had no practical consequence for the Fund's ability to meet the demand for its loans during this intense phase of the crisis in 2008–09.[39]

Of course, it is still possible that the London announcement was significant in boosting general confidence in a way that lessened the need for countries to borrow from the Fund. But it is interesting to note that, in advance of the London summit, lead G20 officials had in fact acknowledged that "the Fund has the capacity to meet members' expected financing needs." They had called for a doubling of the Fund's resources only because it seemed "prudent" because "the environment is highly uncertain and members' demands for Fund financing could increase significantly."[40] In the end, however, new demand for IMF loans in the immediate aftermath of the London summit was limited. G20 officials had been right that the IMF already had enough funds on hand to meet it. The main barrier to the IMF playing a larger role in balance of payments lending during the crisis was not a funding constraint but rather one relating to demand for its loans.

A key reason why demand remained low was the enduring stigma attached to borrowing from the IMF, particularly among large countries in East Asia and Latin America. This stigma had encouraged reserve accumulation that helped protect many countries in these regions from the need to borrow from the IMF. Indeed, protected by their reserves, many Southern countries were able to engage in counter-cyclical expansionary policies that contributed to the global recovery. If these countries had borrowed from the IMF, this contribution might not have been made because IMF lending programs often required austerity rather than counter-cyclical expansionary policies during the crisis.[41] In other words, the ability of large Southern countries to fulfill the G20 mandate to expand their economies was dependent on their self-insurance policies rather than their access to IMF lending. It was their desire to distance themselves from the Fund in the pre-crisis years—rather the G20's boosting of Fund resources at the London summit—that allowed these countries to contribute to the global economic stimulus.

Even many countries that did feel the need for external assistance refused to go to the Fund because of the stigma involved. For example, when the South Korean currency experienced strong downward pressure after the collapse of Lehman Brothers, the country's finance minister Kang Man-Soo made it very clear that he would never apply for an IMF loans because of Koreans' "sentiment" toward the Fund.[42] Instead, as noted later, he relied on a swap line from the US Federal Reserve. The Fund's new FCL program and commitment to streamline conditionality had been designed to address the stigma problem, but the distrust toward the Fund remained.

The Fund's image was not helped by the failure of significant reforms to its governance aimed at giving Southern countries more influence. The latter had long resented the fact that the G7 countries had enormous influence over the institution because of their large voting shares (which are determined largely by quota size) and representation on the

Fund's twenty-four-member Executive Board. As the weight of large Southern countries in the global economy grew, these resentments and demands for governance reform only increased. At the 2007 IMF annual meetings, Brazil's finance minister Guido Mantega had highlighted the link between self-insurance and the absence of IMF governance reform. In the absence of the latter, he noted developing countries "would go their own way [. . .]. We will seek self insurance by building up high levels of international reserves, and we will participate in regional reserve-sharing pools and regional monetary institutions. The fragmentation of the multilateral financial system, which is already emerging, will accelerate."[43]

Southern governments used the opportunity of the first G20 summit to push for IMF governance reform and the final communiqué noted the following: "We are committed to advancing the reform of the Bretton Woods Institutions so that they can more adequately reflect changing economic weights in the world economy in order to increase their legitimacy and effectiveness. In this respect, emerging and developing economies, including the poorest countries, should have greater voice and representation."[44] But officials from the United States and Europe resisted substantial change. By the time of the London summit, the G20 leaders could only reach consensus on a commitment to implement some very modest reforms to quota and voice already agreed in April 2008 and to complete the next quota review by January 2011. When they promised to increase the Fund's resources, the G20 leaders also did so in a manner that did not affect voting shares. Instead of endorsing a new quota increase, many countries simply expanded their commitments to existing credit lines. In the absence of governance reform, others, such as Brazil, Russia, and China, also invested in bonds issued by the Fund to avoid making a longer commitment. The lack of progress on IMF governance did little to increase trust in the institution among potential Southern borrowers.[45]

The dramatic boosting of the IMF's resources was thus much less important to the management of the crisis throughout 2008–09 than the hype at the London summit suggested. Of course, it may have

influenced confidence in a general way. But its material significance for
the IMF's actual lending was negligible because lingering Southern distrust of the Fund left the institution without many customers. Few of
the countries that received IMF loans were "systemically significant"
to the world economy at the time. Even among the borrowers, the contribution of IMF lending to the global recovery was undermined by the
fact that the Fund often continued to insist on pro-cyclical policies. The
countries that self-insured instead were freer to pursue expansionary
domestic policies.

THE US AS INTERNATIONAL LENDER-OF-LAST-RESORT

The IMF was also not the only game in town when it came to the provision of balance of payments lending. Some of its loans were supplemented
by considerable support from other sources. For example, loans from the
EU and Nordic countries supported the IMF's program in Latvia on a
scale that was larger than the IMF contribution. In the cases of Hungary
and Romania, the IMF's large loans were also accompanied by substantial
EU funds.[46]

Much more significant in size was the bilateral support offered by the
US Federal Reserve during the crisis. In late October 2008, the Federal
Reserve established $120 billion worth of swap lines with four systemi-
cally important emerging market countries: Brazil, Mexico, Singapore,
and South Korea ($30 billion each). The swaps enabled these central
banks to sell their national currency to the Fed in exchange for dollars,
with a promise to buy that currency back (along with interest) at the same
exchange rate at a specified future date within the next three months.[47]
From the standpoint of the countries themselves, the Fed's swap line provided access to liquidity in a manner that was much more attractive than
an IMF loan because it came quickly and without conditions, and was
free of the IMF stigma.

Neither Brazil nor Singapore used their swap, and Mexico drew only
$3.2 billion in April 2009.[48] Some analysts argue, however, that the swaps

did immediately help strengthen the exchange rates of all four countries.[49] In South Korea's case, the impact was particularly significant because it drew on the swap extensively—up to $16.3 billion.[50] The country faced not just a depreciating national currency but also a situation where its banks had enormous problems refinancing dollar denominated debt at the time. The government addressed their dollar shortages through a large infusion of liquidity drawn from the country's foreign exchange reserves, which fell $42 billion between the end of August and the end of December to an overall size of just over $200 billion. In this context, the swap helped restore confidence and the Korean currency soon stabilized by 2009.[51] It is worth noting that South Korea's economy was more "systemically significant" to the world financial system than any of the countries receiving IMF support between the Washington and Pittsburgh summits.

The Fed extended even larger swaps to other regions that were even more systemically significant. Two swap arrangements were created with the European Central Bank (ECB) and Swiss National Bank (SNB) in December 2007. Although their initial limits were $20 billion and $4 billion respectively, these swaps were increased several times until in late September 2008 when they totaled $240 billion (ECB) and $60 billion (SNB). In mid-September 2008, the Fed also established swaps with Bank of England and the Bank of Japan at $40 billion and $60 billion respectively, and their size was quickly doubled at the end of the month. In mid-October, the Fed threw caution to the wind and allowed all four of these swaps to be unlimited in size. In September and October, the Fed also created swaps with the central banks of Australia, Canada, Sweden (each initially capped at $10 billion but increased quickly to $30 billion), Denmark, Norway (each starting at $5 billion but soon enhanced to $15 billion), and New Zealand ($15 billion). All of these swaps expired in February 2010.[52]

These swaps were designed to provide emergency financial assistance during the crisis, but the goal was not to cover balance of payments problems. Instead, they were designed to help foreign authorities provide dollar liquidity to troubled firms and markets within their jurisdictions. Since 2000, many foreign private banks, especially European banks, had accumulated large dollar-denominated assets (including mortgage-backed securities) by borrowing dollars cheaply in short-term markets (or by borrowing short-term funds domestically and converting them to dollars via foreign exchange swaps). When sources of short-term dollar funding dried up as the financial crisis intensified, these banks could not secure necessary funds unless their central banks provided liquidity.[53] If the monetary authority provided liquidity in domestic currency, it would provoke a depreciation of the local currency because the funds would need to be traded for dollars to be useful. Alternatively, the central bank could provide dollars from the country's foreign reserves (as in the Korean case), but those reserves might temporarily illiquid, too small, or even prohibited for use for the purpose (and the move also risked undermining confidence in the country's currency). In this context, borrowing dollars from a Fed swap line was the most attractive option.[54]

When the Fed first raised the idea of a swap with the ECB in August 2007, the latter rejected the proposal. In David Wessel's words, "the plan ran up against a strong effort to pin the Great Panic on the United States".[55] The ECB's go-it-alone attitude at the time had also been apparent when it neglected to notify the Fed in advance of its important announcement on August 9 to provide unlimited funding for banks, a neglect that Tett notes "seriously irritated" the Fed.[56] But as the crisis worsened, the ECB and other foreign central banks began to see the virtue of the Fed's initiative. The Fed swaps were not just accepted but also used extensively as many authorities flooded their domestic markets with liquidity to stem the crisis. Indeed, foreign drawing on all Fed swap lines peaked at almost $600 billion in November and December 2008—far higher than any IMF lending during the crisis. The largest drawers included the ECB (whose top borrowing reached $310 billion), the Bank of Japan ($128 billion), the Bank of England ($95 billion), the SNB ($31 billion), the Reserve Bank of Australia ($27 billion), Sweden's Riksbank ($25 billion), and Denmark's central bank ($20 billion).[57] Not until August 2009 did aggregate drawing on the lines fall below $100 billion. Of these various countries, only Canada and New Zealand did not draw funds from their Fed swaps.[58]

In taking the initiative to create this network of bilateral swaps between 2007 and 2010, the Fed was effectively acting as an international lender-of-last-resort. The experience was very different than that during the Great Depression. Inadequate provision of international liquidity greatly exacerbated the financial stresses of the early 1930s.[59] By contrast, the Fed's bilateral swaps of 2007–2010 helped to ensure that sufficient international liquidity was available in ways that also allowed domestic monetary authorities in all the leading financial centers to provide adequate domestic liquidity to stressed domestic firms and markets.

It is also worth noting that the Fed provided liquidity directly to troubled foreign financial institutions by allowing their US branches and subsidiaries access to its discount window and enormous emergency facilities during the crisis. While the sums involved in the dollar swap lines were more significant, foreign institutions—particularly European banks—did borrow heavily from the Fed's discount window and they received more than half of the funds from Fed facilities such as Term Auction Facility and Commercial Paper Funding Facility.[60] The US Treasury also helped foreign financial institutions by allowing some of the public bailout funds from the Congressionally approved Troubled Asset Relief Program (TARP) to be channeled to them. Considerable portions of the enormous American International Group (AIG) bailout, for example, ended up in the hands of European banks that had been AIG counterparties, such as Société Génerale, Deutsche Bank, Barclays, and UBS.[61]

The Fed was not the only central bank to extend swaps in the crisis. In April 2009, the Fed itself accepted swap arrangements from the ECB, SNB, Bank of England, and Bank of Japan, allowing it access to the currencies they issued in case shortages in the United States emerged. These swaps were never drawn upon.[62] In the European context, the ECB and SNB also created swap facilities for a few nearby countries—Poland (ECB, SNB), Hungary (ECB, SNB), Sweden (ECB), and Denmark (ECB)—that faced potential shortages of euros or Swiss francs, often because loans (such as domestic mortgages) had been denominated in those currencies. But the scale of these swaps was much more limited—$35 billion in aggregate for the ECB and $57 for the SNB—and actual drawings were small.[63]

One month and half after the Fed extended its swap to South Korea, both the Bank of Japan and the People's Bank of China also expanded existing swap lines to the same country (to a level of $20 and $26 billion, respectively), but neither was used.[64] In addition, the Bank of Japan set up small swaps in 2008–09 for India ($3 billion) and Indonesia ($12 billion).[65] The Chinese central bank was more ambitious, signing swaps with eighteen other countries between late 2008 and mid-2012. They included countries across the East Asian region (Australia, Hong Kong, Indonesia, Malaysia, New Zealand, Singapore, Thailand) as well as many countries further afield (Argentina, Belarus, Brazil, Iceland, Kazakhstan, Mongolia, Pakistan, Turkey, UAE, Ukraine, Uzbekistan). Some of these Chinese swaps were designed to help countries cope with financial stress, but many had the primary purpose of promoting bilateral commerce and the greater international use of the RMB for reasons discussed in Chapter 3.[66] Because the RMB was used so little in international markets, it is not surprising that these swaps were not activated, with the single exception of Hong Kong's brief use in 2010 in the face of a squeeze in the RMB market in that territory.[67]

In East Asia, a broader network of bilateral swaps among the central banks of China, Japan, South Korea, and Association of Southeast Asian Nations (ASEAN) countries had also already been created much earlier in 2000 under the Chiang Mai Initiative (CMI) as a response to the 1997–98 East Asian crisis. During the 2008 crisis, however, no country drew on these swaps. The failure of the CMI to be used was striking to those who had seen it as an effort to lessen East Asia's dependence in Western assistance. But one reason for its neglect was quite clear: the CMI included a rule that no more than 20% of its funds could be drawn upon without an IMF program in place. This IMF link had been included to enhance the credibility of the new scheme and reduce the political exposure of creditors such as Japan and China.[68] But because no East Asian country was willing to borrow from the Fund during the crisis, the funds available under CMI were very limited. As one analyst put it, the CMI had been "more symbolic than truly effective."[69]

The international leadership role of US authorities was thus critically important to the international management of the crisis. In Moessner and Allen's words, "it seems likely that had the Fed not acted as it did, global financial instability would have been much more serious, and the recession would consequently have been deeper."[70] The US leadership role reflected the fact that it had a unique ability to produce unlimited amounts of the currency that many people needed because of the dollar's prominent role in international financial markets. This enduring structural power of the United States in global finance—rather than the creation of the G20 leaders' forum—was what underpinned the most important form of international financial cooperation during the crisis.

If US authorities had a unique capacity to act as an international lender-of-last-resort, what explains their willingness to take on this role? Their interest once again reflected more continuity with the past than change: US officials had usually taken a lead role in managing international financial crises in the postwar period. Indeed, the Fed's swap program itself had an important historical precedent. In the 1960s, as a response to growing pressures on the Bretton Woods exchange rate system, the Fed had built a bilateral swap network involving eleven central banks.[71] The aggregate size of the swaps had risen from $2 billion in 1963 to $30 billion by 1978. The swaps fell into disuse after the early 1980s when the IMF assumed the more central role in managing international crises that stemmed from sovereign debt problems in Southern countries.[72] In the context of a crisis centered in industrialized countries and the unwillingness of many Southern countries to borrow from the IMF, the Fed simply revived its swap network diplomacy, albeit with more countries and on a grander scale.

In the past, US authorities were usually motivated to assume a lead role in managing international crises because of concerns about the potential vulnerability of US financial institutions, US markets and/or the dollar to international instability, given their central role within the global financial system. The same kinds of concerns encouraged the US to act decisively in this crisis. For example, in explaining the swap program, a number of analysts have argued that the Fed was particularly concerned about the impact of foreign instability on major US banks. They point to the fact that the countries chosen for swap arrangements were ones where major US banks had the highest loan exposures.[73] McDowell high-lights how the Fed was also concerned about broader systemic risks in the US financial system. If foreign banks did not receive dollar funding, Fed officials were very aware that defaults by those banks on US borrowing would have generated wider financial instability at home at the time. In addition, US officials hoped that the provision of dollars to foreign central banks might discourage foreign banks from demanding dollars in the United States and thus relax dollar funding market pressures at home. Lowering offshore eurodollar interest rates could also affect domestic short rates; indeed, many US contracts (including the majority of US adjustable rate mortgages) were indexed against the London interbank borrowing rate. US officials may have also seen the swaps as a means of containing upward pressure on the dollar after it began to spike in the summer of 2008 (see Chapter 3).[74] The willingness of the US Treasury to allow foreign firms to access American bailout funds reflected similar concerns about domestic financial instability. As Pauly notes, "the first draft of the US bailout plan in the fall of 2008 made US taxpayer funds available to 'American' banks only. That changed within 24 hours, after the US Treasury was reminded that 25% of the US banking system was now controlled by 'foreign' intermediaries."[75]

In short, it was the US capacity and willingness to act as international lender-of-last-resort role that was critical to the international management of the crisis. The significance of its leadership provides one more reason not to overstate the G20's crisis management role. At their first summit, the G20 leaders declared that they were ready "take whatever further actions are necessary to stabilize the financial system," a statement that highlighted their commitment to provide liquidity to distressed firms and markets.[76] But the G20 leaders' forum played no role in organizing the most significant international initiative that allowed national authorities to provide liquidity to their own markets: the creation of the Fed's swaps. All of these swaps were established before the first G20 summit and they resulted from bilateral negotiations between the Fed and foreign central banks. It was US authorities—rather than the G20 forum—that played the key role in ensuring adequate liquidity was available.

At their second summit in London, the G20 leaders applauded themselves for supporting their banking systems not just through liquidity provision but also by recapitalizing financial institutions. It is important to recognize that their cooperation played no role in fostering the key initiatives in that area either. Those initiatives took place one month before their first summit when the United States, Britain, and other European countries injected capital directly into their troubled banks. These recapitalization moves of October 2008 marked a crucial turning point in the management of the crisis, but they reflected unilateral choices rather than cooperation. British Prime Minister Gordon Brown had in fact made extensive efforts in September 2008 to persuade US policymakers of the merits of a cooperative initiative to inject public capital into the banks. When they rejected his overtures, he reluctantly chose to launch this initiative unilaterally. Brown considered the risks of this unilateral approach so high that he told his wife to be prepared to leave the Prime Minister's residence within hours if markets responded badly. When the markets responded positively, other countries quickly followed the British lead.[77]

Failed Global Reform Initiatives

The limitations of the role of the G20 leaders' forum were apparent in one other way. When the Fed swaps expired in February 2010, the South Korean government—as chair of the G20 at the time—urged G20 members to create a more regularized and global swap regime. Rather than simply allow the successful cooperative mechanisms developed during the crisis to lapse, the Korean proposal sought to expand and institutionalize them in a permanent way that was no longer ad hoc or reliant on the goodwill of one country. This initiative was part of broader G20 discussions at the time about how to build a better global "financial safety net" that drew on the lessons of the crisis. But the G20 leaders refused to back the initiative at their Seoul summit in November 2010 and it vanished from the global reform agenda.[78]

While many Southern countries were supportive of the Korean pro-posal, US officials were concerned about the burdens and risks that it might place on the Fed, as the issuer of the main currency that everyone might need.[79] Indeed, even strong supporters of the Fed swaps recognized that there were some risks involved in the lending. One was the sovereign credit risk associated with lending to other central banks. A second was a "moral hazard" problem that the lending—particularly given the absence of conditionality—might encourage irresponsible behavior abroad. Both the Fed and ECB were concerned that any initiative to make their swap lines permanent would exacerbate this problem.[80] As Moessner and Allen put it more generally in discussing proposals to institutionalize swaps, "how could the Federal Reserve be sure that the funds it provided would be used for the purposes intended? Could the funds be used by coun-tries to finance unsustainable domestic policies and postpone necessary macro-economic adjustments? And to make the swap lines conditional, in order to meet this concern, would undermine their purpose, since con-ditional swap lines would not provide the beneficiaries with the required assurance of access to funds in an emergency."[81] To minimize these kinds of problems, Fed officials preferred swaps to be temporary, bilateral, and extended on a discretionary basis. Not until October 2013 did they finally agree to keep in place some swap arrangements indefinitely but they did so then outside of the G20 context and only with a very select group of monetary authorities: the ECB, SNB, the Bank of Canada, the Bank of England, and the Bank of Japan. For everyone else, the Fed would make no future commitments.[82] Indeed, it is noteworthy that the Fed had already rejected requests for a swap from at least one G20 member—Indonesia—in early 2009. When India requested a swap in October 2012, Fed officials were also very reluctant to discuss the idea.[83]

The political difficulties involved in creating a global swap regime were apparent on a smaller scale in the East Asia region, where coun-tries reformed the CMI in the wake of the crisis. After detailed negotia-tions, CMI members transformed their network of bilateral swaps into a self-managed multilateral fund that opened in March 2010 with $120 billion (doubled to $240 billion in June 2012) under the name of CMI

Multilateralization (CMIM) and that was now backed by a new regional surveillance mechanism. This initiative appeared to represent a strengthened swap regime, but it had some key limitations. Loans would now be decided by the members as a whole according to a weighted voting system and most of the funds were still available only with an IMF program (the portion available was raised from 20% to 30% in June 2012 and will rise to 40% in 2014). In other words, the CMIM was missing key attractive features of the Fed swaps, such as their automaticity and lack of conditionality. Because of these features, critics argued that CMIM was unlikely to be used and that "in the event of another crisis, it would be back to a series of ad hoc bilateral swaps or the much-maligned IMF."[84]

That same status quo outcome existed at the global level as well. The failure of Korea's G20 initiative to institutionalize the Fed swap regime meant that the G20 failed to create a permanent legacy from the most significant cooperative initiative in crisis management during the crisis. Because Fed decisions would presumably continue to be driven primarily by considerations of US interests, the access of future crisis-afflicted countries to these swaps would remain ad hoc and uncertain, outside of a very select few monetary authorities that the Fed committed to October 2013.[85] This situation may encourage further mini-multilateral initiatives of the CMIM kind.

For example, at an informal meeting in advance of the June 2012 G20 summit, the leaders of the BRICS countries (Brazil, Russia, India, China, and South Africa) declared that they "discussed swap arrangements among national currencies as well as reserve pooling" and asked their finance ministers and central bank governors to work on the issue. At their March 2013 summit meeting, they declared that their officials had "concluded that the establishment of a self-managed contingent reserve arrangement would have a positive precautionary effect, help BRICS countries forestall short-term liquidity pressures, provide mutual support and further strengthen financial stability." They directed their finance ministers and central banks to work toward the creation of an arrangement with an initial size of $100 billion that they argued would "contribute to strengthening the global financial safety net and complement existing international arrangements as an additional line of defence."[86] When they met in September ahead of the formal opening of the G20 leaders meeting in St. Petersburg, they announced that plans for creating a $100 billion "Contingent Reserve Arrangement" were progressing with China agreeing to contribute $41 billion, while Brazil, India and Russia contributed $18 billion each and South Africa gave $5 billion.[87] Few other details were released and the negotiation of this arrangement will raise many of the same issues that the CMIM has faced.

As an alternative, the IMF's lending capacity could have been strengthened in a way that ensured that the Fed's initiatives left a more lasting legacy in global financial governance. In December 2008, a creative proposal of this kind was advanced by Edwin Truman, who worked briefly in the US Treasury during the early Obama administration. Truman was concerned the extensive Fed swap program was undermining the IMF's crisis management role and encouraging "the development of regional, lower-conditionality substitutes for the IMF, which is not healthy for the longer run." To restore the IMF's centrality, he suggested that the IMF's charter be amended to allow it to swap SDRs for unlimited amounts of dollars for up to two years with the Federal Reserve (and other central banks issuing national currencies used extensively in international financial markets). With these funds, the IMF would be able to "centralize the responsibility and risk of extending the type of liquidity support that the Federal Reserve has been providing to other central banks over the past 12 months...and that other central banks such as the Swiss National Bank (SNB) and the European Central Bank (ECB) have been providing on a much smaller scale as well." He continued: "This authority would help to support the central role of the IMF in the international financial system and discourage countries from setting up bilateral or regional arrangements in order to bypass IMF policy conditionality."[88]

Truman reiterated his proposal during the 2010 debates about a global financial safety net.[89] To be implemented, his initiative would have required US Congressional support to approve both an amendment to the IMF Articles of Agreement and the Fed's authority to engage swaps with the Fund. It is not surprising that the initiative went nowhere given the concerns generated within the United States by the provision of support to foreigners during the 2008 crisis. Even on the Fed's Federal Open Market Committee, one member—William Poole—had opposed offering swaps to the ECB and SNB in December 2007 on the grounds that foreign central banks had adequate dollar reserves to satisfy domestic needs.[90] The fact that some AIG bailout funds ended up paying off foreign counterparties of the failed firm also generated controversy in Congress. In July 2009, Democratic Congressman Alan Grayson grilled Fed Chair Ben Bernanke more generally about why the Fed was lending so actively to foreigners—as far away as New Zealand—given the pressing needs at home. This kind of sentiment only grew when detailed figures about the extent of Fed support for foreign banks were revealed in late 2010. Members of Congress such as independent senator Bernie Sanders expressed surprise about the "huge sums of money going to bail out large foreign banks" and he asked: "Has the Federal Reserve of the United States become the central bank of the world?"[91] Much of the consternation also came from conservative Republicans who had long opposed the IMF's international lending. Indeed, concerns about Fed's international lending encouraged longtime Fed critic Ron Paul, with the support of most Republicans, to push for greater permanent transparency of its activities.[92]

Other less ambitious proposals involving the IMF were also put forward during the 2010 discussions about a global financial safety net. In March of that year, IMF staff suggested the creation of "Multicountry Swap Line mechanism" in the Fund that could be activated temporarily "to *offer* financial assistance to systemic countries with good fundamentals that face short-term liquidity pressures during systemic events."[93] As they put it, "such a mechanism would play a similar and, possibly, complementary role to that played by the Fed and other central banks at the height of the recent crisis. In fact, given the ad hoc nature of central bank swap lines, and uncertainty about the breadth of their availability in the future, a predictable multilateral framework for handling future systemic crises could help mitigate demand for self-insurance in good times."[94] When the issue was discussed at the IMF executive board in April, however, a number of countries "had reservations about publicly identifying a set of qualified countries, and many expressed concerns about the operational complexity of such an instrument and its uncertain resource requirements."[95]

In June, the IMF staff proposal was refined around the concept of a "global stabilization mechanism" (GSM) that could be activated by majority vote in the Fund's board during a systemic crisis. In addition to enabling new IMF lending, the GSM would trigger Fund coordination "with monetary authorities and regional financing arrangements to put in place a multilayered web of bilateral swaps, and regional and Fund lending."[96] The GSM was supported by the British and French governments, but German officials were concerned that it would undermine policy discipline by making access to loans too easy.[97] Even more politically problematic was the idea that the IMF would play some kind of coordinating role vis-à-vis central bankers. As Suominen notes, the Fed and other central banks were "unlikely to want to relinquish their authority over swap lines to the finance-minister-run IMF."[98] In their Seoul summit in November, the G20 leaders welcomed the IMF's creation of a new "Precautionary Credit Line" (PCL) in August, but the idea of an IMF role in coordinating central bank swaps was dropped.

Even if the proposals of either Truman or the IMF staff had been supported by the United States and European governments, they would have encountered the enduring resistance of many Southern governments to IMF borrowing. Indeed, during its first year of operation, only one PCL arrangement was created (with Macedonia), prompting the IMF to replace the scheme with yet another one—the Precautionary and Liquidity Line—in November 2011. As IMF staff acknowledged that month, the limited interest in both the FCL (created in March 2009) and PCL likely reflected not just features of these programs but also "ongoing concerns regarding stigma" and "a preference for self insurance through reserves."[99]

To be sure, the G20 made some further efforts to increase trust in the Fund among Southern countries through more governance reforms. At their Seoul summit in late 2010, the G20 leaders committed to double IMF quotas and backed reforms that would see a shift of roughly 6% of voting shares to emerging market and developing countries (with China's share alone increasing from 4% to 6.39%, leaving it in third place). As part of this deal, European chairs on the Executive Board would also be reduced by two to make room for more emerging market and developing country representatives. But as of early 2014, US Congress had yet to approve the new reforms, despite the fact that they were meant to be ratified in late 2012. Needless to say, the situation has done little to enhance the popularity of the Fund among potential borrowers in Southern countries.

CONCLUSION

It is far from clear that the G20's reputation as a successful global crisis manager is deserved with respect to the financial dimensions of the management of the crisis. The high-profile summits and the G20 leaders' apparent willingness to cooperate may have contributed in a general way to boosting confidence.[100] But it is certainly an exaggeration to give the G20's primary credit for preventing another Great Depression. Although some analysts credit the G20 with marshalling national macroeconomic stimulus programs in 2008–09, these programs more reflected distinct national choices emerging in response to domestic pressures in the context of global economic crisis. Their temporal congruence across leading powers reflected the simultaneous and global nature of the economic shock rather than successful economic cooperation.

The significance of the G20's $1.1 trillion rescue plan is also easily overstated. Some of the funds were not new money, while others were not available until after the crisis had subsided. The largest portion of the funds—that given to the IMF—also remained unused in the immediate months following the London summit because of limited demand for the Fund's loans.[101] The ability of many Southern countries to stimulate their economies did not rest on their access to Fund lending, but rather on the fact that they accumulated reserves during the pre-crisis years as a way of distancing themselves from the Fund.

Perhaps the most important reason to question the narrative about the G20's importance is that it had no hand in fostering the key international initiative in the financial management of the crisis: the Fed swaps of 2007–2010. Through its bilateral swap program, the Fed played an important international lender-of-last-resort role, providing critical international emergency assistance to many countries. The capacity of US authorities to play this leadership role reflected the dollar's dominant standing in the global financial system. Their willingness to lead also stemmed from their country's centrality in the system, a position that generated concerns about the potential vulnerability of US financial institutions, markets, and the dollar to instability abroad. Although the scale of the Fed's activities was unprecedented, both the US capacity and its willingness to take a lead role in managing the international dimensions of the crisis were reminiscent of the handling of previous postwar international financial crisis. This continuity in global financial governance—rather than the innovation of the G20's leaders' forum—was critical in explaining the successful international financial management of the crisis.

After the crisis, the G20's international financial reform agenda has also done little to change this status quo. The Korean initiative within the G20 to create a multilateral swap regime that built on the Fed's crisis activities failed. Truman's innovative proposal to empower the IMF to take on the role the Fed had played also went nowhere, as did less ambitious IMF staff proposals. The G20's efforts to restore trust of potential Southern borrowers in the Fund's lending role remained largely unfulfilled. Reticence from US (and often European) policymakers has blocked serious reform in most of these cases. The consequence is that the crisis management dimensions of global financial governance will likely continue to rely heavily on ad hoc US leadership.

There is one final aspect of the management of the crisis that this chapter has neglected: the absence of a dollar crisis. The US financial meltdown unfolded at a moment when the country had become unusually dependent on foreign capital inflows to fund large current account deficits. In this context, many policymakers and analysts worried that the crisis might generate a loss of foreign confidence in US investments and downward pressure on the US dollar. A collapse in the greenback's value would have greatly exacerbated the global crisis because of the dollar's role as a dominant international currency. In addition to causing greater global instability, it might have forced the US Federal Reserve to hike US interest rates dramatically (as it had in 1979 when faced with a dollar crisis), contributing further to the country's domestic financial upheaval and the world's financial troubles. US authorities would also have encountered greater difficulties in financing the massive bailouts and fiscal stimulus programs.

This disaster scenario did not materialize for reasons explored in Chapter 3: the support provided to the dollar by private investors and a number of foreign governments. The support of foreign governments was particularly interesting because it reveals another international dimension of the official management of the crisis. Interestingly, it is a dimension never mentioned by those who trumpet the role of the G20's crisis management role. The reason is straightforward. Foreign official support for the dollar emerged out of set of uncoordinated and unilateral government choices rather than any kind of G20-led international cooperation. This fact only reinforces the need for skepticism about claims of the G20's centrality in preventing a repetition of the Great Depression.

Was the Dollar's Global Role Undermined?

At the start of the crisis, many analysts and scholars predicted that the dollar's position as the dominant international currency would be severely challenged by the global financial crisis. If these predictions had been borne out, the crisis would indeed have revolutionized global financial governance. Throughout the entire post–World War II period, the dollar has been the foundation of the world monetary system. A serious challenge to this foundation would have had enormous consequences for both the United States and the world as a whole.

The predictions were understandable. As the first section of this chapter describes, scholars were already arguing before the crisis that foreign confidence in the dollar's global role was increasingly precarious. The fact that the 2008 crisis was then centered in US markets only heightened concerns that there might be a sudden flight from the dollar. In the end, however, these concerns were entirely misplaced. Rather than collapse in value, the dollar appreciated dramatically at the height of the crisis. The crisis not only failed to shatter confidence in the dollar but also highlighted the centrality of the dollar within the global financial system.

The second and third sections of this chapter describe how new challenges to the dollar's international role subsequently appeared in the wake of the crisis. Many policymakers and analysts around the world began to express in quite explicit ways their dissatisfaction with the existing dollar-centered international monetary and to propose reforms such as a strengthening of the reserve function of the International Monetary Fund (IMF)'s Special Drawing Rights (SDRs) and the greater internationalization of other existing currencies. It soon became clear, however, important political barriers stood in the way of significant challenges to the dollar's global role. In the end, then, neither the crisis nor the post-crisis reform discussions did much to undermine the dollar's status as the world's dominant currency. Indeed, if anything, they showed very effectively key reasons why the dollar remains at the top of the world's currency pyramid.

THE SURPRISING ABSENCE OF A DOLLAR CRISIS

Just before the outbreak of the global financial crisis, the position of the US dollar as the world's preeminent currency was clear. Its status as the leading international medium of exchange was apparent from the fact that the dollar was used on one side of 85.6% of all foreign exchange transactions. Its two nearest rivals, the euro and the yen, were well behind at 37% and 17.2% respectively.[1] As an international store of value, the dollar also comprised 64% of the foreign exchange reserves held by governments, while the euro's share was just 26.5% and the yen's was below 5%. The dollar was also used much more extensively as a unit of account to denominate international trade than any other currency, with more than half of all exports invoiced in dollars. More countries pegged their currency to the dollar than any other as well.[2] The only areas where the dollar was seriously challenged by the euro were in its share of cross-border bank claims (41.9% vs. 39.6% for the euro) and outstanding international securities issues (36% vs. 47.3% for the euro). In those two areas, the yen was far behind (3.4% and 2.7%).[3]

Why a Dollar Crisis Was Expected

When the global financial crisis began, most of the initial predictions about challenges to the dollar's international role rested on an assumption that the crisis would provoke a collapse in the value of the dollar.

Even before the outbreak of the 2008 crisis, there had been growing questions about the dollar's strength. The large current account deficits of the United States, combined with its growing external debt, had raised serious concerns about foreign confidence in the greenback. There was widespread speculation that foreign creditors of the United States might soon withdraw their funding, generating a "financial meltdown in the dollar" and a "hard landing" for the United States as a whole.[4]

The creation of the euro in 1999 contributed to the predictions of an impending dollar crisis because it appeared to present the dollar with its first serious challenger for international currency status in the postwar period. Analysts argued that the euro was a particularly attractive alternative reserve asset to investors because it was issued by a central bank that was constitutionally protected from political influence and dedicated to price stability, unlike the US Fed. The euro was also backed by an economic zone of a size comparable to that of the US. In addition, euro assets could be held in European financial markets whose combined size rivaled that of their American counterparts. For all these reasons, at the very moment that the US financial crisis began in the fall of 2007, analysts were noting how the euro was rapidly becoming "ever more global."[5]

Analysts also noted the growing dependence of the US dollar on potentially fickle support from foreign governments.[6] Approximately half of the US current account deficit between 2002 and 2007 had been financed by foreign governments through holdings of US dollar assets, particularly Treasury bills and the bonds issued by the two US government-sponsored mortgage lending agencies, Fannie Mae and Freddie Mac ("Fannie and Freddie").[7] Some of the large official dollar holders were close US allies such as Japan and the Gulf states. But others, such as Russia and China, were potential geopolitical rivals. Indeed, at the time that the crisis broke out, China's foreign exchange reserves had become the world's largest, at more than $1.5 trillion (of which approximately 70% to 80% were in dollar-denominated assets). The costs to these governments of holding large dollar reserves were also growing in the context of the dollar's depreciation since 2002. In China's case, each 10% decline in the value of the US dollar generated a loss equivalent to approximately 3% of China's gross domestic product (GDP).[8]

As the costs of reserve holdings rose, some analysts worried that one foreign government might be tempted to sell first in order to minimize its losses before others made the same move. This collective action problem might then trigger a herd-like selling of dollars. The prospects of disorderly dumping of the dollars were said to be enhanced further by the absence of close ties and intergovernmental networks of officials among the main reserve holders as well as between them and the United States.[9] Others speculated that foreign governments might consider strategic reserve selling as a weapon to achieve political goals, as had sometimes been done in the past.[10] Indeed, just before the crisis, Johnson highlighted how Russian officials were already reducing their large dollar reserves as part of a broader distancing from US foreign policy.[11] Others speculated that some key Middle East dollar reserve holders might make similar moves because of dissatisfaction with US foreign policy toward their region.[12]

In the summer of 2007, Chinese analysts also discussed whether their country's enormous dollar reserves could be used as a "bargaining chip" with the United States.[13] US pressure on China to appreciate its exchange rate policy was intensifying at that time. Encouraged by the United States, the IMF had voted in June 2007 to strengthen its exchange rate surveillance, a move that was widely seen as directed at China. Chinese authorities had unsuccessfully opposed the decision in a rare vote of the Executive Board, and the episode had left deep resentments among many Chinese policymakers.[14]

In light of these kinds of considerations, it is not surprising that some scholars had predicted just before the outbreak of the global financial crisis that a major US recession or financial upheaval could act as a "spark" for a withdrawal from US dollar investments.[15] When a massive US financial crisis did actually break out, these fears intensified. Given that the United States was at the epicenter of the financial turmoil, it seemed plausible that the financial crisis would provoke a loss of confidence in US financial assets and the dollar. As US policymakers responded to the

crisis with dramatic interest rate cuts and larger fiscal deficits, the likelihood of this outcome only seemed to grow.

Predictions of a dollar crisis were widespread during the global financial crisis, particularly in its early phases. The media widely reported fears
in the markets about a collapse of confidence in the dollar in late 2007
and early 2008.[16] Top policymakers, such as US Treasury Secretary Hank
Paulson, also worried about this scenario throughout much of 2008.[17]
Prominent investors such as George Soros, too, anticipated a flight from
the dollar and the end of the dollar's dominant role as an international
currency.[18]

Scholars noted other political reasons why China might choose to
withdraw its financial support for the United States. At the time the
financial crisis began, Chinese policymakers were facing growing domestic criticism for the poor performance of US investments. These criticisms
mounted in the early stages of the crisis when US interest rates were cut
dramatically and investments by China's sovereign wealth fund in the
United States lost money.[19] Historians such as Harold James also wondered whether Chinese authorities might question the desirability of
continuing to support a global financial system in which the key institutions were US controlled. He also speculated about whether Chinese officials might see the crisis in broader political terms as a moment to exact
some revenge for the US treatment of East Asia a decade earlier: "might
not 2008 be a payback for the American bungling of the 1997–1998 East
Asian crisis?"[20]

The latter concern was intensified by the fact that the United States
responded to its own crisis with much more lenient policy measures—
such as low interest rates, expansionary fiscal policies, bank bailouts—
than it had demanded of East Asia a decade earlier. Prominent Asian
analysts such as Andrew Sheng noted the contrast: "everything that is
being done to deal with the current crisis is exactly what the Washington
Consensus told us that we should not do during the Asian crisis."[21]
Indeed, some top US officials who had been involved in managing the
East Asian crisis, such as Tim Geithner, even acknowledged the double standard: "There have been moments, certainly, when I understood

better some of the reactions of officials in crisis countries now than one was able to from the outside at the time. It is easier to be for more radical solutions when one lives thousands of miles away than when it is one's own country."[22]

Private Support

In the end, the fears of a dollar crisis were misplaced. Indeed, as the financial crisis became more severe in the second half of 2008, the dollar even strengthened, appreciating as sharply as at any moment since the introduction of floating exchange rates in 1973.[23] In explaining what they call the "surprising" appreciation of the dollar in the second half of 2008, McCauley and McGuire highlight the importance of the heightened international private demand for dollars in this period.[24] As during other postwar international financial crises, investors flocked to US Treasury bills as a kind of safe haven in the storm.[25] Given that the crisis was centered in the United States, it may seem odd that US government debt was perceived as a safer asset during the crisis than others. But the US Treasury bill market was one of the few financial markets that remained liquid and continued to operate smoothly during the crisis. This asset was also backed by the full force of the world's dominant geopolitical and economic power.[26] As Reinhart and Rogoff put it, "world investors viewed other countries as even riskier than the United States and bought Treasury securities copiously."[27]

The dollar's safe haven status also benefitted from the failure of the euro to inspire more confidence at this time. The euro was not helped by the fact that European financial markets were not yet fully integrated and that no central equivalent existed to the uniquely liquid and deep US Treasury bill market because of the absence of a single European fiscal authority. At the end of September 2008, the largest category of outstanding euro-denominated government securities ($1.8 trillion) had been issued by the Italian government, whose fiscal policies did not inspire enormous market confidence. The second largest involved German government securities (at $1.4 trillion) but they were much less liquid than US government securities (which totaled $7.3 trillion) because of a relatively underdeveloped secondary market.[28]

A second problem facing the euro related to its governance. When European countries had committed to the monetary union in the 1991 Maastricht Treaty, they had failed to specify clear procedures for the prevention and resolution of Eurozone financial crises. The consequence of this design flaw quickly became apparent during the crisis. As noted in the last chapter, many European financial institutions were deeply exposed to the subprime crisis because they had been large purchasers of US securities and were deeply involved in US financial markets before the crisis. In the absence of clear rules about bailouts, eurozone governments responded in unilateral ways to the distress facing individual financial institutions in their territories. Seeing the lack of coordination, financial analysts quickly wondered whether European financial integration could unravel and whether Eurozone unity itself might be threatened.[29] Even before the outbreak of the European sovereign debt crises in early 2010, flaws in the euro's governance structure were thus revealed in ways that called into question the broader political credibility of the whole initiative and undermined the euro's ability to compete with the dollar for investor confidence.

The dollar's value was also boosted by several other developments in private markets that were linked to the global importance of US financial markets. Because of their large dollar borrowing to fund the accumulation of dollar assets since 2000, many foreign banks (especially in Europe) required dollars to fund their positions at the height of the crisis. When interbank and other wholesale short-term financial markets froze, the intense demand for dollars in this context of shortage contributed to the currency's appreciation. Also important was the fact that non-US banks and institutional investors had to purchase dollars to square their books and meet collateral needs as the value of their dollar assets suddenly deteriorated during the crisis. In addition, the dollar's value was boosted by the unwinding of trades in which investors had borrowed dollars to invest in higher-yielding instruments in foreign currencies.[30]

Foreign Official Support

The dollar's strength during the crisis resulted from the decisions of not just private investors but also foreign governments that refrained from dumping their large dollar holdings. While some governments did draw down their reserves somewhat to cope with the crisis, Gallagher and Shrestha note many emerging market countries actually increased the size of their official reserves between 2007 and 2009, with growth being particularly large in countries such as Brazil (29.2%), Chile (42.8%). Thailand (56.9%), and China (56.9%).[31] Because of the scale of its reserves, China's decisions were particularly important. At the very height of the crisis in mid-September 2008, US officials received assurances from the top Chinese leadership that they were preventing their own officials and financial institutions from selling US investments.[32] Indeed, from 2007 to 2009, China's stash of overall reserves grew enormously from $1.528 trillion to $2.399 trillion.[33] China thus acted as a stabilizer rather than a destabilizer during the crisis.

Foreign official support for the United States came not just in the form of reserve holdings of US government debt and "agency" bonds. Sovereign wealth funds (SWFs) from countries such as China, Singapore, and the Gulf states also helped to recapitalize US financial institutions directly during the crisis, especially in its first phase. Indeed, Herman Schwartz notes: "Ironically, developing-country SWFs provided the U.S. financial firms with more money—$24.8 billion—in the last quarter of 2007 than the IMF ever lent in any single quarter to bail out troubled LDCs."[34] Some Western analysts had worried that these politically controlled investment funds might "increase the fragility of cooperation in global finance."[35] In the end, however, these firms played an important role in boosting global financial stability.

Why did China and other foreign governments continue to support the United States during the crisis? To answer this question, it is useful to recall why they had accumulated dollar reserves during the immediate pre-crisis years.[36] Part of the rapid reserve growth took place in countries benefitting from a post-2002 commodity price boom. Another key development was already discussed in Chapter 2: reserve accumulation in many developing countries was driven by a desire for "self-insurance." In many countries, the political prominence of this goal reflected a reaction to the 1997–98 financial crises in emerging market countries. In the case of China specifically, self-insurance was also linked more broadly to the protection of security and social stability in the context of the opening of the Chinese economy to a potentially volatile world. Because of its domestic political and economic challenges, the Chinese leadership was particularly risk-averse in this respect.[37]

Why hold these reserves in dollars? One reason was that dollars were the dominant currency used in international financial markets and international trade, and thus they were the key for intervention purposes. Like private investors, foreign governments were also attracted to investing reserve assets in dollars because of the unique depth, liquidity, and security of US financial markets, especially the market for US Treasury securities.[38] In the case of close US allies such as Japan and the Gulf states, many analysts have also linked support for the dollar to these countries' security dependence on the United States.[39]

In some countries, the accumulation of dollar reserves was also designed to serve export-led development strategies. By purchasing dollars to keep their country's exchange rate low, governments could bolster the competitiveness of national exporters. The recycling of reserves into dollar assets also helped keep their major export market—the United States—economically buoyant. Analysts drew a parallel to the strategy of many Western European countries and Japan during the 1960s when they built up dollar holdings in the 1960s to protect export-led growth under the Bretton Woods exchange rate system. This "Bretton Woods II" interpretation thus saw reserve growth more of a by-product of export-oriented growth strategies than as a goal in and of itself driven by self-insurance motivations.[40]

Some scholars also have also identified the domestic interests in the reserve accumulating countries that benefitted from these arrangements and supported the policy. For example, Steinberg and Shih show how China's exchange rate policy during 2003–08 was strongly influenced by Chinese interest groups in export industries.[41] Vermeiren also argues that support for reserve accumulation in China came from the country's powerful state-owned enterprises (SOEs) that benefitted from the investment-led, export-dependent growth model and its associated financial repression.[42] Similarly, Hung notes the "symbiotic relation" between the Chinese coastal elite and Wall Street financial interests, the latter benefitting from the recycling of Chinese surpluses through American financial markets.[43] In explaining China's pre-crisis reserve accumulation, Schwartz points more generally to the interests of the Community Party elite who derived private profits from their control—or their children's control—of export industries, while deflecting to the mass Chinese public the costs of supporting the US (e.g., losses on dollar holdings, inflationary pressures from sterilizing the enormous reserves).[44] That elite also faced fewer challenges to their rule by maintaining high levels of growth and employment through support for the Bretton Woods II arrangement.

Continuity in Foreign Official Preferences

Given these various motivations for the accumulation of the dollar reserves before the crisis, it is easier to see why the crisis did not lead to a foreign pullout, as many of these motivations for dollar reserve accumulation were in fact reinforced by the crisis. This was certainly the case with the self-insurance rationale for reserve holdings. The global financial meltdown represented a moment when the war chest of reserves was finally proving its worth as a bulwark against external instability. Rather than dumping reserves, governments sought to preserve and even increase them. The appeal of self-insurance as an economic strategy was also greatly enhanced by the fact that developing countries that had accumulated large reserves appeared better equipped to cope with the crisis than those that had not.

Like private investors, official reserve holders were also discouraged from switching their dollar holdings to euros by the instability of the Eurozone and the lack of an equivalent euro product to US Treasury securities. As one Chinese official, Luo Ping, put it in early 2009 when explaining why China continued to buy US Treasury bills during the crisis: "Except for US Treasuries, what can you hold?...US Treasuries are the safe haven. For everyone, including China, it is the only option.... Once you start issuing $1 trillion-$2 trillion...we know the dollar is going to depreciate, so we hate you guys but there is nothing much we can do."[45]

Turning to the Bretton Woods II story, foreign governments whose economies were heavily dependent on exports to the United States—particularly China—also faced strong incentives to maintain and even increase dollar reserves during the crisis. With the global economic downturn, countries were more concerned than ever to keep their major foreign market afloat financially and to prevent exchange rate appreciation from undermining the competitiveness of their export sector. As Schwartz put it, "steering a different course would have required painful changes in the domestic political structures of U.S. foreign creditors."[46]

China, for example, stopped the gradual appreciation of the renminbi (RMB) in July 2008 and kept its exchange rate pegged to the dollar until mid-2010. Indeed, Chinese leaders were often quite explicit about their concerns about social unrest stemming from unemployment in the export factories. As Premier Wen Jiabao put it in 2010, "if the yuan is not stable, it will bring disaster to China and the world. If we increase the yuan by 20 per cent or 40 per cent...many of our factories will shut down and society will be in turmoil."[47] Some scholars initially wondered whether the crisis might provoke China's leadership to radically reconsider the benefits of their export-oriented development model in favor of a more inward-oriented approach that was less vulnerable to the unstable global economy.[48] The government's massive fiscal stimulus program announced just before the first G20 summit in November 2008 appeared at first to be an initiative that might have this intention. In fact, however, the content of the program continued to promote the same investment-led, export-dependent model growth as well as the interests of the SOEs and export sector linked to it.[49]

What about the danger identified by analysts before the crisis that reserve holding countries might generate a run on the dollar through unilateral dumping because of collective problems? This danger was minimized by the problems of the euro, the desire for self-insurance, and concerns about the need to maintain export competitiveness during the crisis. The latter motivation deserves particular attention since it highlights how the collective action problem could even be reversed. Many exporting countries continued to support the dollar during the crisis because they did not want to see their exchange rate rise in ways that would undermine the competitiveness of their exports vis-à-vis those of China. As Setser puts it, "as long as China limited the RMB's appreciation, any country that allowed its currency to appreciate against the RMB paid a price."[50] The Bretton Woods II logic, in other words, trumped any collective action problems that might have encouraged individual reserve holding countries to dump reserves for short-term financial gain.

The risk of a deliberate selling of dollar reserves to achieve more strategic goals also deserves some discussion. This possibility was remote for large reserve holding countries that were close US allies. But in his memoirs of the crisis, US Treasury Secretary Hank Paulson notes that he received a "deeply troubling" report in the summer of 2008 that Russian authorities tried to encourage their Chinese counterparts to sell their Fannie and Freddie bonds jointly in order to force the United States to prop up the companies.[51] Russian and Chinese authorities had purchased large sums of these agency bonds before the financial crisis under the assumption that they were implicitly backed by the US government, despite repeated denials from US officials.[52] When Fannie and Freddie's financial problems mounted in mid-2008, these foreign authorities became increasingly worried about whether the US would indeed bail the firms out. Indeed, prominent Chinese analysts such as Yu Yongding were warning at the time: "If the U.S. government allows Fannie and Freddie to fail and international investors are not compensated adequately, the consequences will be catastrophic....If it is not the end of the world, it is the end of the current international financial system."[53]

In the end, Chinese and Russian officials were reassured when the United States placed Fannie and Freddie under a public conservatorship in early September (even though the US officials still refused to provide an explicit guarantee of the agencies' debts, despite Chinese pressure[54]). Even before this decision, however, Paulson reports that the Chinese government had already rebuffed the Russian initiative. China's unwillingness to dump its dollars no doubt reflected not just the factors previously mentioned but also the fact that the country already had so much invested in dollar assets. In this context, any effort to diversify its reserves out of dollars risked triggering market reactions that undercut the value of its remaining investments. With Chinese claims on the United States equal to approximately one-third of the Chinese GDP near the start of the crisis, China found itself in a "dollar trap" with its economic well-being tied up with that of the United States.[55] As Premier Wen put it in March 2009, "we have lent a huge amount of money to the U.S. Of course we are concerned about the safety of our assets. To be honest, I am definitely a little worried."[56]

The fact that China and other foreign official dollar holders had many reasons to continue to support the dollar meant that the United States itself did not have to work too hard to cultivate this outcome. To be sure, if the United States had closed off its markets to foreign exports, foreigners might have reconsidered their support for the dollar.[57] Foreign official creditors were also supportive of US decisions such as the rescues of Bear Stearns and American International Group (AIG) and the introduction of the Troubled Asset Relief Program (TARP), even though those decisions were taken primarily with US domestic considerations in mind.[58] A more explicit effort to avoid antagonizing its major creditor was the US support for the burying of an IMF report criticizing Chinese exchange rate policy at the height of crisis in September 2008, a report that stemmed directly from the 2007 decision that had so frustrated the Chinese.[59] US officials also made efforts throughout the crisis to keep in touch with their major foreign official creditors, encouraging their investments in US troubled financial institutions and welcoming support for the dollar.[60] In general, though, it is striking how foreign official support for the dollar emerged less a product of international political cooperation than of unilateral decisions of creditor states. As Setser puts it, "there has been little coordination between debtors and creditors in the crisis…Nor did emerging market governments explicitly coordinate their lending to the United States."[61]

Many of the reasons why foreigners chose to support the dollar were linked to what Susan Strange called the broader "structural power" of the United States in global political economy.[62] This power derived from factors such as the attractiveness of its financial markets, its importance as a destination for foreign exports, its geopolitical dominance, and foreigners' vulnerability to the "dollar trap." Of course, foreigners still had important agency within this structural context. The decision of the Chinese leadership to maintain an outward-oriented development strategy was particularly important. So too were the preferences of many governments for self-insurance and European governments' inability to respond cooperatively to financial distress in the Eurozone. But the absence of a dollar crisis reflected in large part the fact that market actors and creditor states—acting in an uncoordinated manner—made choices within this broader structural environment of US power.

Foreign support for the dollar ensured that America's financial crisis unfolded in a very different manner than crises experienced by many emerging market countries over the previous two decades. Like many of those countries, the US financial bubble of the pre-crisis years had been fueled in part by inflows of foreign capital. When bubbles burst in previous emerging market crises, foreign (and domestic) investors withdrew their funds, triggering exchange rate crises that only exacerbated financial turmoil in these countries. In the US case, the opposite phenomenon occurred: instead of fleeing US investments and the dollar, foreigners plowed into them as the US financial crisis became more severe, thereby lending important support to the country in its time of need. Ricardo Hausman summed up the distinctive US position well in late 2008: "the US has become the only remaining super-borrower, able to issue thousands of billions of dollars in debt at record low rates while the dollar strengthens. People are unwilling to lend to almost anybody except for the US Treasury. This has allowed the US to provide—at record low cost— about $5,000bn (£3,325bn, €3,700bn) to bail out its financial system and organise a Keynesian reflation of its economy."[63]

THE LIMITED STRENGTHENING OF THE SDR

Although the crisis itself did not generate a dollar collapse, new potential challenges to the dollar's international position quickly emerged in its wake. The crisis experience prompted many foreign policymakers, and even some Americans, to openly question whether their countries—and the world as a whole—were well served by the dollar-centered international monetary system. This dissatisfaction generated various initiatives to promote alternative international currencies to the dollar. It quickly became clear, however, that each possible challenge faced many daunting political obstacles. Dislodging the dollar from its top perch in the global currency pyramid was more easily said than done.

Zhou's Proposal

One of the most prominent early expressions of dissatisfaction with the dollar's international role came from the Chinese central bank governor Zhou Xiaochuan. On March 23, 2009, just in advance of the second G20 leaders summit, Zhou published a short four-page paper titled "Reform the International Monetary System."[64] Although the paper did not in fact mention the dollar explicitly, Zhou's target was clear.

In his view, the crisis and its spread across the entire world had demonstrated "the inherent vulnerabilities and systemic risks in the existing international monetary system." Invoking the Triffin dilemma of the 1960s, Zhou argued that "issuing countries of reserve currencies are constantly confronted with the dilemma between achieving their domestic monetary policy goals and meeting other countries' demand for reserve currencies." A better system, he suggested, would be based on "an international reserve currency that is disconnected from individual nations and is able to remain stable in the long run." Such a "super-sovereign" reserve currency could be "anchored to a stable benchmark and issued according to a clear set of rules" in order to allow global liquidity to be managed more effectively and in a manner "disconnected from economic conditions and sovereign interests of any single country."[65]

Zhou noted how the idea of international reserve currency was not new. John Maynard Keynes had unsuccessfully promoted it during the Bretton Woods negotiations. In 1969, the IMF had also created the Special Drawing Right (SDR) as a supranational reserve asset to address the Triffin dilemma. Zhou noted, however, that the SDR's subsequent use had been inhibited by "limitations on its allocation and the scope of its uses."[66] Indeed, allocations of SDRs could be approved only with the support of IMF members with 85% of votes, and this approval had been granted only in 1970–72 and 1979–81, bringing the total cumulative amount to SDR 21.4 billion, or less than 1% of the world's non-gold official reserves by 2008.

The SDR's usefulness was also undermined by the fact that it was used only in very limited ways to settle accounts among IMF member governments and with the IMF. Because a private market for SDRs did not exist (and private holding of official SDRs was not permitted), the SDR could not be used directly for market intervention purposes or the provision of liquidity to private actors. For these purposes, member governments had to exchange SDRs for national currencies with another government either via a voluntary trading scheme or via a designation mechanism (under the IMF instructs a member government to make the trade). The former took at least five days, while the latter had not been used in more than two decades (and the IMF was reluctant to activate it). In this context, the SDR was a relatively illiquid and unattractive reserve asset.[67]

Despite its limitations, Zhou argued that the SDR "serves as the light in the tunnel for the reform of the international monetary system" and he proposed a "gradual process" of giving it a more prominent international role. One step was to increase the allocation of SDRs, a move that he noted would have the added benefit of providing the IMF with greater resources. Zhou also suggested a number of initiatives to encourage the SDR's wider use, such as the creation of "financial assets denominated in the SDR" and a "settlement system between the SDR and other currencies" as well as actively promoting the SDR's use in "international trade, commodities pricing, investment and corporate book-keeping."[68] In addition, he recommended expanding the basket of currencies (which included just the dollar, euro, yen, and sterling) forming the basis for SDR's value.

Zhou also recommended that the SDR allocation rules could "be shifted from a purely calculation-based system to a system backed by real assets, such as a reserve pool, to further boost market confidence in its value." This idea seemed to relate to his suggestion that the IMF could manage a portion of countries' reserves by setting up "an open-ended SDR-denominated fund based on the market practice, allowing subscription and redemption in the existing reserve currencies by various investors as desired."[69] This proposal resurrected an idea widely discussed in the late 1970s to create an IMF "substitution account" under which national monetary authorities could deposit dollars in exchange for SDRs. At that earlier time, this idea appealed to many dollar reserve holding countries in the Western alliance because it would have enabled them to diversify reserves in a manner that did not trigger dollar depreciation at the time (because the exchange was off-market).[70] It now held the same appeal for Chinese officials: it would allow them to offload the exchange rate risks that China had assumed by accumulating such large dollar reserves. As Paul Krugman put it, Zhou's proposal was "a plea that someone rescue China from the consequences of its own investment mistakes."[71]

Although Zhou's paper was seen by many analysts to be a rather sudden challenge to US monetary dominance, Chinese advocacy of a strengthened SDR was in fact nothing new. Greg Chin has detailed how Zhou and other Chinese officials had been calling for this for a number of years before the crisis as well as in advance of the first G20 summit in November 2008 (albeit without level of detail of Zhou's March 2009 paper). Their longstanding interest in a strengthened SDR reflected frustrations with their vulnerability to dollar fluctuations and unilateral US monetary policy choices.[72] For this reason, they had also urged strengthened IMF surveillance over US economic policies. Indeed, in a speech shortly after his March 2009 paper was released, Zhou reiterated this idea, calling for the IMF "to strengthen the surveillance on the economic and financial policies in major reserve currency countries."[73]

It is true, however, that the crisis experience greatly intensified Chinese concerns about their vulnerability to US policy choices and the dollar's instability. From a Chinese standpoint, the crisis demonstrated how the dollar's international role enabled the United States to live recklessly beyond its means and then to deflect costs of adjustment onto others, with adverse systemic consequences.[74] The dramatic US monetary easing in response to the crisis only heightened concerns about risks of China's exposure to dollar depreciation among both Chinese policymakers and the general public. Indeed, when US Treasury Secretary Tim Geithner attempted in June 2009 to reassure a student audience at Peking University of the value of their country's US assets, one reporter noted that he was met with "loud laughter."[75] Although their country's vulnerability to exchange rate risks left Chinese officials with strong incentives in the short term to defend the dollar, it has also encouraged them to explore ways of reducing their dependence on the dollar over the longer term.

The G20 Initiatives and Wider Politics

Although Chinese calls for a strengthening of the SDR's role were not new, they suddenly found a more receptive audience. Just over a week after the release of Zhou's paper, the G20 leaders at their London summit supported a new allocation of SDRs—the first in almost three decades—valued at SDR150 (approximately $250 billion). After approval by the IMF's Executive Board in July, the new SDR allocation took place in August. In addition, the G20 leaders supported urgent ratification of the 1997 Fourth Amendment of the IMF Articles of Agreement, which had endorsed a special one-time allocation of SDR 21.5 billion in order to compensate members that had joined the IMF since 1981 (including China and Russia). This recommendation was also quickly implemented; ratification by the US Congress in June paved the way for the special SDR allocation in September. In June 2009, the IMF also issued SDR-denominated bonds for the first time that were purchased by a number of governments such as Brazil ($10 billion), Russia ($10 billion), and China ($50 billion).

But the significance of these moves should not be overstated. After the increase, outstanding SDRs still represented less than 4% of global reserves, a share lower than it had been for most of the 1970s and 1980s.[76] The IMF's SDR bonds were also non-marketable. These various initiatives were also not followed up with any further moves. Neither the G20 nor the IMF membership endorsed more SDR allocations. Zhou's proposal for a substitution account went nowhere. The G20 also did not undertake any efforts to encourage the SDR's wider role through reforms relating to its official use or by collectively issuing SDR-denominated bonds (as analysts such as Barry Eichengreen suggested they could[77]).

What explains the inaction? It is worth noting that the cause of strengthening the SDR did find some important sources support outside China. Just a few days before Zhou's paper was released, a high-profile UN Commission of Experts chaired by Nobel Prize–winning economist Joseph Stiglitz had called for a new SDR-centered "global reserve system." The Stiglitz Commission argued that new SDR issues could help meet the growing demand for reserves without generating the kinds of global imbalances that the dollar-centered system did. If reserves were created by a supranational institution instead of the United States, the seigniorage earned from their issuance could also be more widely shared.[78] These ideas were more fully developed in the Commission's final report in September 2009 that called for an annual SDR emission of US$150 to $300 billion, with the possibility of larger emissions in crisis periods or to help finance global public goods and development goals. That report also recommended that SDRs no longer be allocated according to IMF quota sizes (a system that ensured most SDRs went to rich countries that needed them least) but rather according to GDP or countries' needs ("some estimation of the demand for reserves").[79]

The other BRIC countries were also supportive of strengthening the SDR's role. In advance of the first G20 leaders meeting in November 2008, Indian prime minister Manmohan Singh had already raised the possibility of a new SDR allocation.[80] At a meeting just before the release of Zhou's paper, the finance ministers of the BRICs countries had also called collectively for "a substantial SDR allocation."[81] At the London

G20 meeting soon after, Russian officials were particularly enthusiastic about the new SDR allocation, which they saw as a first step toward the creation of a global currency to replace the dollar.[82] Brazilian officials were also quite critical of the dollar's international dominance and they shared China's annoyance about the lack of discipline on US policymaking, particularly when US monetary easing began to generate destabilizing capital flows to their country.[83] When the BRICs leaders met for their first summit in June 2009, the final communiqué also included a statement about the need for a "stable, predictable and more diversified international monetary system."[84] Other G20 countries such as Argentina also supported Zhou's ideas when they were first put forward.[85]

When the French government assumed the chair of the G20 in late 2010, it also prioritized the cause of international monetary reform, including an expanded role for the SDR.[86] The position was in keeping with longstanding French complaints about the dominant role of the dollar in the international monetary system dating back to the 1960s. As part of building support for his goals, President Sarkozy reached out to China at this time. Chinese officials initially appeared quite receptive to the French overtures, with Chinese President Hu Jintao agreeing to hold a seminar in China on the subject.[87] But they soon became more wary and did not consider France a reliable partner. Their distrust, it appears, stemmed from the fact that the French were allying with the United States and others at the time to press for Chinese exchange rate policy reform.[88] Even if the French–China partnership had been stronger, however, opposition from other G20 countries would have blocked any serious initiative in this area.

This opposition had been apparent when the IMF Executive Board held a discussion in late January 2011 of an IMF staff discussion paper that discussed proposals such as increasing SDR allocations, encouraging greater use of the SDR to denominate trade and financial assets, and issuing SDR-denominated bonds.[89] A published summary of the Board discussion noted that "many remained unconvinced at this stage that there is a key role for the SDR in the process [of reform]." It also noted that directors felt that the cultivation of a market for SDR-denominated assets was "likely to be a very long-term process" and a number of them "expressed doubts that regular SDR allocations would reduce reserve accumulation, and many pointed to potential moral hazard implications."[90]

A few months earlier, these doubts had been expressed publicly by Bank of Canada governor Mark Carney, who had noted that a strengthened SDR would do nothing to change "incentives for the surplus countries that have thwarted adjustment" and that a "substitution account would create considerable moral hazard, since reserve holders would be tempted to engage in further accumulation."[91] Since the London summit, other close US allies, such as Britain, Japan, and South Korea, had also signaled at various moments their lack of enthusiasm for discussions of initiatives to strengthen the SDR's role.[92] It was the opposition of the United States itself, however, that was most important because of its dominant voting share in the Fund.

US Opposition

The Obama administration had supported the decision to boost SDR allocations at the London G20 summit and secured Congressional ratification of the Fourth Amendment. But the US interest in these SDR allocations was driven largely by short-term imperatives rather than the cause of longer-term international monetary reform. Like British officials organizing the London summit, US policymakers saw these moves as part of their broad initiative to boost quickly the IMF's resources and buffer countries from balance of payments shocks in the context of the crisis.[93] The SDR allocations did this cheaply and without involving complicated debates about reforming IMF quotas—a point Zhou himself had also highlighted in his March paper. Indeed, it is important to note that British and American officials had already been developing plans for a new SDR issue well before Zhou's speech.[94] But in the lead-up to the subsequent G20 summit in Pittsburgh in September, US officials resisted efforts from the BRICs to place the issue of international monetary reform on the agenda of the meeting.[95]

There were in fact some prominent US analysts who were supportive of longer term reform proposals. Stiglitz was one and his Commission went out of its way to highlight the costs to the United States of supplying the world's reserves, such as growing current account deficits and constraints on US policy autonomy. Prominent US economist Fred Bergsten also urged the US government to welcome Zhou's initiative and he suggested an annual issuance of SDRs totaling $1 trillion over five years. From his standpoint, the crisis experience had shown that US policymakers now "must recognize that large external deficits, the dominance of the dollar, and the large capital inflows that necessarily accompany deficits and currency dominance are no longer in the United States' national interest."[96] Because an IMF substitution account could help minimize the risks of disorderly selling of dollars by large reserve holding countries, Bergsten also supported that proposal.

These arguments were fascinating because they contrasted so sharply with the view in China (and elsewhere) that dollar provided the United States with an exorbitant privilege. From the standpoint of these US analysts, the dollar's role was more of a burden that they hoped to shed. The arguments also had some parallels with the past. As far back as the 1960s, US officials complained about the constraints on their macroeconomic policy stemming from the link between the world's growing demand for reserves and US payments deficits. Their support for the creation of the SDR in 1969 reflected their desire to partially shed this burden of providing liquidity to the world. When foreign flight from the dollar in the late 1970s again threatened US policy autonomy, a number of US policymakers—including Bergsten himself—were supportive of proposals to strengthen the SDR and create a substitution account.[97]

But the arguments of these analysts did not gain as much traction in US official circles as they had at these earlier moments. At the core of Bergsten's argument was the idea that the United States needed to reject the pre-crisis pattern of US growth characterized by large current account deficits, foreign capital inflows, and accumulating foreign debt. Some US domestic economic groups might have benefitted from this change, such

as firms and workers in manufacturing sectors that had faced intensified foreign competition before the crisis. But the highly technical and
abstract nature of the SDR reform debates inhibited societal mobilization
in support of these proposals in any politically significant way.

The pre-crisis pattern of growth, on the other hand, had some clear
supporters who benefitted directly from it. In the political arena, the dollar's global role and foreign capital inflows allowed the country to live
beyond its means in ways that allowed politicians to postpone difficult
and unpopular political decisions. US multinational firms also partici-
pated actively in the "Bretton Woods II" arrangement, relying on export
platforms in China to sell cheap products to the US consumer market. In
addition, powerful private financial firms on Wall Street gained "denomi-
nation rents" from the dollar's international role, a role that put them at
the center of the selling of dollar-denominated securities to foreign investors as well as other global financial flows.[98] There was, in fact, a strange
complementarity between these various US domestic interests and
domestic groups within the major creditor countries—such as China's
export interest and SOEs—that also favored the status quo.

US dependence on foreign capital also provided some more immediate
incentives for US officials to avoid endorsing China's proposals, a lesson
that Geithner learned in late March 2009. When asked about the Chinese
proposal soon after Zhou's paper had been released, the newly installed
Treasury Secretary stated that the US government was "quite open" to it.
The statement caused immediate selling of the dollar in global markets.
As one currency trader explained, "the mere fact that the US Treasury
Secretary is even entertaining thoughts that the dollar may cease being the
anchor of the global monetary system has caused consternation." To reassure the markets, Geithner quickly clarified that the dollar would remain
the "world's dominant reserve currency . . . for a long period of time." Even
President Obama felt the need to emphasize at a news conference shortly
afterwards that "I don't believe that there is a need for a global currency."[99]
The episode highlighted the concrete risks for American policymakers
of signaling their support for explicit efforts to downgrade the dollar's
global role.

Collapse of the Proposal

In the face of opposition from the United States and others, very little came from Sarkozy's initiative. In the November 2011 G20 summit communiqué, the only reference to the SDR concerned its potential role in boosting IMF resources, a review of its valuation, and a vague commitment that the G20 "will continue our work on the role of the SDR."[100] As the prospects for reform dimmed, the enthusiasm of China and the other BRICS countries for SDR-related reforms appeared to wane. At their April 2011 summit (which now included South Africa), the BRICS leaders had welcomed discussion about the SDR's role and called for "the reform and improvement of the international monetary system, with a broad-based international reserve currency system providing stability and certainty."[101] But when they met again in March 2012, their communiqué did not refer to the SDR and simply called for "the establishment and improvement of a just international monetary system that can serve the interests of all countries and support the development of emerging and developing economies."[102] By June, the Russian finance minister declared there was no prospect for the SDR to become an international reserve currency "at the current moment."[103]

While the Russian disappointment appeared very genuine, the Chinese perspective was less clear. Although Zhou's paper had helped trigger the debate, the seriousness of Chinese commitment to strengthening the SDR was open to question. At any time, China could have helped promote the development of a private SDR market by committing to issue its own SDR-denominated bonds.[104] China was also very well placed to generate demand for SDR-denominated assets in ways that would have boosted private markets. As the IMF staff paper noted in 2011, "a public statement of interest in such assets by large reserve holders would mitigate the liquidity premium likely to be demanded initially by investors."[105] Although these initiatives would have involved some costs, they would have signaled the seriousness of China's intention. The costs could also have been mitigated somewhat through joint action with the other BRICS countries. But no such initiatives were undertaken..

The Stiglitz Commission also noted that smaller groups of states—in the face of resistance to SDR reform—could proceed on their own to create 'Reserve Currency Associations' whose members pooled their reserves and held a new common reserve currency that they committed to exchange for their own currencies. Some analysts have gone further to argue that these Associations could then proceed to create agreements among themselves, building what Ocampo calls 'a new global reserve system bottom-up'.[106] As noted already in Chapter 2, the BRICS leaders did commit at their March 2013 summit to a form of reserve pooling, but no link was drawn between that initiative and the creation of a common reserve currency.

The absence of these kinds of initiatives—when combined with the China's wary reaction to French overtures—reinforces the perception that China's support for the SDR, both before the crisis and after, may have had more to do with what Eichengreen calls "symbolic politics" than genuine commitment.[107] At the international level, China's SDR support served the international purpose of signaling discontent with the dollar's dominance and steering foreign attention away from its exchange rate policies and reserve accumulation. Domestically, it also helped address growing anger about the management of China's dollar reserves.[108]

THE PUSH FOR A MULTIPOLAR CURRENCY ORDER

Post-crisis challenges to the dollar came from advocates not just of the SDR but also of a more multipolar currency order involving the internationalization of other currencies. The goal of creating a more multipolar currency order has long been prominent in Europe, where one of the motivations for creating the euro was to reduce dependence on the dollar and challenge the latter's international dominance.[109] In the immediate wake of the crisis, many European officials and analysts reiterated this objective. As President Sarkozy put it a July 2009 speech, "We cannot stick with one single currency...we've still got the Bretton Woods system of 1945...60 years afterwards we've got to ask: shouldn't a politically multipolar world correspond to an economically multi-currency world?"[110]

The Collapse of the Euro Challenge

Like his push for a strengthening of the SDR, however, Sarkozy's hopes that the euro would challenge the dollar proved unrealistic. The difficulties caused by the uncoordinated responses to financial institutions in distress within the Eurozone in 2008 have already been noted. Even more serious problems became apparent with the outbreak of the debt crises in the periphery of the Eurozone a few months after Sarkozy's speech. The debt crises revealed deeper flaws in the political foundations of the euro.

Since the euro's creation a decade earlier, critics had argued that the Eurozone was not what economists call an "optimum currency area" and that its architecture did not make adequate provisions for adjustments to intra-zone payments imbalances. Many of the euro's supporters had long been well aware of these economic weaknesses, but had felt that broader political benefits of the euro outweighed the economic risks that its creation entailed. They anticipated that European policymakers would strengthen the euro's institutional foundations over time as the economic consequences of the weaknesses of the initial design became more evident.

Those economic consequences became particularly apparent in the wake of the financial crisis, with costs to the euro project that were higher many had anticipated. During the first decade of the euro's existence, Germany accumulated large surpluses while payments deficits emerged in a number of poorer Eurozone countries (e.g., Greece, Ireland, Italy, Portugal, and Spain) in response to differing rates of productivity growth, asymmetric shocks, and other diverging economic trends. Within large national currency zones such as the United States or Canada, imbalances of this kind between regions of the country are paved over by mechanisms such as labor migration and large fiscal transfers from the national government. In the Eurozone, however, large labor migration was unlikely and no Europe-wide authority existed with a mandate to mobilize large-scale fiscal transfers of this kind.

A monetary union could still function effectively under these circumstances if countries adjusted to imbalances through wage and price flexibility, as happened during the era of the international gold standard. Many designers of the euro had in fact hoped the currency would encourage such flexibility, with deficit countries adjusting via lower wage and prices. But those kinds of adjustments are slow, painful, and politically difficult in an era of mass democracy. Many deficit countries found it easier simply to finance payments deficits through private and public borrowing from investors outside their country. Indeed, large external borrowing often financed domestic consumption booms, property bubbles, and/or government deficit spending that only contributed to the country's payments problems as well as to high levels of private and public debt.

The 2008 global financial crisis brought this external borrowing to a halt, exposing the underlying payments imbalances as well as unsustainable levels of private and/or public debts in a number of countries. The severe global economic downturn only contributed further to the difficulties of servicing debts, particularly for governments that saw tax revenues collapse and spending increase (including for bank bailouts). Greece was the first Eurozone country to face a severe debt crisis, but others soon experienced troubles too, as private investors reacted to the new context as well as to the slow and bumbling European management of the crisis.

In this context, it became clear to all that, rather than challenging the dollar's global role, the very survival of the euro was now at stake. European policymakers scrambled to solve the immediate sovereign debt crises of a number of its poorer members and the associated problems of exposed European banks. After much debate and delay, financial assistance packages, supported by the IMF, were extended first to Greece (May 2010 and again in the summer of 2011), and then to Ireland (November 2010), Portugal (May 2011), and Spain (June 2012). At the same time, European authorities set out to address the flaws in its governance that had been so bluntly revealed, including the need for region-wide financial regulation and supervision, clearer provisions for the extension of emergency liquidity, and greater (and more automatic) fiscal transfers.

Because the focus of this book is on *global* financial governance, an analysis of these various regional initiatives is beyond its scope. What is crucial, however, is that their slow negotiation and uncertain outcomes led many to question the political coherence and strength of the Eurozone after early 2010. Those uncertainties, in turn, undermined the euro's ability to challenge to the dollar's international role. Indeed, by the end of 2012, the share of the reserves of developing countries held in euro had fallen from 30% at the start of the crisis to 24%, its lowest level since 2002 (while that of the dollar remained at around 60%).[111] The share of all foreign exchange transactions in which the euro was used on one side also fell from 37% in 2007 to 33% in 2013.[112] European policymakers recognized that a more politically consolidated Eurozone would accelerate the euro's internationalization and the move towards a more multipolar currency order.[113] But the initial responses of European policymakers to the Eurozone crisis highlighted how the political roadmap for getting from here to there would be, at best, a long and winding one.

RMB Internationalization and Its Limits

In the wake of the crisis, Chinese authorities also backed the goal of promoting a more multipolar currency order as a way of addressing their frustrations with the dollar's international role. Like their support for the SDR, Chinse officials had embraced this stance already before the crisis.[114] Because of their frustrations with dollar dependence, Chinese leaders had welcomed the euro's creation at the turn of the century, arguing that it would "establish a more balanced international financial and monetary system."[115] With the outbreak of the European debt crises in 2010–2011, their backing of the euro took a even more tangible form when they helped boost confidence in the currency through public expressions of support and targeted purchases of the government bonds of troubled Eurozone countries. In addition to supporting the euro's role as a counter-weight to the dollar, these moves helped defend the value of their existing euro assets and the health of a major export market for Chinese products.[116]

To promote a more multipolar currency order after the 2008 global crisis, however, the main focus of Chinese policy came to be centered on the internationalization of their own currency, the RMB, whose global role had remained extremely limited despite China's growing size in the world economy. From a Chinese perspective, RMB internationalization could address the problems associated with dollar dependence in a manner that—unlike SDR reform—did not require US support.[117] For example, greater use of RMB in trade payments would allow the country's exporters and importers to minimize exchange rate risks associated with dollar-denominated transactions. Vulnerability to the kind of dollar shortages experienced in the 2008 crisis could also be minimized if China's financial institutions conducted international financial transactions in RMB. If more external Chinese lending could be done in RMB, the country could avoid the enormous exchange risks stemming from the fact that the vast bulk of China's foreign assets were held in US dollar-denominated assets. More generally, RMB internationalization might also boost China's power and prestige abroad, particularly in the East Asian region.[118]

To promote RMB internationalization, Chinese officials recognized that they had to relax the tight regulations they had in place on its international use. The initial post-crisis initiatives liberalized restrictions on the use of RMB in the settlement of trade payments. In July 2009, the government allowed 365 firms in five cities to use RMB for the first time to invoice and settle trade with Hong Kong, Macau, and Association of Southeast Asian Nations (ASEAN) countries. This pilot scheme was then expanded rapidly several times, culminating in a 2012 decision to allow all firms in China to invoice and settle all current account transactions in RMB. As part of this initiative, foreign banks and firms were also allowed to make greater use of Chinese banks for RMB deposits and clearing.[119] A number of bilateral agreements with foreign governments were also struck to encourage use of each other's currencies in bilateral trade.

In a flurry of moves in 2010–2011, the government also encouraged greater use of the RMB in the realm of international investment.[120] Constraints on the use of RMB in foreign direct investment into and out of China were loosened. The Chinese government also relaxed some rules on the issue of RMB-denominated bonds in China by foreign entities and the sending of their proceeds abroad. Particularly important was the government's cultivation of the growth of the offshore RMB financial market in Hong Kong. While Hong Kong banks had accepted some RMB deposits since 2004 and RMB bonds had been floated in Hong Kong since 2007, restrictions on these activities were now liberalized. Although this offshore market was still cordoned off from the domestic Chinese financial system by capital controls (so that interest rates and even the value of RMB in the offshore market differed from those in the mainland China), the government did begin to allow some firms to invest offshore Hong Kong RMB proceeds in Chinese stock markets and interbank bond markets.

The RMB's international use was promoted in some other ways as well. One of these was described in the last chapter: the proliferation of swaps agreements between Chinese monetary authorities and foreign counterparts from late 2008 onwards. In 2010, central banks which had swaps with China were also allowed to invest RMB funds in the Chinese interbank bond market. In addition, the Chinese government began to extend more overseas aid in RMB as well as to encourage RMB-denominated foreign loans from state-owned banks such as the China Development Bank.[121]

These various initiatives encouraged some RMB internationalization, but only to a very limited degree. Although the share of China's cross-border trade settled in RMB quickly rose from below 1% to 10.2% by the second quarter of 2011, this still left approximately 90% of the country's trade settled in foreign currencies (primarily the dollar).. The growth in RMB trade settlement then suddenly slowed after mid-2011 when exchange rate and interest rate differentials between the offshore RMB market and that within China narrowed, highlighting how much of the volume had been linked simply to arbitrage activity.[122] The same was true of the size of RMB deposits in Hong Kong, which actually fell between mid-2011 and mid-2012.[123] Foreign exchange trading involving the RMB grew considerably between 2010 and 2013 from $34 billion to

$120 billion, but its share of overall foreign exchange trading volume was still only 2.2% (compared to 87% for the dollar).[124] Despite the growth in RMB trade settlement, the RMB's role as a world's payments currency also continued to be quite small, ranked in 2013 behind that of currencies such as the Thai baht or the Swedish krona.[125] The RMB's use in international bank deposits, bond issues, and official reserves also remained extremely limited in comparison to those of the dollar (and euro).[126]

Further RMB internationalization was held back by the absence of more far-reaching financial reforms. One key barrier was the unwillingness of the Chinese authorities to make the RMB fully convertible. Extensive state control of the domestic financial system also prevented the emergence of deeper, more liquid financial markets—including government bond markets—that would be attractive to foreigners. As Eichengreen put it, if the euro's problem was that it was a "currency without a state," the RMB was a "currency with too much state."[127]

These kinds of significant financial reforms were resisted for an important reason. They would undermine the government's tight grip over finance that is at the core of the Chinese development model. Through capital controls and domestic financial regulations, China's central government is able to maintain a competitive exchange rate and ensure that domestic savings are channeled to industry at cheap rates via the banking system. The reforms necessary to promote more significant RMB internationalization would threaten these arrangements.[128] It is thus not surprising that these reforms had powerful opponents within the Chinese government and broader society, including among state-owned enterprises. In other words, many of the same groups that encouraged the Chinese state to support the dollar during the crisis were also inhibiting the RMB's challenge to the dollar in the post-crisis period.

Currency Internationalization Elsewhere?

What about the internationalization of other currencies? We have seen how the other BRIC countries supported a more "diversified international monetary system" at their initial 2009 summit. In their 2010 summit, they repeated the call and noted they would "study feasibilities of monetary cooperation, including local currency trade settlement arrangement between our countries."[129] But their subsequent initiatives have been very limited. At the March 2012 summit of the BRICS countries, their development banks signed a cooperation agreement to extend credit facilities to each other in their respective local currencies. The intended goal of this initiative was "to reduce the demand for fully convertible currencies for transactions among BRICS nations, and thereby help reduce the transaction costs of intra-BRICS trade."[130] The initiative falls short even of the limited goal of creating an intra-BRICS local trade settlement arrangement.

The Russian leadership was, however, strongly committed to goal of ruble internationalization after the crisis. The Russian leadership's support for currency internationalization reflected frustrations with dollar dependence and it was also linked to the cause of broader economic and financial reforms and the cultivation of Moscow as an international financial center. In addition, the promotion of the ruble's international role was linked to their broader quest for Great Power status; indeed, Russian officials highlighted their concerns that China was using BRICS cooperation to promote the RMB's use in central Asia at the expense of their efforts to spread the ruble's influence in that region.[131] But little progress was made after the crisis, as ruble internationalization was inhibited by the country's limited trade network, inflationary history, shallow and opaque financial markets, and commodity dependence.[132]

There was also some discussion in Brazil about promoting the internationalization of the real as a way of reducing dollar dependence. In May 2009, Brazil's finance minister Guido Mantega predicted that currencies "such as the Brazilian real and the Chinese yuan will gain in importance" as international currencies vis-à-vis the dollar as a result of the crisis.[133] That same month, Brazil's President Lula traveled to Beijing to discuss how more trade between China and Brazil could be denominated in the two countries' currencies.[134] In June 2009, Lula pressed the other BRIC leaders as a whole to consider initiatives to promote the settlement of trade

among themselves in local currencies. Brazil also supported the creation
in October 2008 of a new payments system between Brazil and Argentina
to encourage settlement of bilateral trade in their respective currencies
instead of dollars.[135] Leading Brazilian financial institutions also signaled
their interest in 2010 in the goal of the internationalization of the real and
of transforming São Paolo into an international financial center.[136]

But these initiatives had little impact. Between October 2008 and March
2010, the volume of trade under the Argentine-Brazilian payments system
consisted of approximately 1% of bilateral trade.[137] The prospects for a more
significant internationalization of Brazil's currency were also curtailed by
the government's decision to introduce and strengthen capital account
restrictions from October 2009 onwards. As discussed in Chapter 4, the
controls have been designed to protect Brazil from the effects of US monetary easing, which have generated large capital inflows to Brazil that
threaten to drive up the real's value and generate an inflationary credit
bubble domestically. With these moves, Brazilian officials have made clear
that their desire to protect policy autonomy in this context trumps any
commitment to the internationalization of Brazil's currency.[138] Ironically,
then, it has been the very exercise of US monetary unilateralism that has
undermined Brazil's enthusiasm to challenge the dollar.

The Brazilian experience highlights a broader point. As a 2011 IMF
staff paper pointed out, currency internationalization in an emerging
market context "involves a number of potential risks to monetary and
financial stability; including complicating monetary management...and
straining the financial system's ability to adequately absorb capital flows
(due to increased volatility of capital flow and susceptibility to surges and
sudden stops)."[139] These risks have discouraged serious pursuit of this policy goal in many countries. For example, neither of the other two BRICS
countries—South Africa and India—have shown the kind of enthusiasm
for currency internationalization demonstrated by their Russian and
Chinese counterparts.

East Asia, South Korea, and some ASEAN countries expressed some
support for the internationalization of their currencies after the crisis. But
it was clear that they had very limited goals in mind. They were willing to

support only modest regional initiatives to promote local currency trade settlement in order to minimize transaction costs and reduce their vulnerability to the dollar's fluctuations and the kinds of shortages of dollar liquidity shortages experienced at the height of the financial crisis. Many of them also introduced capital account restrictions after the crisis, highlighting that they—like Brazil—valued the protection of their policy autonomy over a more significant internationalization of their currencies.

Because of its size in the world economy, it is also worth noting the position of the Japanese government. After the East Asian financial crisis of 1997–98, the Japanese government had become more supportive of the yen's internationalization than in the past. But the yen's international use continued to be held back by regulatory barriers, problems in the Japanese financial system, resistance from some Japanese firms, and foreign wariness of Japanese monetary leadership in the East Asian region.[140] By the time of the 2008 financial crisis, the interest of Japanese authorities in tackling these issues and promoting yen internationalization more aggressively was not much apparent. As Cohen noted, "even the most ardent of the currency's supporters [in Japan] appear to have lost their enthusiasm for the struggle."[141] Japan's broader dependence on the United States for security and an export market may have helped to keep their ambitions in check and inhibited the kinds of criticisms of the dollar's international role that were heard in policymaking circles in China and elsewhere.[142]

Challenges from Within?

Finally, what about support within the United States itself for a more multipolar international currency system? We have already seen how the 2008 crisis generated arguments within the United States that the dollar's international role no longer served US interests. In addition to backing a strengthened role for the SDR, critics such as Bergsten urged the United States to support "the further evolution of a multiple-currency system in which other monies increasingly share the international position of the dollar in private markets." As part of this goal of "downsizing" the dollar's international role, he suggested that the United States encourage the internationalization of other currencies such as the euro and RMB.[143] Other US analysts went further to suggest that the US government could accelerate the de-internationalization of the dollar by actively restricting China's purchasing of US financial assets and thus its accumulation of dollar reserves.[144]

Any explanation of the dollar's enduring international role after the financial crisis must explain why these views did not have more influence on US policymaking after the crisis. In discussing US views of the SDR, we have already discussed a core reason: powerful US public and private interests benefitted from the dollar's international role and the pre-crisis growth model. Any initiative to introduce US capital controls would also have provoked strong opposition from these interests as well as foreign investors on whom the United States had become increasingly dependent.

Although the US government did not support the goal of de-internationalizing the dollar, it is worth noting that some of its post-crisis policies unintentionally encouraged foreigners to continue to press for this outcome. As noted previously, US monetary easing encouraged further resentment of the dollar's role abroad. Equally important was the US budget stalemate in the summer of 2011 that almost generated a default on US government debt and that was followed in August by a decision from Standard and Poor's to downgrade the US government debt. The episode only encouraged further foreign criticism of the US-centered international monetary order and more foreign interest in insulation from US policymaking. In the wake of the move by Standard and Poor's, China's official news agency even called for "international supervision over the issue of US dollars" and it noted that "a new stable and secured global reserve currency may also be an option to avert a catastrophe caused by any single country".[145]

Even if US policymakers had been more supportive of the goal of de-internationalizing the dollar, however, the British historical experience with sterling suggests that this objective would not necessarily be easily realized. During the 1960s, British officials became increasingly critical of sterling's international role, leading them to try to curtail it through initiatives such as tightening controls on the currency's international commercial use and the launching of bilateral negotiations with foreign countries aimed at reducing official holdings abroad. But the de-internationalization of sterling ended up being a long and cumbersome process that stretched well into the 1970s because of enduring foreign political support for the currency's international role.[146] For many countries, the holding of sterling reserves was linked to benefits they sought to preserve such as export relationships with the United Kingdom or the preservation of British security ties. Countries holding large sterling reserves also worried that their efforts to diversify might trigger sterling's devaluation, thus undermining the value of their remaining reserves.[147]

If the United States had tried to de-internationalize the dollar after the 2008 crisis, these kinds of motivations might well have played a similar role in encouraging foreign governments to slow the decline of the dollar's international standing. As noted previously, many foreign governments held large dollar reserves for some similar reasons as well as because of their desire for "self-insurance." Private economic actors might well have continued to support the dollar's international role as well because of inertia. When a well-established transactional network already exists, the switching of currencies can be economically costly. Inertia may also be a product of conservative and risk-averse behavior among economic actors when faced with uncertainties involved in choosing an alternative currency.[148] During the decline of sterling, private actors also had an attractive alternative international currency to embrace: the dollar. In the contemporary context, given the euro's troubles and the issues identified previously relating to the internationalization of other currencies, an attractive alternative was hard to see. As Eichengreen puts it, "the dollar has its problems, but so do its rivals."[149] When market actors fled to dollar investments during the 2008 crisis, they were signaling their judgment that the former was less serious than the latter. The Fed's willingness to act as an international lender-of-last-resort in dollars also likely enhanced the attractiveness of the currency to international market actors.[150]

CONCLUSION

The crisis of 2008 and its immediate aftermath resulted in remarkably little change in the dollar's international role. The dollar's share of all official foreign exchange reserves, for example, declined only slightly from 64% at the start of the crisis to 62% by the end of 2012.[151] In 2013, the dollar also continued to be used on one side of 87% of all foreign exchange transactions, a figure that was slightly higher than the 85.6% share in 2007.[152] Between 2007 and 2010, there was also a slight increase in the dollar's share of all cross-border bank claims (from 41.9% to 43.7%) and international securities issues outstanding (36% to 37.8%).[153]

This status quo outcome is remarkable given the widespread predictions at the start of the crisis. Instead of challenging the dollar's international role, the 2008 crisis ended up demonstrating its international dominance very effectively. Private demand for the dollar at the height of the crisis—and the dependence of many central banks on Fed dollar swaps—revealed quite starkly the centrality of the currency in private international financial markets. The willingness of foreign governments to back the dollar, even in the face of this major upheaval in US financial markets, also demonstrated the durability of the political basis of this official support. In the wake of the crisis, many foreigners and Americans expressed very public frustrations with various consequences of the dollar's international role, but the weak results of the push for a strengthened SDR and multipolar currency order revealed the limitations of these potential challenges to the dollar's dominance.

Each of these phenomena provided new insights about the sources of the dollar's international preeminence. They revealed that the dollar's global role stemmed in part from the broader structural power of the United States within the global political economy arising from factors such as its uniquely attractive financial markets, the dependence of foreigners on the United States as an export market, its geopolitical power, its veto power in the IMF, and foreigners' vulnerability to the "dollar trap." Although US structural power set the environment within which many market and foreign government decisions were made, the agency of emerging market governments was also significant in bolstering the dollar, notably their enduring risk-averse commitments to self-insurance, policy autonomy, and export-dependent development strategies. As Kahler noted more generally, "the developing world remained invested in the existing order and served as a key constituency in its defense."[154] The dollar also benefitted from the weaknesses of the governance of its major potential competitor, the euro.

Also important was the agency of US policymakers. Their role was significant in a number of ways, including through blocking of further SDR reform, keeping US financial markets open, and maintaining the support of foreign official creditors through various activities (e.g., maintaining open US markets for foreign exports, bailing out troubled US firms in which foreign governments had heavy stakes, burying the IMF report on China's exchange rate policy). In some cases, US decisions reflected domestic concerns about financial stability (e.g. domestic bailouts). But the agency of US officials also reflected the country's dependence on foreign capital and the lack of a significant challenge to the pre-crisis US growth model and the interest groups who benefitted from it.

Was the Market-Friendly Nature of International Financial Standards Overturned?

At their very first summit in Washington, the G20 leaders committed to reform international financial regulation to reflect lessons learned during the crisis. In fact, the final communiqué of that summit focused very heavily on this issue, outlining a detailed international regulatory reform agenda. At every subsequent G20 summit, this topic remained a top priority and the issues covered widened considerably. The result was a flurry of initiatives to reform both the content and the governance of international financial regulation. The consistent focus devoted to often very technical regulatory issues by the G20 leaders was impressive.

Watching this buzz of activity, it is tempting to conclude that the crisis generated a dramatic strengthening of the international financial regulatory regime. But five years on, what has actually been accomplished? Chapter 5 addresses this question from the standpoint of the governance of international financial regulation. This chapter examines the content of the new international financial regulatory standards, with a special focus on the question of whether the reforms overturned the "market-friendly" nature of international standards that existed before the crisis.

At the height of the crisis, many predicted such a transformation. This chapter highlights, however, how the reforms to international financial standards were much less significant than many anticipated. Rather than overturning the pre-crisis "neoliberal" model, the G20 leaders merely tweaked it in incremental ways. This argument is developed through an analysis of core aspects of post-crisis reforms that are most relevant to the issue of the market-friendly content of international standards: the Basel III agreement; the governance and content of international accounting rules; international standards for credit rating agencies, hedge funds, over-the-counter (OTC) derivatives; and the treatment of cross-border capital mobility. The chapter concludes with an explanation of why change was so limited in this area of global financial governance.

PREDICTIONS OF CHANGE

The outbreak of the 2008 financial crisis generated many predictions that the age of free markets was over. Joseph Stiglitz, for example, argued that "September 15, 2008, the date that Lehman Brothers collapsed, may be to market fundamentalism…what the fall of the Berlin Wall was to communism."[1] Within the field of international political economy, Benjamin Cohen made a similar case: "Like the collapse of the Soviet Union, the crash of the global financial structure has all the earmarks of a genuine systemic transformation—the end of an age of vast, untrammeled market expansion and neoliberal deregulation."[2] From the world of finance itself, George Soros argued that, while crises of the early 1980s and late 1990s had reinforced "market fundamentalism," this latest crisis "constitutes the end of an era."[3]

The Rise of Market-Friendly International Financial Standards

Predictions of this kind often focused specifically on the financial sector because it was at the core of the crisis. Since the 1980s, many countries—with the United States and United Kingdom in the lead—had liberalized regulations over financial markets. A backlash against this trend seemed very likely in the wake of the crisis, particularly given the massive tax-payer support for financial institutions in many countries. As the prominent financial journalist Martin Wolf put it after the Bear Stearns bailout of March 2008: "If we accept that we are going to bail out the financial system when it gets into trouble, regulation is inevitable."[4] Indeed, he saw this bailout as a key turning point: "Remember Friday March 14 2008: it was the day the dream of global freemarket capitalism died. For three decades we have moved towards market-driven financial systems. By its decision to rescue Bear Stearns, the Federal Reserve, the institution responsible for monetary policy in the United States, chief protagonist of free-market capitalism, declared this era over."[5]

By the time the crisis intensified in the fall of 2008, these kinds of predictions had become commonplace. They were particularly relevant to the content of international financial regulatory standards. Since the mid-1970s, Western powers—again led by the United States and United Kingdom—had been developing increasingly elaborate international standards to foster the harmonizing of national financial regulatory and supervisory practices. The initial steps had been taken by leading bank supervisors working within a body called the Basel Committee on Banking Supervision (BCBS).[6] Created in 1974, the BCBS had initially negotiated an agreement in 1975—the Basel Concordat—that clarified national supervisory responsibilities for international banks. In the wake of the international debt crisis of the early 1980s, the BCBS then created the 1988 Basel Accord, which established a common minimum capital adequacy standard for international banks for the first time.

The 1994 Mexican and the 1997–98 East Asian financial crises then acted as a catalyst for much more ambitious initiatives. As part of their efforts to create a "new international financial architecture" at the time, G7 policymakers encouraged supervisors and regulators to develop a much wider set of international prudential standards relating to issues such as bank supervision, securities regulation, insurance, accounting, and payments systems. They created a new body in 1999, the Financial Stability Forum (FSF), to help coordinate this process and promote internationally the standards that were developed. The new international standards promoted what Walter calls a model of "regulatory neoliberal-ism" based on (idealized) Anglo-American practices.[7] They encouraged regulators and supervisors to be politically independent technocrats enforcing transparent rules, thereby minimizing discretionary state interference in the market. G7 policymakers also invoked global financial markets as a positive force that could help discipline governments that refused to accept these market-friendly standards. Underlying the "inter-national financial standards project" of this period was a belief that the crises of the 1990s had been caused not by malfunctioning global markets but by policy failures in the afflicted countries, including poor financial regulatory and supervisory practices that fell short of Western practices.[8]

From the mid-1990s onwards, the content of other international finan-cial standards also reflected the increasingly market-friendly thinking.[9] For example, while the initial 1988 Basel Accord had set a minimum 8% capital-to-assets ratio for international banks, the BCBS amended the Accord in 1996 to allow large banks to use their own internal value-at-risk models to calculate capital charges for market risk. When the BCBS renegotiated the Basel Accord entirely between 1998 and 2004, this "self-regulatory" approach was reinforced: the new "Basel II" agreement allowed large banks to rely more on their own data and internal models in determining the amount of capital to put aside for overall credit risk. In the words of one US regulator who was critical of this reform, the new framework "let big banks essentially set their own capital requirements."[10] Alongside capital requirements and adequate supervision, Basel II also placed emphasis on "market discipline" as a third "pillar" that would pro-mote financial stability.

The willingness of G7 governments to delegate regulatory functions to private market actors was also apparent in their promotion of inter-national accounting standards created by the International Accounting Standards Board (IASB). The IASB was a London-based private sector body with no public oversight. Moreover, it backed the use of "fair value" accounting that forced institutions to value assets at their market value at any given moment rather than more traditional approaches that used historic costs. Favored by investors, this market-oriented accounting system left firms and managers much more exposed to the fluctuations and judgments of financial markets.[11]

The G7 also refrained from endorsing international standards that would support government regulation of credit rating agencies. Instead, they backed a voluntary code for the firms developed by the International Organization for Securities Commissions (IOSCO) in 2004. Similarly, when criticisms of hedge funds emerged in the late 1990s, the G7 governments explicitly chose not to endorse any international standard backing direct regulation of the industry by governments. They chose an alternative strategy of welcoming some indirect measures as well as private sector initiatives to develop self-regulatory standards. The G7 embraced a similar approach vis-à-vis OTC derivatives markets that grew dramatically in the 1990s and 2000s.[12]

The Crisis as Potential Turning Point?

There were many reasons to expect that the crisis of 2008 would seriously challenge these market-friendly international financial standards. To begin with, the very private financial institutions that had been among the strongest advocates for market-friendly regulation now found themselves on the defensive and politically weakened. Indeed, many of the institutions that had been allowed to self-regulate were now identified as key culprits in triggering the crisis such as international banks, credit rating agencies, OTC derivatives dealers, and accountants. The ability of these private actors to resist stronger regulation seemed likely to be severely compromised by their sudden dependence on state support during the crisis.

Second, the financial meltdown appeared very likely to undermine the credibility of ideas that had played a major role in encouraging the creation of market-friendly international financial standards. These ideas included not just free market ideology but also more technical economic concepts such as the efficient markets hypothesis in finance that was popular among the transgovernmental networks of regulators that dominated international financial standard-setting in the pre-crisis period.[13] As the crisis deepened, many signs of this ideational crisis began to appear, even within the financial industry itself. For example, days after the bailout of Bear Stearns, Joseph Ackermann, chief executive of Deutsche Bank, told the world: "I no longer believe in the market's self-healing power."[14] By October 2008, even Alan Greenspan, who had been among the most enthusiastic supporters of free market finance during his tenure as chairman of the US Federal Reserve from 1987 to 2006, famously acknowledged that "those of us who have looked to the self-interest of lending institutions to protect shareholders' equity, myself especially, are in a state of shocked disbelief."[15]

Finally, because the financial crisis was centered on US and British markets, it seemed likely to undermine the influence of Anglo-American officials who had been the strongest backers of market-friendly international financial standards in the pre-crisis period. Before the crisis, continental European policymakers from countries such as France and Germany had often demanded tighter international financial regulations, only to be thwarted by Anglo-American opposition. The crisis presented the former with a political opportunity that they seemed keen to seize. In May 2008, the German president (and former IMF Managing Director) Horst Köhler attracted headlines with his declaration that crisis had "made clear to any thinking, responsible person in the sector that international financial markets have developed into a monster that must be put back in its place."[16] The next month, German Chancellor Angela Merkel also expressed her interest in seeing the euro-zone secure more influence vis-a-vis the "strongly Anglo-American-dominated system" of international rules governing financial markets.[17] A few months later in September, German finance minister Peer Steinbrück also blamed the crisis on "the irresponsible overemphasis on the 'laissez-faire' principle, namely giving market forces the most possible freedom from state regulation in the Anglo-American financial system." Noting that the US had mocked past German proposals to tighten regulation, he predicted that a more "multipolar" global financial system would now emerge from the crisis in which "America will not be the only power to define which standards and which financial products will be traded all over the world."[18] In the same month, French President Nicolas Sarkozy outlined his priorities for international financial reform in a blunter manner: "The idea of the all-powerful market that must not be constrained by any rules, by any political intervention, was mad. [....] Self-regulation as a way of solving all problems is finished. Laissez-faire is finished. The all-powerful market that always knows best is finished'.[19] Analysts anticipated that German and French policymakers could use the European Union's new market power in finance—strengthened over the past decade by the consolidation of regulation at the regional level—to force change in global rules.[20]

In the pre-crisis period, many officials from developing—or "Southern"—countries had also favored stronger controls over international financial markets that they held at least partly to blame for the crises they had experienced in the 1990s.[21] As the 2008 crisis unfolded, they too appeared now willing to challenge Anglo-American leadership and ideas. As early as May 2008, senior Chinese banking regulators were arguing that "the western consensus on the relation between the market and the government should be reviewed... they tend to overestimate the power of the market and overlook the regulatory role of the government and this warped conception is at the root of the subprime crisis."[22] At a meeting with Indian and South African officials in October 2008, Brazilian President Luiz Inácio Lula da Silva also openly chastised "the irresponsibility of speculators who have transformed the world into a gigantic casino."[23] Soon thereafter, China and other emerging powers were invited to become members of the new G20 leaders group and key international standard setting bodies for the first time, providing them with new opportunities to influence the content of international financial standards. Just before the first G20 summit, the BRIC countries coordinated their position and signaled a determination to push for tighter financial regulation in their joint statement: "The crisis revealed weakness in risk management, regulation, and supervision in the financial sectors of some advanced economies. Therefore we call for reform of regulatory and supervisory frameworks, as well as clearer rules and transparency."[24]

This combination of developments—the political weakening of private financial interests, the lost credibility of free market ideas, and challenges to the Anglo-American leadership—provided some solid reasons to anticipate that the market-friendly nature of international financial standards would be severely challenged by the crisis. Predictions of change were bolstered by the fact that leading policymakers very quickly made high-profile commitments to reform existing international financial standards. As early as September 2007, the G7 governments—led by the United Sates—asked financial officials working within the FSF to develop an agenda for international regulatory reform.[25] By April 2008, the G7 backed a very detailed reform agenda developed by the FSF, despite the opposition of private international bankers who proposed various new self-regulatory initiatives as an alternative.[26] Indeed, when top bankers pressed their case at a private dinner with G7 ministers and central bankers at this time, the exchange between the bankers and officials was described as a "testy affair". Jean-Claude Trichet, the head of the European Central Bank, appeared to sum up the new determination of public officials to tighten regulation: "We all have to take our responsibilities very seriously and displease the private sector, where necessary."[27] At their first November 2008 summit, the G20 leaders then built directly on the FSF agenda and quickly took over from the G7 the role of driving the content of international regulatory reform. At their next two summits in April and September 2009, the G20 leaders also widened the focus and ambition of the reform agenda, prompting scholars to speculate that pressure from countries such as France, Germany, and China might usher in a "changing paradigm of global financial governance" involving the "end of the liberal finance."[28]

Were such predictions borne out? To what extent was the market-friendly nature of pre-crisis international financial standards overturned? The rest of this chapter addresses these questions. The analysis does not pretend to provide a comprehensive analysis of all post-crisis international regulatory reforms. That task would require a book-length study.

Instead, it aims to provide an overview of those aspects of post-crisis international regulatory reform that are most relevant to the question of the fate of market-friendly international financial standards.[29]

BASEL III

A prominent aspect of post-crisis international regulatory reform has been the negotiation of a new set of minimum international prudential standards for banks. Although many BCBS members had yet to implement Basel II by the time of the 2008 crisis, the latter immediately generated demands for its renegotiation. When the G20 leaders met in November 2008, they called for a number of reforms that reinforced initiatives the BCBS had already committed to in July 2008. By the time of the Pittsburgh summit in September 2009, the G20 leaders endorsed a more comprehensive reform of Basel II and they set a quick deadline of the end of 2010 for the overhaul. The BCBS—whose membership widened between March and June 2009 to include all G20 countries (see Chapter 5)—then quickly negotiated Basel III, the results of which were announced in September 2010 and then endorsed by the G20 leaders at their November 2010 summit. The agreement was to be phased in gradually between 2013 and 2019.

This new agreement increased the quantity and quality of capital required for banks. It also included rules on liquidity to help buffer banks from times of market stress, a provision that the BCBS had been unable to reach agree upon at the time of the negotiation of Basel 1. Basel III also broke new ground by supporting the use of minimum leverage ratios that the G20 leaders noted could "serve as a backstop to the risk-based capital measures."[30] The agreement also endorsed for the first time the use of counter-cyclical buffers that encourage banks to build up extra capital in boom times that can be drawn down in times of economic stress.

The new liquidity rules, leverage ratio, and counter-cyclical buffers all supported not just the "microprudential" objective of strengthening the stability of individual banks but also a "macroprudential" goal of containing the accumulation of system-wide risk. While pre-crisis international financial regulation had been focused on the former, a new consensus began to emerge in G20 circles from the fall of 2008 onwards about the need to give more attention to the latter. The strength of this new consensus was apparent by the time of the second G20 summit at which the leaders committed "to reshape our regulatory systems so that our authorities are able to identify and take account of macro-prudential risks."[31] As Baker notes, this ideational transformation was largely a kind of "insiders' coup d'etat" that emerged from the transgovernmental networks of financial officials concerned with international regulatory issues.[32] In these technocratic circles, the new macroprudential thinking offered a critique of the efficient markets hypothesis by highlighting phenomena such as pro-cyclicality, herding behavior, and complex externalities within financial markets. It highlighted very effectively how unregulated or self-regulated financial markets could generate systemic risks that had not been well anticipated by pre-crisis thinking. The logic was outlined well by the G20's Working Group 1 in advance of the London summit in April 2009:

> while each financial crisis is different, the crises over history generally share some key common elements including excessive risk taking, rapid credit growth and rising leverage. This points to the need for regulators, supervisors, and central bankers to supplement strong microprudential regulation with a macroprudential overlay to more effectively monitor and address the build-up of risks arising from excess liquidity, leverage, risk-taking and systemic concentrations that have the potential to cause financial instability.[33]

As part of the macroprudential agenda, Basel III also included a provision for the imposition of extra capital charges on "systemically important financial institutions" (SIFIs), whose failure would cause significant disruption to the wider financial system. This provision to regulate SIFIs more rigorously than other banks was prompted by the massive economic costs associated with the collapse and/or bailouts of large institutions. As the G20 leaders put it at their September 2009 summit, "our prudential standards for systemically important institutions should be commensurate with the costs of their failure."[34] At their Cannes summit in November 2011, the G20 leaders then endorsed the release of a list of 29 banks that were designated as "global SIFIs" and that would be subject to "more intensive and effective supervision" as well as additional capital requirements from 2016 onwards.[35]

Despite these various provisions, the Basel III agreement has been widely criticized. One key criticism has been that the agreement continued to allow large banks to use their internal models for risk weighting of assets. This provision was one of the most important "market-friendly" features of Basel II and its consequences had been revealed starkly by the crisis. The risk of banks using choices of models that deliberately lowered their capital requirements endured after the crisis. Indeed, a study commissioned by the BCBS revealed in early 2013 enormous variations in capital held against the same assets by different banks because of contrasting assumptions made in models, leading some regulators to worry openly that banks were continuing to distort the intention of the rules.[36] As the vice chair of the US Federal Deposit Insurance Corporation (FDIC) Thomas Hoenig put it, "you can game Basel II and Basel III, and the fact is they are gamed in every instance."[37]

The formal capital requirements themselves have also been strongly criticized. Although minimum capital ratios were set at a higher level than before the crisis, the new levels were not higher than ratios held by many financial institutions that got in trouble during the crisis. As Boone and Johnson put it, "Basel III will end up with capital requirements for systemically important institutions no higher than that reported by Lehman the day before it failed."[38] For this reason, leading financial columnists such as Martin Wolf of the *Financial Times* have referred to the new capital standards as "the capital inadequacy ratio."[39] The head of Britain's Financial Services Authority and senior economists at the Bank of England have all argued that the minimum Tier one capital ratio should be at least twice as high.[40]

The "backstop" of the minimum leverage ratio is also very unlikely to serve as much of constraint in this context as it has been set only at 3%. The ex-chair of US FDIC Sheila Bair describes this as "paltry," while the existing chair Martin Gruenberg also noted in July 2013 that it "would not have appreciably mitigated the growth in leverage among these organizations [large institutions] in the years preceding the recent crisis."[41] The Bank of England's executive director for financial stability, Andrew Haldane, was much blunter in June 2013, admitting that the idea of an adoption of the 3% ratio as long-term goal for financial stability "sends shivers down my spine."[42] When the details of the new international leverage standard were announced in January 2014, journalists also noted that "ferocious" bank lobbying had succeeded in watering down the regulators' initial proposals about how even this limited leverage ratio would be calculated. As one bank analyst acknowledged, the outcome was "more of a win for the industry than I was expecting."[43]

The size of the capital surcharge on SIFIs that the BCBS agreed to in mid-2011 was also quite small and it was placed in a part of the agreement—Pillar II—that leaves its implementation up to the discretion of national supervisors.[44] The implementation of the counter-cyclical capital buffers was also left up to the discretion of national authorities. Many analysts questioned whether authorities will be willing to take the unpopular move of raising capital requirements during boom times in ways that curtail lending (and also hurt the international competitiveness of national banks).[45] Even if authorities do use counter-cyclical buffers, their implementation may be hindered by complicated voluntary reciprocity agreements that have been established for international banks. Under these agreements, host regulators will be reliant on home authorities to impose buffers on international banks operating in the boom country that are calculated on the basis of a weighted average of a bank's domestic and international exposures. As one British official put in early 2011: "Reciprocity is key. It only works if overseas banks entering a market have a similar increase in capital requirements."[46] But whether foreign authorities will play along with the preferences of host authorities was a very open question since their cooperation will be entirely voluntary. In the words of one financial journalist, "the deal is also remarkable for the trust implied by the reciprocal arrangements."[47]

It was hardly surprising, then, that analysts such as Lall describe the new Basel III standard as a "failure" that did not impose significant new constraints on banks and is unlikely to prevent bank collapses in the future.[48] What explains this failure? Lall himself attributes the result to the enduring influence of powerful international banks working through transnational lobby groups such as the Institute of International Finance. Although these banks strongly opposed many of the initial proposals, he argues that they were able to dilute those proposals to serve their interests because of their close access to, and cozy relationships with, regulators.

Others are more skeptical of the dominant influence of the private international bank lobby.[49] Indeed, insider accounts make clear that stricter regulation was precluded by sharp disagreement between representatives of different countries within the BCBS. Interestingly, the fiercest resistance within the BCBS did not come from the US and British officials; indeed, faced with domestic demands for tighter standards at home, many officials from these two countries (along with Switzerland) championed tighter standards at the international level. All the new members of the BCBS from emerging market countries also favored stronger regulation because of their domestic practices and the fact that their own banks held high levels of capital. The strongest resistance to reform came ironically instead from French and especially German authorities.[50]

This resistance partly reflected some distinctive features of their financial systems. For example, the greater reliance of non-financial firms in these two countries—particularly small and medium-sized businesses— on bank credit meant that the new rules would impact the wider economy more substantially than in Britain or the United States. The new Basel rules would also impose particularly high burdens on distinctively structured institutions such as the German Landesbanken and French mutual banks. More generally, French and especially German banks had been slower to write down bad assets and were more undercapitalized than their British and American counterparts at the time of the negotiations. Authorities in those countries were thus concerned about the impact of imposing tighter requirements quickly, particularly given the exposure of many banks to the European sovereign debt crisis at the time.[51]

ACCOUNTING, HEDGE FUNDS, AND CREDIT RATING AGENCIES

In addition to reforming bank regulation, the G20 leaders also signaled their concern about public oversight of international accounting rules. At their November 2008 summit, in addition to calling for convergence on a single set of global accounting standards by the IASB and its US counterpart the Financial Accounting Standards Board (FASB), they urged reforms to the governance of the IASB "to ensure transparency, accountability, and an appropriate relationship between this independent body and the relevant authorities."[52] Soon thereafter in January 2009, the IASB announced a new public accountability mechanism in the form of an international "monitoring board" that would approve the appointment (or reappointment) of the 22 trustees who oversee its operations. The board's members included the US and Japanese regulators, the European Commission, and representatives from the International Organization of Securities Commissions (for this body, see Chapter 5).

This move was quickly heralded as an example of how the crisis was generating reforms that overturned "private governance" mechanisms in global finance. But it is important to recognize that this governance reform had already been in the works before the crisis began as part of efforts to encourage worldwide harmonization around IASB standards.[53] Indeed, it was the IASB trustees who formally proposed the idea to the G20 leaders in advance of the November 2008 summit.[54] Even more important is the fact that, under IASB governance reforms announced in February 2012, the Board clarified that it could refer issues to the trustees and IASB chair for consideration, but it "did not intend to infringe upon IASB independence…In all cases, it is understood that the Monitoring Board will neither influence the decision-making process nor challenge the decisions made by the IASB with regard to substantive standard-setting."[55] Given this very limited role for the Board, it is understandable why critics such as Nölke have argued that the new Board may simply "shield the IASB against direct political influence, similar to the SEC's shielding function between Congress and FASB."[56] More generally, at this time, the Board also outlined a very narrow conception of public accountability, arguing that the IASB should exercise "its independence in a manner that serves the public interest by remaining accountable to investors, markets, and other market participants."[57] In other words, the "public" being invoked was simply investors and market participants, rather than the wider society affected by the accounting rules.

It is also noteworthy that the G20 leaders did little to challenge market-oriented fair value accounting despite widespread criticisms that it had exacerbated the crisis by encouraging a self-reinforcing downward spiral of declining prices and fire sales of assets. To be sure, the G20 leaders did call at their first summit for a review of how "valuation" may "exacerbate cyclical trends" and in April 2009 they welcomed a FSF report that argued that "the extensive application of fair value accounting" was one of the factors that had "contributed to an increase in the procyclicality of the system."[58] But their actual recommendations signaled an ongoing commitment to fair value accounting. They agreed that "the accounting standard setters should improve standards for the valuation of financial instruments based on their liquidity and investors' holding horizons, while reaffirming the framework of fair value accounting."[59] The issue then vanished entirely from the communiqués of the next G20 summits.

Its disappearance reflected a stalemate between the European Union and the United States. In October 2008, the European Union had pressured the IASB to relax its fair value rules because of concerns that they were reinforcing contractionary pressures. When IASB announced a new draft standard in mid-2009 on the issue, the European Union delayed its adoption because some members did not think the proposal went far enough in limiting the use of fair value accounting. While British interests remained staunch defenders of fair value accounting, the European Union's stance was heavily influenced by lobbying from German and French banks and insurers that hoped to avoid booking losses on troubled assets they held.[60]

Many US banks were also very critical of fair value accounting at the height of the crisis and they successfully lobbied for a temporary relaxation of FASB fair value rules just days before the G20 summit in April

2009—a fact that helps to explain the appearance of this issue in that summit communiqué.[61] But that decision was very controversial domestically, particularly among investor groups. Indeed, in May 2010, FASB then released proposed reforms that would force fair value accounting to be used *more* widely than in the past, although that proposal was subsequently dropped.[62] In May 2011, the IASB issued a new standard—IFRS 13—concerning fair value measurement that was developed as a result of a joint project with FASB. The standard sought to reconcile disagreements to some extent by focusing more on the issue of how to measure fair value than on when to apply it, and the European Union finally endorsed it in late 2012. Because of some of its specific provisions, Campbell-Verduyn argues that IFRS 13 actually "exemplifies the entrenchment of FVA and Anglo-Saxon principles in transnational accounting standards post-2008."[63]

While the G20 initiatives vis-à-vis accounting were very limited, the leaders promised more serious efforts to widen the focus of public regulation in some other sectors. At their first summit, they called for "a review of the scope of financial regulation, with a special emphasis on institutions, instruments, and markets that are currently unregulated, along with ensuring that all systemically-important institutions are appropriately regulated."[64] At their next summit, they were even more ambitious in agreeing "to extend regulation and oversight to all systemically important financial institutions, instruments and markets."[65] This goal was linked to their efforts to strengthen macroprudential regulation and it provided the justification for the G20 leaders to extend regulation and supervision to cover institutions and sector that had previously been subject to little or very weak official international rules.

One such set of institutions was credit rating agencies. These agencies were widely seen to have contributed to the crisis through their overly generous ratings of mortgages-backed securities and other structured finance products. Their mistaken ratings were attributed to flawed analyses and assumptions as well as to potential conflicts of interest stemming from the fact that they were paid by the underwriters of the securities they rated. At their first summit in November 2008, the G20 leaders promised that all rating agencies providing public ratings would be registered and that regulators would ensure that agencies complied with IOSCO's code of conduct that had been updated in May 2008.[66]

Like the accounting reforms, however, these moves were not terribly significant. Since 2006, authorities within the United States—home of the world's dominant rating agencies—had already required all rating agencies used for regulatory purposes to be registered and subjected to regulatory oversight. The G20 statement simply reflected the fact that the European Union caught up with US preferences on this approach. The IOSCO code also focused more on issues such as the need for information disclosure from the agencies (e.g., information about their methodologies, the historical track record of their ratings) than direct regulation of their funding model or the content of their ratings and ratings methodologies.[67] Perhaps not surprisingly, by 2013, accusations had already began to surface again that major US credit raters were resuming the practice of trying to capture more business through favorable ratings. As one investor put it, "You can see that we are slipping our way back to 2007."[68]

At their second summit in April 2009, the G20 leaders also endorsed "for the first time" the extension of official regulation and oversight to "systemically important hedge funds."[69] The rationale for tightening regulation of hedge funds was their potential systemic significance as well as concerns that their short-selling and deleveraging amplified the intensity of the crisis.[70] In specific terms, the G20 leaders committed that "hedge funds or their managers will be registered and will be required to disclose appropriate information on an ongoing basis to supervisors or regulators, including on their leverage, necessary for assessment of the systemic risks that they pose individually or collectively." They added that hedge funds "will be subject to oversight to ensure that they have adequate risk management."[71] A few months later in June, IOSCO recommended more specifically that hedge funds be required to follow rules concerning issues such as information disclosure to investors, conflicts of interest, and internal organization and operational conduct (e.g., protection of client funds, recordkeeping, the need for comprehensive risk management frameworks, and annual independent audits).[72]

Once again, these initiatives did not mark much of a change from the market-friendly pre-crisis international regime. To be sure, these standards endorsed the idea that public authorities should have a greater ability to monitor the ways in which hedge funds might contribute to systemic risks or market manipulation. But much of the focus of the new standards was once again on disclosing information to public authorities and investors. The G20 leaders did not endorse any actual constraints on the trading activities of hedge funds through measures that critics were calling for at the time such as caps on leverage, capital requirements, limits on positions or concentration, or restrictions on short-selling or the trading of derivatives. As Pagliari puts it, "the regulation that has emerged could be better described as 'enhanced oversight' of hedge funds managers than a 'granular approach' to closely regulating and constraining their investment activities."[73]

Within the G20 and IOSCO, some policymakers—particularly those from Germany and France—did indeed favor tighter regulation.[74] Ever since the East Asian crisis and the 1998 collapse of the hedge fund Long-term Credit Management, the German and French governments had pressed for tighter international regulation of hedge funds because of the latter's growing systemic significance and the challenges posed to corporate governance structures in their "organized market economies." But their regulatory goals had been thwarted by opposition from Britain and the United States, which together were home to about 85% of all hedge fund assets under management.[75] The new international standard reflected the fact that the United States and Britain became more supportive of official regulation.

But the limited nature of this support explains the weak content of the new international rules. In the US case, policy changed because of new domestic political circumstances rather than German and French lobbying. The crisis experience—including the high-profile arrest of Bernard Madoff in December 2008 for fraud in activities linked to hedge funds—strengthened the hand of regulators in the SEC who had sought in the pre-crisis period to better protect investors' interests. This relatively narrow objective, when combined with strong hedge fund lobbying, ensured that the appetite of US policymakers for radical reform was limited. Faced with the changed US position, the British came to see the G20 statement as a means to preempt stronger EU-wide regulation as well as trade-off for securing German and French support for ambitious British plans to boost the IMF's resources at the London G20 summit.[76]

OTC DERIVATIVES

More extensive initiatives were launched to bring the massive over-the-counter (OTC) derivatives markets under the official international regulatory umbrella for the first time. These markets had been a poster child for pre-crisis market-friendly regulation, but they quickly because the subject of official scrutiny because of their role in the crisis. The collapse of Bear Stearns in March 2008 and then Lehman Brothers and American International Group (AIG) in September 2008 revealed how the OTC market for credit default swaps (CDSs), in particular, had concentrated risk rather than dispersed it. Because large financial institutions had become extensively interconnected as counterparties to CDS contracts, a collapse of any one of them risked triggering a chain reaction. The lack of transparency of the markets also contributed to the severity of the financial panic because the scale of counterparty exposures to firms in distress was unknown. The fact that AIG had sold hundreds of billions of dollars worth of CDS contracts without adequate capital to back them also highlighted how the opacity and lack of regulation of the markets had allowed firms to hide risk and accumulate excessive leverage.[77]

As part of their macroprudential agenda, the G20 leaders made a number of commitments at their first meetings that were consolidated into four core objectives by the time of the Pittsburgh summit. First, to enhance transparency, market participants would have to report all contracts to "trade repositories" (which act as centralized electronic databases recording information about who has traded what and with whom). Second, transparency would be enhanced further by requiring all "standardized" OTC derivatives contracts to be traded on exchanges or electronic trading platforms (in which participants could gain a broader view of market prices and trading volumes). Third, all such contracts would also be cleared through regulated central counterparties (CCPs) that would reduce counterparty risks by serving as an intermediary between seller and buyer. Finally, contracts that were not centrally cleared would be subject to higher capital requirements that would help to protect the firms involved against counterparty risk.[78] Of all the reforms developed by the G20, these were the most ambitious in changing existing market practices. By steering trades through various central nodes—such as clearing houses, organized trading platforms, and trade repositories—the G20 leaders were committing to create what one analyst called a new kind of "ecosystem" for the markets.[79]

The content of the reforms closely followed core features of US domestic legislative proposals outlined by the Obama administration after it came into office in early 2009, proposals that were soon implemented under the Dodd–Frank bill passed in July 2010 by US Congress.[80] The Obama administration's commitment to reforms reflected both new skepticism of unregulated OTC markets among elite officials and experts as well as strong popular demand for regulation in the context of the severity of the crisis and anger at the fact that US taxpayer support of firms such as AIG was directly linked to their OTC CDS activities. Indeed, previously obscure topics such as the regulation of credit default swaps suddenly became the subject of public debate and legislative discussion.

To prevent its new tighter domestic rules from driving derivatives business offshore, US officials pressed for new international standards that would encourage foreign jurisdictions to follow its lead. To secure foreign compliance, the United States threatened to deny access to US markets to firms not complying with new US rules. In fact, many policymakers in other countries welcomed the US initiative and its new willingness to support tighter regulations over OTC derivatives. European officials also faced similar domestic pressures for reform as their US counterparts and quickly launched similar legislative initiatives that echoed those in the United States.

While the G20 action on derivatives was quick, the ambition of the reforms was diluted by the vagueness of key terms such as "standardized" contracts or "electronic trading platforms" that enable market actors to find loopholes, allowing them to continue pre-crisis trading patterns. The wording reflected both the caution of lead US officials such as Tim Geithner as well as compromises made by US officials in their domestic legislative initiatives in the face of strong private sector lobbying. The strongest opponents of tighter controls were the large dealer banks that had dominated pre-crisis trading and earned enormous revenue from its large volume and high margins. Pressure for vaguer language also stemmed from other private sector groups, including non-financial groups that worried that tight new rules would increase the cost of their use of derivatives products.[81]

It is worth noting, however, that not all private financial interests have opposed reforms. For example, financial exchanges backed the G20 push for greater exchange trading and clearing, seeing these as a way to capture more of the expanding derivatives markets away from the dealer banks. "Buy-side" investors were also keen on official initiatives to reduce the opacity and dealer-controlled nature of OTC markets in ways that would benefit them and encourage more participation in the market. These distributional benefits for powerful private sector actors help to explain why regulatory change vis-à-vis OTC derivatives reforms was more extensive than in some other sectors.

From the standpoint of the theme of this chapter, the most significant limitation of the G20 derivatives reform agenda was its market-friendly character. The central goal of the reforms was to make the markets more resilient and transparent to regulators and other market participants. Little was done to restrict their growth. Indeed, the new ecosystem is likely to encourage even more derivatives trading than before the crisis as products are standardized and trading becomes less opaque. Some of the private sector support for the reforms was driven by precisely this goal.

It is also noteworthy that the G20 refused to endorse widespread calls for more anti-market forms of regulation, such as restrictions on some kinds of OTC derivatives contracts. For example, the Bank for

International Settlements (BIS) and others suggested all new financial products be registered and evaluated on an ongoing basis by a consumer financial products regulator for the systemic risks they might pose.[82] Like pharmaceutical drugs, some products could be endorsed for everyone's use (such as over-the-counter drugs), others could be restricted to authorized users (such as prescription drugs), still others could be available only in limited amounts to prescreened users (such as drugs on experimental trials), while a final category could be banned. Advocates of this system of precautionary regulation argued that it would help officials to evaluate and regulate OTC derivatives such as CDS in a more comprehensive and nuanced way.

Many critics of the CDS market focused particular attention on the need for restrictions on "unattached" CDS contracts that permit investors to speculate on the likelihood of default on the underlying bond without actually owning that security. In the words of New York insurance superintendent Eric Dinallo, these products—which made up the bulk of the CDS market—were the equivalent of "taking out insurance on your neighbour's house and maybe hoping it blows up."[83] Because insurance law bans the purchase of insurance where there is no underlying interest, many joined Dinallo in asking why this product was allowed.[84] George Soros reinforced these calls with a high-profile argument about how CDS contracts had worsened the crisis by offering speculators convenient ways to short-sell bonds with limited risk. This feature, he argued, encouraged self-reinforcing bear raids, a phenomenon that he believed helped to explain the collapse of Lehman and AIG. Many analysts concluded along with Soros that CDS contracts were intrinsically "toxic" and should be banned.[85]

Speculation against Greek sovereign bonds in 2010 rekindled interest in this issue, prompting European governments to approve the use of temporary bans on trading of unattached CDS on sovereign debt in emergency situations in the fall of 2011. Earlier, Germany and Luxembourg had pressed for wider international action, but the idea was rejected by the United States, where domestic legislative initiatives to ban the product had been defeated in the face of strong opposition from the financial sector.[86] At their November 2011 summit, the G20 leaders called for fur-ther study of "the functioning of credit default swap (CDS) markets and the role of those markets in price formation of underlying assets", but no further action was taken.[87]

The G20 also did not challenge the profit-seeking mandates of institu-tions such as CCPs that they had now placed at the center of the mar-kets. With all standardized OTC trades now being steered through CCPs, counterparty risks were becoming concentrated in these bodies in ways that transform them into systemically important institutions. Authorities recognized the risk that privately owned, profit-maximizing CCPs might be tempted to compete for business by relaxing their prudential rules.[88] Indeed, in 2010, the Bank of England argued that "user-ownership and not-for-profit governance arrangements provide the strongest incentives for effective risk management, aligning CCPs' interests with suppliers of capital."[89] After leaving his position as deputy governor of the Bank of England, Paul Tucker was much blunter in early 2014: "Were a clearing-house to fail in a disorderly way, I am certain that legislators would ask why on earth the authorities had allowed them to be for-profit entities."[90] But the G20 made no effort to mandate nonprofit governance arrange-ments—let alone public ownership—for this core infrastructure of the markets.[91] Instead, the G20 reforms had the effect of encouraging a rather intense competitive scramble among the world's leading banks and exchanges to capture the new clearing business.

The only area where the G20 endorsed significant anti-market regula-tion was with respect to the regulation and supervision of commodity derivatives. At their Cannes summit in late 2011, the G20 leaders backed new IOSCO principles in this area that included support for trading restrictions—such as ceilings on the positions that market participants can take in specific contracts—in order to limit market manipulation, volatility, and concentration.[92] Indeed, the G20 leaders went out of their way to state that "market regulators should have, and use formal position management powers, including the power to set ex-ante position limits."[93] Like other aspects of the G20 derivatives agenda, this initiative emerged largely from US domestic priorities. In the wake of severe food and oil price volatility during 2008, a very broad-based coalition of US advocacy groups and businesses in the agricultural, food, and energy sectors had pressed successfully—despite strong opposition from financial interests— for position limits to be imposed on OTC commodity derivatives markets in the July 2010 Dodd–Frank bill.[94] US policymakers then quickly pressed for international harmonization via the new IOSCO standards, an initiative that was supported in Europe and elsewhere.

The international endorsement of position limits in commodity derivatives markets represented an exception to the general tenor of post-crisis international regulatory reforms.[95] As we have seen, these reforms certainly extended official oversight to new markets and institutions, but they generally did so in a very limited, market-friendly way. The focus was on enhancing transparency rather than banning products, restricting market activity, or directly interfering with firms' activities. As Pagliari puts it, the shift in the public–private divide has pertained "more to the consolidation of the authority to regulate and oversee these markets and institutions in the hands of public regulatory than a change in the purpose and content of their regulatory intervention."[96]

CONSTRAINING CAPITAL MOBILITY?

A final regulatory issue deserving discussion was potentially the most anti-market one: constraints on cross-border capital movements. Because large-scale international financial flows contributed to the US financial bubble, prominent analysts such as Dani Rodrik and Arvind Subramanian argued as early as January 2008 that restrictions on capital mobility should be part of the international regulatory reform agenda. In their view, restrictions on capital mobility were in fact more likely to minimize future crises than efforts to strengthen international prudential regulation, given the difficulties regulators encounter keeping up with market innovations: "if the risk-taking behavior of financial intermediaries cannot be regulated perfectly, we need to find ways of reducing the volume of transactions ... What this means is that financial capital should be flowing across borders in smaller quantities, so that finance is "primarily national," as John Maynard Keynes advised."[97]

Rodrik subsequently called for two specific international reforms. The first was the introduction of a "Tobin tax." Named after economist James Tobin, who first proposed it in the early 1970s, this small tax would be imposed on all international financial transactions as a means of discouraging speculative flows while not interfering with productive, long-term international capital movements. Rodrik also urged the International Monetary Fund (IMF) to provide more proactive support for the efforts of Southern governments to control financial flows for prudential purposes. In his view, the experience of the previous two decades had demonstrated the usefulness of restrictions on excessive foreign borrowing in good times and controls on capital flight during crises.[98]

Rodrik was not the only person calling for these kinds of policies to be added to international reform agenda after the outbreak of the crisis. In their formal statement to the spring 2008 meetings of the IMF and World Bank, an international coalition of labor unions called for "measures to protect national economies against destabilizing speculative capital movements, including Tobin tax and capital controls put in place by national governments."[99] Some politicians such as Germany's Oskar Lafontaine – former finance minister and now leader of the newly created Left Party - also called in early 2008 for the worldwide reintroduction of regulation to control capital flows, arguing "we need investments in the real economy, not speculative transactions."[100]

The issue was hardly discussed, however, by the G20 leaders at their first three summits. In the hundreds of pages of international official documents associated with these summits, I have found only three places where the regulation of cross-border capital flows received any attention on the international reform agenda. The first was a vague reference in the formal communiqué from the first G20 summit: "Regulators should enhance their coordination and cooperation across all segments of financial markets, *including with respect to cross-border capital flows.*"[101] The second was a sentence in a G20 working group report at the time of the second G20 summit in London. After tasking international financial institutions with analyzing the causes of the crisis and drawing lessons, the Working Group noted simply that "they should also give attention to the impact of global capital flows on global financial stability."[102] The third and more substantial mention was the G20 leaders' support for ongoing initiatives to clamp down in illicit capital outflows from developing countries, such as the World Bank's Stolen Asset Recovery program and other various multilateral efforts to curtail outflows linked to tax evasion, corruption, and bribery.[103]

The relative lack of attention to this issue contrasted with the experience of the East Asian crisis a decade earlier. At that time, the contribution of capital mobility to the crises experienced in the region had immediately been the subject of heated debates in international policy circles.[104] While US and IMF officials strongly defended financial openness, many East Asian analysts and policymakers openly attacked foreign speculators for contributing to the crises they experienced, and some governments, such as Malaysia, reimposed capital controls to protect their policy autonomy.

The country at the core of the 2008 crisis—the United States—had less reason to raise the issue than East Asian countries had a decade earlier. As discussed in Chapter 3, its financial crisis had unfolded in a very different manner than those in East Asia in the late 1990s. While capital inflows contributed to its domestic bubble, the United States did not experience capital flight and an exchange rate crisis when the bubble burst. Instead, demand for the dollar increased and the United States continued to receive large foreign capital inflows that helped to ease the burden of adjusting to the crisis. US policymakers thus saw restrictions on international financial flows in a negative rather than positive light. Indeed, US structural power within global financial markets had encouraged US policymakers to favor financial liberalization for several decades, a preference reinforced by neoliberal ideas and the interests of powerful internationally oriented US financial institutions.[105]

It was not until the lead up to the June 2010 G20 summit that the proposals Rodrik and others had advanced began to appear on the international reform agenda. In the case of the Tobin tax, it began to attract more official attention, not so much as a tool to reduce capital mobility but rather as a revenue-raising device in the context of debates about forcing financial institutions to share more of the costs of bailouts. At the September 2009 G20 summit, Britain—supported by France and Germany—had pressed successfully for the inclusion in the final communiqué of a request for the IMF to report on "the range of options countries have adopted or are considering as to how the financial sector could make a fair and substantial contribution toward paying for any burdens associated with government interventions to repair the banking system."[106] The resulting IMF report surprised many by providing a detailed rationale—drawing in part on macroprudential thought—for types of internationally coordinated levies/taxes on the financial sector.[107] The previous fall, prominent officials such as Adair Turner, the chair of Britain's Financial Services Authority, had also noted approvingly that a Tobin tax could constrain "excessive activity and profits" in the financial sector, which had, in his view, "grown beyond a socially reasonable size."[108] At a meeting of G20 finance officials in November 2009 in the United Kingdom, British Prime Minister Gordon Brown had also called for an international tax on financial transactions.[109] The French and German governments were also keen on such a tax.[110]

At their June 2010 summit, however, the G20 refused to endorse the IMF's report. While the United States was interested in discussing bank levies (which Obama had proposed domestically in January, but that were removed from the final Dodd–Frank bill in Congressional bargaining in late June[111]), top US officials such as Geithner made clear their opposition to an international transaction tax. A number of other G20 members were also opposed, including the host of the summit, Canada, as well as Australia, Brazil, China, India, Japan, Mexico, and others.[112] At their November 2011 summit in Cannes, the G20 leaders considered proposals for a financial transactions tax (FTT) once again, but agreement remained elusive despite some high-profile advocacy of the issue by Bill Gates and others. In the end, a number of countries implemented levies and taxes on the financial sector on their own, and eleven EU countries agreed in early 2013 to introduce a coordinated FTT in their markets in 2014. But no coordinated action was endorsed at the global level.

Also attracting more attention at this time was Rodrik's other proposal for the IMF to become more supportive of Southern capital controls. The issue of Southern governments' efforts to regulate cross-border capital flows appeared on the G20 agenda at the November 2010 summit in Seoul when the leaders called for "further work on macro-prudential policy frameworks, including tools to mitigate the impact of excessive capital flows."[113] At this time, the leaders had also made a broader commitment to "better reflect the perspective of emerging market economies in financial regulatory reforms."[114] Up until this point in time, Southern countries had let the advanced industrial countries set the agenda of international regulatory reform. This deference partly reflected their newcomer status within the inner club of international regulatory politics as well as their recognition of the dominant market power in the financial sector of those countries. They also generally welcomed any new willingness of the G7 countries to tighten controls over their financial systems. A decade earlier, the G7 countries had seen the creation of new international financial standards as a way to contain negative externalities arising from poor regulation in Southern countries. Now the shoe was on the other foot, as the poor regulatory practices in the United States and Europe undermined financial stability in the developing world. Southern officials were also very supportive of the macroprudential agenda, which many saw as reflective of similar goals they already pursued domestically.[115] As one BIS official noted, "emerging market representatives bring useful macroprudential experience to the table."[116]

The one issue that Northern countries were not discussing, however, was the use of capital controls. While Southern governments lacked power to force Northern countries to accept tighter regulations, many were intent on defending their autonomy to implement controls themselves. Many Southern policymakers felt very strongly that such controls had an important role to play in macroprudential policy because financial crises in their countries were often preceded by capital inflows and/or exacerbated by large-scale capital flight. These views were strengthened by the experience of the 2008 crisis in which countries with capital controls—such as China and India—were often more insulated from the severe financial turmoil in US and European markets. After investors initially fled emerging markets during the crisis, financial flows soon reversed in 2009–2011 when US and European monetary easing prompted investors to seek higher returns in many emerging markets. In the latter context, capital account restrictions also came to be seen in emerging market countries as a key tool for preventing very large capital inflows from driving up their exchange rates and/or generate domestic financial bubbles.[117]

This new circumstance encouraged Southern members of the G20 to become more assertive in demanding that the usefulness of capital controls be discussed on the international regulatory agenda. A debate had already been promoted on the topic by the October 2009 decision of Brazil—a country that was attracting large capital inflows because its domestic interest rates were far higher than those of the United States—to impose a tax on short-term financial inflows. Writing in the *Financial Times*, Subramanian and Williamson urged the IMF to actively support Brazil's initiative: "The world needs a less doctrinaire approach to foreign capital flows. Helping Brazil in its decision last week rather than issuing a negative response would signal that the IMF is playing a constructive role in facilitating this shift."[118] Soon after, IMF Managing Director Dominique Strauss-Kahn declared that the IMF was not opposed to capital controls: "I have no ideology on this."[119] Indeed, the Fund had already supported the use of capital controls in some of its crisis lending programs, most notably in Iceland which—like Malaysia a decade earlier—imposed controls on financial outflows.[120]

But Southern policymakers were also acutely aware that many Northern policymakers—particularly US policymakers and US financial interests—remained skeptical of capital account restrictions. The competing Northern and Southern perspectives were apparent in a set of non-binding "conclusions for the management of capital flows" that G20 finance officials endorsed in October 2011 in advance of the leaders' summit in Cannes. On the one hand, the statement reflected Southern governments' concerns by noting that "there is no one-size-fits-all approach or rigid definition of conditions for the use of capital flow management measures." But it also stressed the long-term goal of putting in place conditions "that allow members to reap the benefits from free capital movements" and it was not accompanied by any significant policy initiative to help countries strengthen their counter-cyclical capital account restrictions.[121] Reflecting the ongoing disagreements on the issue, the G20 finance officials chose instead to support a quite different initiative to develop and deepen local currency bond markets in developing countries as a way to bolster resilience against shocks induced by capital flows.[122]

In late 2012, the IMF announced its new institutional view on the question that would help to inform its surveillance activities. The new view explicitly built on the G20 statement as well as IMF staff work and some heated discussions on the Fund's executive board. Much media attention was given to the fact that it endorsed the use of "capital flow management measures." But it was hardly a ringing endorsement. The document stressed the need for controls on inflow surges or disruptive outflows to be *temporary*, and it noted that capital flows management measures "should not be used to substitute for or avoid warranted macroeconomic adjustment." After noting that "there is no presumption that full liberalization is an appropriate goal for all countries at all times," the document also argued that "careful liberalization of capital flows can provide significant benefits, which countries could usefully work toward realizing over the long run."[123]

These G20 and IMF statements certainly fell well short of the ambitions of many supporters of capital controls. For example, Brazilian officials, who had been playing a leading role among the BRICS (Brazil, Russia, India, China, and South Africa) in pressing the issue, complained that the IMF position was still too cautious and had a "pro-liberalisation bias."[124] It is also easy to overstate the extent of the shift of international policy on the issue. Even at the height of the IMF enthusiasm for financial liberalization in the 1990s, the institution had sometimes been sympathetic to the use of capital controls.[125] When IMF management had sought more of a mandate to promote capital account liberalization in the late 1990s, a wide coalition of Southern governments—backed by some officials from G7 countries— had also successfully resisted the initiative. That outcome had ensured that all countries continued to retain an unrestricted right to control capital movements under Article 6 of the IMF's Articles of Agreement, as they had since the 1944 Bretton Woods conference. In other words, free market ideology had never been firmly entrenched in this aspect of global financial governance. Brazil and the other BRICS and developing countries continued during the post-crisis discussions to resist any effort to amend the IMF Articles of Agreement. The G20 and IMF statements also reiterated this existing right to use capital controls, even if they did signal a greater willingness to allow the IMF itself to endorse their use.[126]

One way that they could have gone further was suggested by a few IMF staff members who resurrected some innovative ideas from the time of Bretton Woods during the lead-up to the institution's December 2012 statement. During the Bretton Woods negotiations of the early 1940s, both John Maynard Keynes and Harry Dexter White had noted that the efforts of countries to control financial movements would benefit from international cooperation between sending and receiving countries. As Keynes had put it, controls would be less effective "by unilateral action than if movements of capital can be controlled *at both ends*."[127] In an IMF "staff discussion note" of September 2012, Ostry, Ghosh, and Korinek had supported Keynes' and White's idea of enlisting the help of source countries in controlling capital flows, noting that recipient countries "would welcome attacking the problem of volatile capital flows at both ends of the transaction."[128] Specifically, they had noted that source countries could regulate the cross-border activities of financial institutions headquartered in their countries. The IMF's institutional document of December did note that "source countries should better internalize the spillovers from their monetary and prudential policies," but it did not explicitly endorse controls "at both ends."[129]

CONCLUSION

Taking these various initiatives as a whole, the G20 leaders certainly deserved applause for tackling a wide range of issues in their efforts to reform international financial regulatory standards. But the content of the reforms endorsed by the G20 fell well short of the predictions of transformative change made when the crisis began. Basel III did not impose strong new constraints on banks and it continued to rely on their internal models for risk weighing of assets. Although the G20 endorsed greater public oversight over international accounting standards, credit rating agencies, and hedge funds, the market-friendly content of international standards in these sectors was not overturned. The same is true of the extensive initiatives vis-à-vis OTC derivatives, with the exception of the endorsement of position limits vis-a-vis OTC commodity derivatives. The expressions of support for capital controls from the G20 and IMF were also far from enthusiastic and simply reiterated longstanding international commitments.

Rather than turning their back on the "market-friendly" nature of the pre-crisis international financial regulatory regime, the G20 leaders merely tweaked its content.What explains this outcome? Each specific case discussed in this chapter had some unique dynamics, but it is possible to draw some generalizations across the cases by returning to the three developments identified near the start of the crisis as opening the possibility of more radical change: the political weakening of private financial interests; eroding credibility of free market ideas, and challenges to the Anglo-American leadership. Why were these developments not more influential?

To begin with, the challenges to Anglo-American leadership were more muted and less significant than many anticipated at the start of the crisis. As we have seen, China and other emerging Southern powers were very supportive of tighter international standards and macroprudential approaches to regulation, but they recognized their lack of market power and took a back seat in the international negotiations over most of these issues, with the exception of the debates on capital controls (which touched directly on their capacity to protect policy autonomy). Their preference for market-constraining regulation was also not consistent, as witnessed by the opposition of some Southern countries to the international FTT initiative in mid-2010.[130]

Despite their strong criticism of Anglo-American lax regulation at the start of the crisis, German and French officials were also not consistent in pressing for tighter regulation. As we have seen, they ended up blocking tighter international standards for bank regulation favored by the United States, Britain, and others during the Basel III negotiations. The impact of the European sovereign debt crisis on their banks helped to encourage a more chastened position.[131] Policymakers from these two countries did press for more anti-market regulation in areas such as accounting, hedge funds, the FTT, and unattached CDS, but their ability to coerce the United States into agreement by flexing the European Union's collective market power was constrained by the difficulties of securing EU-wide agreement on these goals—often because of British opposition.

The limited nature of international regulatory reforms in many areas also reflected the enduring ability of the United States to shape outcomes in this field. To be sure, there were limits to their ability to get their way, as European resistance to US preferences in the Basel III negotiations revealed. But it is striking that the United States both launched the process of international reform in September 2007 and then subsequently set many of its core parameters. Because of the enduring importance of US financial markets, US officials were able to shape the reform agenda and veto international initiatives that went beyond their preferences.[132] They also gained influence from the fact that their domestic regulatory reforms were often developed more quickly than in Europe and elsewhere, giving them a kind of "first-mover" advantage in setting the agenda with an existing "regulatory template" for international negotiations.[133]

From the very start, US preferences toward international regulatory reform were closely tied to the politics of its domestic reforms (although its reticence to back capital controls was linked more to its continuing dependence on foreign capital inflows and the preference of private financial interests for financial openness). One month before it asked the FSF in September 2007 to develop a reform agenda, the Bush administration had begun preparing its own proposals for domestic regulatory tightening. In this context, US officials recognized that internationally coordinated regulatory tightening would help minimize competitive disadvantages for US markets and firms that could result from unilateral US action. From the fall of 2007 onwards, they worked closely with the FSF to coordinate the content of US and international reform proposals.[134] The desire of US policymakers and regulators to foster this kind of coordination only intensified when the proposals for domestic reform became increasingly ambitious with the deepening of the crisis in 2008 and the intensifying domestic pressure for action. This coordination was remarkably successful. Most of the issues addressed in the international reform process paralleled US domestic reform priorities, and their content usually went no further than US legislative initiatives.

To explain many post-crisis international regulatory outcomes, it is thus important to examine the limited nature of US domestic regulatory reforms. A number of policy insiders and analysts have argued that the content of many of those reforms was watered down by strong private sector lobbying.[135] Indeed, it quickly became clear that the predictions at the height of the crisis of a political weakening of private financial interests had been overstated. To be sure, the crisis experience and massive bailouts generated demands among US politicians and wider societal groups for a range of tighter regulations that private financial interests opposed. But the very generosity and success of the public rescues and liquidity provision during the crisis ensured that many private financial interests rebounded quickly from the experience and retained enormous clout. As Barofsky puts it, "Paulson and Geithner hadn't just saved the banks, they'd also preserved a status quo that was dangerously broken."[136]

As in the pre-crisis period, financial institutions continued to shape outcomes through well-organized and well-financed lobbying, and by their technical expertise in an issue area that others often found complex.[137] Analysts also often point to their unique access to regulators, particularly in the context of shared norms and extensive networks between the financial industry and regulators.[138] Many analysts have focused particularly on the enduring clout of the largest banks. In the wake of various mergers and acquisitions, the top US banks emerged from the crisis even larger and potentially more powerful than before.[139] The public bailouts and support were not used to confront their power, but rather to socialize their losses. Indeed, some analysts had been skeptical from the very start about whether the bailouts signaled a political weakening of the banks

for this reason. From this standpoint, the public support of the banks signaled the continued ability of these institutions to manipulate the state to
serve their interests rather than an erosion of their influence.[140]

Despite their extensive reform agenda, the G20 made little effort to
develop international standards that might tackle the issue of the potential "capture" of regulatory process by private financial actors. Despite
widespread discussion of this issue in the media and scholarly community, there was what Andrew Sheng called a "deafening silence" about it
in official circles.[141] Sheng contrasts this experience with the discussions
after the Asian crisis when Western policymakers were quick to blame
the crisis on "crony capitalism" and to prescribe governance reforms as
a solution. Indeed, the post-1998 international standards regime itself
was designed in part to address this governance issue. When crisis struck
countries at the core of global financial system, however, the issue was
not given the same official profile. No effort was made, for example, to
develop standards for regulators that minimize the problem of "revolving
doors" by banning regulators from working for firms they have regulated,
or requiring mandatory public disclosure of all past and present industry
ties of regulators.[142] As Barth, Caprio, and Levine note more generally,
important initiatives such as the Dodd–Frank Act and Basel III steered
clear of "*the* central financial regulatory challenge: how to get regulators
to act in society's best interest."[143]

The lead role of the large banks in fending off challenges to
market-friendly regulation should not be overstated, however.[144] In the
cases analyzed in this chapter, other private sector actors were also active
in lobbying against market-constraining regulatory reforms, such as
credit rating agencies, hedge funds, accounting firms, exchanges, investor groups, and even non-financial firms. As we have seen, large US banks
were also sometimes *supportive* of market-constraining regulation, such
as when they lobbied for a relaxation of fair value accounting. The latter
case also highlights the need to recognize that the views of the private
financial community were not homogeneous. In the case of accounting, investor groups objected strongly to banks' efforts to relax fair value
accounting. Buy-side investors and exchanges also clashed with the large

dealer banks over the content of OTC derivatives reform. In addition, some institutional investors favored tighter controls over hedge fund operations. Similarly, some banks backed tighter regulation of credit rating agencies against the latter's wishes.

More generally, it is clear that the limited ambition of US financial reforms reflected more than just the lobbying of private sector interests. As in the pre-crisis period, the ideas of policymakers were also significant. Before the crisis, the content of US regulation—and international financial standards—had been strongly influenced by the fact that many important US policymakers embraced neoliberal ideas and technical concepts such as the efficient market hypothesis. There is no question that those ideas were challenged by the crisis experience, but why did that phenomenon not have more impact on the regulatory reforms?

Some analysts have suggested that the absence of a major shift in economic policy paradigm after the wake of the crisis can be attributed to the lack of a clear alternative to neoliberal ideas.[145] In the specific case of the financial regulatory realm, however, this argument is hard to sustain because the crisis did result in the sudden political prominence of a clear alternative: the new macroprudential regulatory philosophy. Particularly striking was the rapid conversion to this new philosophy of financial officials working within the influential transgovernmental networks associated with the G20 process and various international financial institutions and standard setting bodies. Within these circles, macroprudential ideas provided a broad intellectual justification for many of the regulatory initiatives discussed in this chapter such as counter-cyclical buffers, tighter controls on liquidity and SIFIs, the extension of public oversight to new sectors, transaction taxes, and support for capital controls.

But the content of macroprudential ideas also helped to explain the limits of the US regulatory response (and by extension, many international regulatory outcomes). Although these ideas offered a critique of the efficient market hypothesis, they backed constraints on markets only insofar as the latter contributed to systemic risk. Because the latter concept was rather vague and hard to identify precisely, its meaning and policy significance were hotly contested.[146] For some, the new macroprudential thinking could rationalize quite anti-market regulations. For others, how-ever, it was invoked to defend the more limited international regulatory reforms undertaken involving extension of greater public oversight over markets with a focus on supervision and monitoring, without actually constraining private activities in significant ways. Many US officials were attracted to this latter approach. As one BIS official noted in late 2011, the US acceptance of macroprudential ideas "was always half-hearted and, even now, sometimes quite partial, at least in policy, I presume partly for 'philosophical' reasons."[147]

In this more restricted form, macroprudential ideas in fact provided policymakers with a perfect cover for responding to demands for tighter regulation but in a manner not too radical from the standpoint of the financial sector. The containment of systemic risk became the rallying call for policymakers and regulators rather than values that might have led to stronger controls on markets, such as distributive concerns relating to wealth and power of the financial sector vis-à-vis public authorities and other societal interests.[148] Indeed, it is often forgotten that, in this limited form, macroprudential ideas were less new to the global financial regula-tory order than some suggested. They had even been invoked as one of the central rationales for the creation in 1999 of the body at the center of the pre-crisis international financial standards project: the FSF. In an important report from 1999 commissioned by the G7 that led to the FSF's creation, former Bundesbank president Hans Tietmeyer had argued that the FSF was needed for authorities to take wider view that would over-come "the separate treatment of micro-prudential and macro-prudential issues" and enable "a better understanding of the sources of systemic risk."[149] This link between macroprudential ideas and the market-friendly international financial standards of the pre-crisis period highlights the ambiguity of the philosophy and its limitations as a challenge to pre-crisis order.[150]

Was a Fourth Pillar of Global Economic Architecture Created?

One issue neglected in Chapter 4 was the question of how the new post-crisis international financial standards will be enforced. Before the crisis, analysts often complained about the weak nature of the governance of international financial standards. In contrast to the international trade agreements, international financial standards have long been "soft law" with which compliance is entirely voluntary.[1] They have been developed by relatively obscure international standard setting bodies with no formal power and little capacity to encourage compliance. Left to the discretion of national authorities, past compliance with international financial standards was frequently uneven at the national level.[2]

One of the accomplishments of the G20 was to bring a new organization into existence—the Financial Stability Board (FSB)—to help strengthen the governance of international financial regulation. Established at the London G20 summit in April 2009, the FSB was in fact the only new institution to emerge from the post-crisis global financial reforms (aside from the G20 leaders forum itself). Its creators heralded it as an innovation of major importance. US Treasury Secretary Tim Geithner described the FSB's significance in the following way:

> the important thing we did in London…is to add, in effect, a fourth pillar to the architecture of cooperation we established after the second

world war. After the second world war, we came together and established
the IMF, the World Bank, the GATT which became the WTO. But the
Financial Stability Board is, in effect, a fourth pillar of that architecture.[3]

Geithner's comments came in response to a reporter's question about
how the new post-crisis international regulations would be enforced.
Others quickly picked up this ambitious image of the FSB as a new
fourth pillar of the architecture of global economic governance that
would promote compliance with international financial standards. In
the words of the FSB's charter itself, the goal of the institution was to
create a "level playing field" internationally in which the G20's regulatory reforms were implemented in coherent fashion that generated
regulatory convergence rather than fragmentation. Did the FSB live up
to this ambitious billing in its first few years? How much did the FSB's
creation represent an innovation in the governance of international
financial standards?

This chapter addresses these questions, focusing on the issue that
Geithner was addressing: the FSB's role in enforcing the implementation of the new international financial standards.[4] I argue that the
FSB's creation represented a much less significant innovation than
Geithner was suggesting. Rather than being created *de novo*, the FSB
built directly on an organization that had been created a decade earlier—the Financial Stability Forum (FSF)—whose history is described
in the first section of this chapter. The second and third sections of
the chapter then highlight how the FSB—like its predecessor—was
given very little power to enforce the implementation of international
financial standards. As the fourth section notes, this weakness was
particularly problematic given the extensive political challenges associated with the implementation of post-crisis international regulatory
reforms, but it reflected a deep-seated resistance of many states—
including the United States—to abandoning regulatory sovereignty.
The final section of the chapter then argues that this resistance was
in fact even reinforced by various crisis and post-crisis experiences
that increasingly encouraged policymakers to back greater financial

market and regulatory fragmentation along national lines rather than an internationally level playing field.

THE EVOLUTION OF THE GOVERNANCE OF INTERNATIONAL FINANCIAL STANDARDS

It is important to recognize that the governance of today's international financial standards initially emerged outside of the 1944 Bretton Woods' legal and institutional framework. Discussions surrounding international financial regulation during the Bretton Woods negotiations were focused almost exclusively on the issue of the use of controls over cross-border financial flows. The question of designing international standards for governing globally integrated financial markets was largely ignored for the simple reason that few policymakers anticipated the dramatic globalization of financial markets that took place from the 1960s onwards.[5]

When the first international bank standards—the 1975 Basel Concordat and the 1988 Basel Accord—were created, the forum in which they were negotiated was the Basel Committee on Banking Supervision (BCBS) rather than the Bretton Woods institutions. The BCBS was located within the Basel-based Bank for International Settlements (BIS), an institution that predated the 1944 Bretton Woods conference. Created by the 1930 Hague convention to facilitate German reparations payments and broader central bank cooperation, the BIS' founding members included six central banks (from the United Kingdom, France, Italy, Germany, Japan, and Belgium) as well as a private US banking group. At the Bretton Woods conference, a resolution had in fact been passed calling for the liquidation of the BIS "at the earliest possible moment" because of its association with private financial interests as well as concerns about its possible links to Germany during the war. But the BIS had survived and it emerged in the 1960s as an important body facilitating central bank cooperation, particularly among the G10 countries of the United States, Canada, Japan, West Germany, France, Italy, the United Kingdom, Sweden, the Netherlands, and Belgium. It was bank supervisors from those G10 countries—plus

Luxembourg and Switzerland—that created the Basel Committee on Banking Supervision in 1974.

The Bretton Woods agreements were legally binding commitments between governments that were approved by national legislatures. By contrast, both the Concordat and the Basel Accord were simply informal agreements among BCBS members that were not legally constraining in any way (indeed, the Concordat was not even made public until 1981). Despite this soft-law character, however, these standards were widely implemented among BCBS members and beyond. Compliance with the Basel Accord was encouraged by threat that the United States and Britain might deny access to their important markets to noncomplying states.[6] Some scholars also argue that compliance was fostered by the desire of bank supervisors to maintain relationships, trust, and reputations vis-à-vis each other as their networks of cooperation intensified (including among bank supervisors from countries outside of the BCBS member-ship to which the BCBS increasingly engaged in outreach activities). In the case of the Basel Accord, there were also market incentives to comply as the Accord came to be seen as symbol of banking stability.[7]

When the G7 set out to create a "new international financial architec-ture" in the late 1990s, the governance of international financial stan-dards became more complex. The complexity was partly a product of the fact that the new international financial standards endorsed by the G7 at this time were created by a wider set of international standards-setting bodies (SSBs) than just the BCBS. For example, international stan-dards for securities regulation were developed by the Madrid-based International Organization for Securities Commissions (IOSCO) that had been established in 1983 (initially in Montreal). International standards for insurance supervision were created by the International Association of Insurance Supervisors (IAIS), established within the BIS in 1994. A BIS-based body established in 1990—the Committee on Payment and Settlement Systems (CPSS)—generated the core principles for "systemati-cally important payments systems." Finally, as we saw in Chapter 4, the G7 also endorsed international accounting standards developed by the London-based International Accounting Standards Board (IASB) that had been established in 2001. Like the BCBS, none of these SSBs had been created by formal international treaties, and they all had very few staff and little formal power. Their main purpose was to facilitate networks of informal cooperation and information sharing.

To bring greater coherence to this cluttered institutional landscape, the G7 created one more institution in 1999: the Financial Stability Forum (FSF). Housed in the BIS, this body brought together in one place for the first time the key international standard setters (the BCBS, IAIS, IOSCO, IASB, CPSS), other key international bodies (the IMF, World Bank, Organisation for Economic Co-operation and Development [OECD], BIS, and a G10 central bank forum called the Committee on the Global Financial System), as well as the European Central Bank and financial authorities from the G7 countries (with each country represented by a delegation of three, including representatives from its central bank, finance ministry, and supervisory authority). Membership in the FSF was expanded slightly within a few months to include one member from each of Australia, Hong Kong, the Netherlands, and Singapore, and then also one from Switzerland in 2007.

The FSF reported to the G7 finance ministers and central bank governors, and it was assigned an ambitious but rather vague mandate to "assess issues and vulnerabilities affecting the global financial system and identify and oversee the actions needed to address them, including encouraging, where necessary, the development or strengthening of international best practices and standards and defining priorities for addressing and implementing them." In addition, it was meant to "ensure that national and international authorities and relevant international supervisory bodies and expert groupings can more effectively foster and coordinate their respective responsibilities to promote international financial stability, improve the functioning of the markets and reduce systemic risk."[8] But the FSF's formal capacity to meet these goals was extremely limited. It had no founding charter, no legal status, and no formal power of any kind. Its staff was never larger than 7.5 full-time equivalent staff, most of whom were seconded temporarily from other institutions with their salary paid by the BIS.[9] The body was designed to bring more institutional coherence to the emerging international financial standards regime, but it could do little more than simply facilitate interactions between all the key actors involved in the international financial standards project. In this respect, it represented a kind of pinnacle of the loose networked form of governance that characterized the various SSBs. As Porter puts it, the FSF really was a kind of "network of networks."[10]

As one of its first tasks, the FSF identified twelve key international standards—including those of the BCBS, IAIS, IOSCO, CPSS, and IASB—that countries around the world were encouraged to embrace. It focused primarily on encouraging implementation in Southern countries where G7 policymakers assumed risks to global financial stability were most likely to emanate. To encourage those countries' compliance with these standards, the FSF held a number of regional "outreach" meetings over the next decade with countries in Africa, Latin America, Asia-Pacific, and Central and Eastern Europe.[11] But the lead role for promoting compliance was assigned to the IMF and World Bank which began to prepare Reports on the Observance of Standards and Codes (ROSCs), summarizing countries' compliance levels with the twelve core international standards and making recommendations. The ROSCs drew on a new Financial Sector Assessment Program (FSAP) created by the IMF and World Bank in 1999 to conduct reviews of national financial sectors.

The creation of the ROSCs and FSAPs marked the first time that the Bretton Woods institutions had been involved in the emerging international financial standards regime. It was still a relatively limited involvement. The IMF and World Bank played no role in the development of the content of the various standards (that task was left to the SSBs) or the overall coordination of international financial standards project (that task was given to the FSF, of which the IMF and World Bank were simply members). But they were seen as useful for encouraging worldwide implementation of the standards because of their near universal membership, the World Bank's expertise in this area, and the IMF's established surveillance mechanism (which had already begun to examine financial sector issues).[12]

The G7 had sought initially to give the IMF a formal mandate to make compliance with the standards a condition of its loans to developing countries. But that initiative was blocked by Southern countries that insisted that participation in the FSAPs and ROSCs be voluntary and that participating governments be allowed to block publication of the results in part or in full.[13] The wariness of Southern governments reflected concerns about the costs of implementing the new standards as well as their appropriateness for poorer countries (given that they were often based on Anglo-American models). Southern governments were also wary of the fact that they had little formal representation in either the FSF or many of the international SSBs that designed the standards.[14] Indeed, the BCBS' membership before 2009 included no Southern countries, while the CPSS was made up of just the G7, Belgium, the Netherlands, Singapore, Hong Kong, Sweden, and Switzerland. The private IASB was also dominated by members from developed countries. Even within the SSBs that had much wider membership such as IOSCO and the IASB, Southern countries had limited influence. For example, IOSCO's regulatory initiatives were developed by a Technical Committee whose membership involved only the G7 countries, Australia, Hong Kong, Mexico, the Netherlands, Spain, and Switzerland before 2009.

Because of these limitations, the G7 came to rely primarily on market discipline to encourage the implementation of international standards. They hoped that international financial markets would reward countries whose ROSCs and FSAPs indicated compliance, while disciplining those countries not complying or refusing to participate (or refusing to publish the results). But G7 policymakers were quickly frustrated to discover that market actors seemed to take little notice of compliance levels.[15] Even when Southern governments worried about market reactions, they often engaged in a kind of "mock" compliance, particularly vis-à-vis standards (e.g., accounting, bank supervision) where third party monitoring was difficult and private sector resistance was high.[16]

There was one additional initiative that FSF members undertook to enforce compliance in a more substantial way. The target was much more specific: encouraging forty-two small "offshore financial centers" (OFCs) to comply with a small number of very basic international standards contained within BCBS, IAIS, and IOSCO principles relating to cross-border cooperation and information sharing, essential supervisory powers and practices, and customer identification and record-keeping. In 2000, the FSF approved a recommendation of one of its working groups that its members could consider using "positive and negative incentives" to promote OFC compliance with these basic standards.[17] While members could employ these incentives individually, the report noted that collective action would be more effective and avoid the competitive disadvantages that might arise from unilateral action.

Employing a "name-and-shame" approach, the FSF then published a list of the OFCs divided into three groups according to the quality of their regulation and supervision, and the extent of their cooperation. It also signaled a willingness in 2000 to endorse tough sanctions by FSF member governments against the twenty-five jurisdictions it placed in the bottom category. These possible sanctions included the following: expulsion from SSBs, withdrawal of financial assistance, increased reporting requirements on financial institutions doing business with individuals or firms from non-complying jurisdictions (NCJs), denial of market access for financial institutions from NCJs, and even restrictions on both home institutions operating in NCJs and financial transactions with counterparties in NCJs.[18] But when the IMF assumed the role of assessing compliance, the focus on sanctions diminished and the FSF itself assumed a more low key role vis-à-vis the initiative. By 2005, the FSF declared that its list of OFCs "had served its purpose and is no longer operative," despite the fact that many observers questioned the degree of progress that had been made.[19]

The FSF's declining involvement in the OFC issue was part of its wider marginalization. After an ambitious start, the FSF played a much more limited role in global financial governance than many of its founders had hoped. In the words of Davies and Green, the FSF came to act primarily "as a clearing house for initiatives and ideas emerging elsewhere" and it was not able to "carve out a distinctive position, integrating the various perspectives of the diverse membership, as was originally hoped." They note that US policymakers in particular "consistently argued that the Forum should not take initiatives of its own."[20]

When the first signs of the subprime crisis appeared in the summer of 2007, however, the attitude of US policymakers toward the FSF began to change. As noted in Chapter 4, US authorities encouraged the G7 in September 2007 to assign the FSF the task of developing the agenda for international regulatory reform that could parallel its domestic proposals for US regulatory tightening. The task gave the FSF new life, and the detailed reform agenda it developed was endorsed by the G7 in April 2008 and became the basis for the communiqué of the G20 leaders' first summit in November.

THE CREATION OF THE FSB

The FSB's creation at the G20 leaders' second summit in April 2009 built very directly on this history. The FSB was not really a new organization but simply a renamed and slightly souped-up version of the FSF. One way in which the new organization differed was in its reporting lines: the FSB reported to the G20 leaders rather than the G7 finance ministers and central bank governors. Its membership was also wider. At their first summit, the G20 leaders had insisted that the FSF "must expand urgently to a broader membership of emerging economies."[21] This reform had been pushed strongly by the emerging market countries that had long resented their exclusion from the narrowly constituted FSF. This resentment had been broadcast clearly at a G20 finance officials meeting one week before the first G20 leaders' summit when the Brazilian hosts refused a request from the head of the FSF, Mario Draghi, to speak in his FSF capacity. He could speak only, the Brazilians told him, in his capacity as governor of the Bank of Italy. Two days before the leaders' summit, Draghi publicly endorsed the idea of expanding the FSF's membership to include "key emerging market economies."[22] When the FSB's creation was announced less than five months later, its membership included all G20 countries along with other jurisdictions that had already become members of the FSF after its creation—Hong Kong, the Netherlands, Singapore, and Switzerland—as well as Spain and the European Commission.[23] The G7 countries along with the BRICS (Brazil, Russia, India, China, and South Africa) were assigned three representatives each in the new body, while Australia, Mexico, the Netherlands, Spain, South Korea, and Switzerland were each given two, and everyone else was left with one (Argentina, Hong Kong, Indonesia, Singapore, Saudi Arabia, South Africa, and Turkey).[24] The other members of the FSB—that is, the SSBs and other international institutions—remained as they had been under the FSF.

Country representation within the SSBs themselves also widened at this time in response to a request from the G20 leaders at their first summit that the "other major standard setting bodies should promptly review their membership."[25] In January 2009, the IASB guaranteed geographical diversity on its board for the first time in a manner that ensured developing country representation.[26] The next month, Brazil, India, and China were invited to join IOSCO's Technical Committee. In an awkward two-step process in March and June 2009, the BCBS also expanded to include all G20 countries along with Hong Kong and Singapore. Finally, in July 2009, the CPSS also welcomed the following new members: Australia, Brazil, China, India, Mexico, Russia, Saudi Arabia, South Africa, and South Korea.[27]

In addition to its wider membership, the FSB was also given a founding charter and much more specific mandates than the FSF. The latter included tasks such as conducting (jointly with the IMF) early warning exercises, setting guidelines for the establishment of international supervisory colleges for private institutions, and supporting contingency planning for cross-border crisis management. The FSB was also assigned the general role of assessing vulnerabilities affecting the global financial system, and identifying and reviewing regulatory and supervisory responses. The charter even gave the FSB a specific mandate to "promote and help coordinate the alignment of the activities of the SSBs" and to "undertake joint strategic reviews" of their policy development work to ensure it was "timely, coordinated, focused on priorities and addressing gaps" (while also noting that the SSB's reporting to the FSB would be "without prejudice to their existing reporting arrangements or their independence").[28] In keeping with this mandate, the FSB quickly became prominent in coordinating the creation of post-crisis international financial regulatory reforms and even developed a number of its own standards.[29]

The FSB also became very involved in the process of encouraging the implementation of international standards. The FSB's charter declared that the body would "promote the implementation of effective regulatory, supervisory and other financial sector policies." The preamble to the charter also highlighted its role in "fostering a level playing field through coherent implementation across sectors and jurisdictions."[30] When the FSB's charter was amended in June 2012, this role was reinforced with the addition of a new formal mandate to "promote member jurisdictions' implementation of agreed commitments, standards and policy recommendations through monitoring of implementation, peer review and disclosure."[31]

What kind of tools did the G20 leaders give to the FSB to encourage implementation of, and compliance with, international standards? To begin with, the FSB's charter noted that all members must commit to "implement international financial standards."[32] Although the charter did not mention which standards had to be implemented, the press release announcing the FSB's creation specified that this obligation included the twelve core international standards that had been promoted since the late 1990s.[33] The FSB has subsequently also focused on the implementation of the various post-crisis international regulatory reforms endorsed by the G20 leaders and developed by the SSBs and FSB itself.

This commitment to implement international standards marked a departure from the FSF; membership in the latter had not been associated with any commitments or obligations. But the provision did not signal the introduction of "hard law" into the international financial standards regime because the G20 leaders had chosen not to address the basic weakness of the FSF's governance model. Although the FSB had a charter and an impressive array of mandates, it still had no formal power. The body had not been ratified by any legislature and did not even have any legal standing of any kind. As the FSB's charter acknowledged, membership in the FSB was "not intended to create any legal rights or obligations."[34]

The consequences of failing to comply with the new membership obligations were also not specified in the charter. The charter did state that "the eligibility of Members will be reviewed periodically by the Plenary in the light of the FSB objectives."[35] But it seemed very unlikely that a country's membership in the body would be suspended because the FSB inherited the internal governance model of the FSF: its ultimate decision-making body (which also explicitly addressed decisions about membership) was a Plenary involving all members and employing a consensus rule.[36] The latter suggested that a country could have its membership revoked for noncompliance only if the country itself supported the decision.

The second tool assigned to the FSB for encouraging implementation of international standards was a peer review process. The charter noted that all members committed to "undergo periodic peer reviews, using among other evidence IMF/World Bank public Financial Sector Assessment Program reports."[37] The latter part of this phrase implied a strengthening of the pre-crisis surveillance regime, as it suggested that FSB members were committing to participate in FSAPs and publicize the results. All G20 countries had in fact already committed to undergo FSAPs at their first summit in November 2008.[38] Soon after the FSB's creation, all FSB members formally committed to undergo a FSAP every five years and to publicize the detailed IMF/World Bank assessments used as a basis for the ROSCs.[39] As a number of FSB members had refused to undergo FSAPs before the crisis—including the United States, China, Indonesia, and Argentina—this signaled a change.[40]

The commitment to undergo peer reviews marked more of a departure from the pre-crisis regime. At the time of the FSF's creation, the potential benefits of peer review in encouraging compliance had been discussed, but the idea had not been taken up, perhaps because the two-way exchange of ideas embodied in the peer review process was less compatible with the G7's conception at the time of offering necessary advice to developing countries in a one-way fashion.[41] With the FSB's creation, the peer review model was now embraced as "a means of fostering a 'race to the top'" by FSB member jurisdictions in terms of adherence to standards."[42]

Through the peer review process, the FSB was placed in a more central role than the FSF ever was in encouraging compliance with international standards. Each peer review drew on a report developed by a team of experts from FSB members with the support by FSB staff (who were expected to take the lead in producing it). The actual review was conducted by the FSB's Standing Committee on Standards Implementation, with a final report generated by FSB staff, approved by the FSB Plenary, and then publicized. Implementation of recommendations was then monitored by the FSB. FSB peer reviews included not just country reviews but also thematic ones. The latter were designed to focus on "the implementation across the FSB membership of policies or standards agreed within the FSB, with particular attention to consistency in cross-country implementation and the effectiveness of the policy or standard in achieving the intended results."[43] Thematic reviews have been completed on various issues such as compensation, mortgage underwriting and origination practices, risk disclosure practices, deposit insurance systems, and risk governance.

The peer review process had some limitations as a tool for encouraging implementation of international standards. One was quickly identified and addressed. Because reviews had to be approved by the Plenary, critics initially highlighted that any reviewed country would be able to veto unwanted criticism because of the Plenary's consensus rule. To get around this problem, the FSB noted the following in a December 2011 *Handbook for FSB Peer Reviews*: "for the purpose of peer reviews, consensus is understood to mean that the views of all members are considered and compromises are sought, but that no single jurisdiction can block a decision supported by a clear majority; compromises are sought, differences are accepted, but dissenters do not stand in the way of a decision."[44]

Even if reviews could not be vetoed, a larger question remained about how candid FSB members are willing to be in highlighting each other's problems. As Pierre Hugues Verdier puts it, the effectiveness of peer reviews "will depend crucially on the willingness of regulators to forcefully question and challenge their peers." He questions the prospects for peer reviews because "regulators have historically been reluctant to breach a deep-seated norm of mutual deference."[45] Paul Blustein is equally skeptical: "international groupings are notorious for conducting peer reviews with kid gloves, because members know that harsh treatment toward others will invite the same on themselves.... Little evidence of a proclivity for such outspokenness has surfaced in the handful of peer reviews conducted by the FSB so far."[46]

Another limitation stemmed from the capacity of the FSB's secretariat. Analysts have noted how the better known OECD's peer review process depends heavily on the role played by OECD staff in drafting initial and final reports and supporting reviewers.[47] The FSB, however, remains severely constrained by the tiny size of its staff. Although the G20 assigned it a full-time Secretary-General and a slightly larger staff than the FSF, its secretariat remains much smaller (twenty-eight staff in mid-2013 and entitled to rise to forty) than that of the OECD (which has approximately 2000 staff) or other institutions in global financial governance such as the World Trade Organization (WTO; more than 600 staff) and IMF (approximately 2400). The refusal of the G20 leaders to provide greater resources to the institution—in contrast to the enormous sums given to the IMF at the very moment that the FSB was created in April 2009—was a telling sign from the start of their limited backing for the vision of the FSB as a serious fourth pillar of global economic architecture. It also inhibits the FSB's ability to lead a thorough and effective peer review process. Indeed, in 2011, the FSB decided that countries would be expected to undergo country peer review only "approximately two to three years after the completion of an FSAP or ROSC."[48] Because FSB members must undergo an FSAP only every five years, country peer reviews would take place with the same infrequency, thereby diluting the ability of the peer review mechanism to provide an ongoing effective means for assessing compliance. Verdier notes another key limitation stemming from the FSB's constrained resources: "Based on the FSB's Handbook, both country and thematic peer reviews will rely primarily on questionnaires filled out by the country's own regulators, and are not expected to include on-site visits. Given this procedure, it seems likely that—like prior efforts—peer reviews will be more effective at assessing formal than substantive compliance."[49]

The most important limitation of the peer review process, however, was that it was still not backed by any "teeth" for addressing noncompliance. In its December 2011 *Handbook*, the FSB noted the following:

> If implementation in a particular jurisdiction is lagging, then the SCSI should be ready to propose exceptional measures for the Plenary's approval, which would be employed on a graduated basis in order to incentivise actions. These could include a letter from the FSB Chair to the relevant member outlining the Plenary's concerns; a discussion by the Plenary with the reviewed jurisdiction; or publication of the Plenary's concerns on the FSB website.[50]

It seems unlikely that these consequences will be terribly effective in "incentivizing" actions from a government intent on avoiding implementation of international standards.

A REGIME WITH TEETH?

At the time that the FSB was created, the G20 leaders did suggest that they were willing to consider more serious initiatives to "incentivise actions" in NCJs. At the London summit, they called on the FSB "to develop a toolbox of measures to promote adherence to prudential standards and cooperation with jurisdictions."[51] In early September 2009, G20 finance ministers and central bank governors also stressed the need for not just "peer review" and "capacity building" but also "countermeasures" to tackle NCJs that fail to meet regulatory standards."[52]

Responding to this call, the FSB launched an initiative in March 2010 promising that NCJs would face "a balance of both positive and negative measures."[53] The wording was reminiscent of the FSF's initiative vis-à-vis OFCs a decade earlier and so were the examples provided by the FSB of what the "negative measures" might be. As a first step, the FSB promised to publish the names of noncomplying jurisdictions by the end of 2010 if positive measures (such as dialogue and technical assistance) were not

achieving sufficient progress. The FSB's list of other potential negative measures was very similar to that outlined by the FSF in 2000, including various
sanctions such as restrictions on market access or on cross-border financial
transactions. While noting that the use of such measures would be subject
to any legal constraints facing member countries, the FSB also highlighted
the relevance of "'prudential carve out' provisions (for instance in international trade agreements), which permit jurisdictions to impose restrictions
for prudential reasons."[54] The FSB made clear that the application of these
negative measures would be "subject to approval by the Plenary and the
judgement of the FSB member jurisdictions in their implementation."[55]

Explicitly building on the FSF's earlier work vis-à-vis OFCs, the FSB
chose to focus initially only on compliance with some very basic international cooperation and information exchange principles embodied in
three key standards of the BCBS, IAIS, and IOSCO.[56] But unlike the FSF's
earlier work, this initiative was much more ambitious in its geographical reach. The FSB aimed to secure compliance worldwide—including
among FSB members—rather than just targeting OFCs. As a first step, it
selected sixty-one jurisdictions—based on their financial importance—to
evaluate for levels of compliance, including all twenty-four members of
FSB. Those judged not fully compliant were invited to join a confidential
dialogue with the FSB to improve their status.

Following the FSF's example, the FSB then published a report just before
the November 2011 G20 leaders summit that divided the sixty-one jurisdictions in three groups according to the degree of their compliance. At
the summit itself, the G20 leaders also noted: "We stand ready, if needed,
to use our existing countermeasures to deal with jurisdictions which
fail to meet these standards."[57] But the size of the list of noncomplying
jurisdictions called into question the seriousness of this threat. Only two
jurisdictions were included—Libya (the former regime) and Venezuela—
both of which were described simply as "not engaged in dialogue with
the FSB."[58] When the list was updated a year later, Venezuela was still on
the list (where it remained in late 2013) and Libya had been temporary
suspended from participation in the process until the FSB could establish
a dialogue with new authorities in the country.[59]

Of the remaining 59 jurisdictions, forty-one were deemed in November 2011 to be demonstrating "sufficiently strong adherence," while eighteen were described as "jurisdictions taking the actions recommended by the FSB and/or making material progress towards demonstrating sufficiently strong adherence."[60] The latter included seven FSB members, although five were on the list simply because they had been "not previously assessed" for a ROSC (Argentina, China, India, Indonesia, Saudi Arabia)[61]. The other two—Russia and Turkey—were described as in dialogue with a FSB evaluation team, as were Greece and Mauritius. The other nine non-FSB countries in this category had a ROSC underway, planned, or requested. By December 2013, China, the India, Saudi Arabia, and the Czech Republic had graduated to the top category.[62]

It remained somewhat unclear whether FSB members would expand this initiative to include a wider group of countries beyond the initial group. In March 2010, the FSB had declared that "the ultimate goal is to promote adherence by all countries and jurisdictions" and promised that "following completion of the first round of evaluations, the Expert Group will engage in a further round of dialogue with a different group of jurisdictions, subject to approval by the Plenary after review by the SCSI [Standing Committee on Standards Implementation]."[63] As of early 2014 this second round of evaluations had yet to take place and it was clear that some FSB members, such as the IMF, were very uncomfortable with the initiative and its threat of coercive measures.[64]

It is tempting to conclude that the FSB had shown some willingness to back their desire to promote adherence to international standards with teeth by threatening the use of serious sanctions against NCJs. But the significance of the initiative was greatly undermined by two factors. First, it was very unlikely that sanctions would be applied against a FSB member because any such measure required the support of the Plenary. If FSB members agreed formally to dilute the meaning of "consensus" within the plenary in the way they had vis-à-vis peer reviews, this limitation would have been overcome.[65] In the absence of that kind of initiative, however, FSB members were subject only to softer forms of influence such as peer reviews and surveillance.

The second limitation of the initiative was that it focused on only some very basic core standards. As Verdier notes, "it focuses on cooperation and information exchange rather than on substantive regulation."[66] In early 2010, the FSB suggested that the initiative could eventually be widened to apply to broader set of international standards, but this idea was not returned to in subsequent reports.[67] Particularly striking was their unwillingness to see this approach used to encourage implementation of the various international regulatory reforms introduced since the crisis. To encourage adherence to the post-crisis international reforms among FSB members, the FSB chose to rely entirely on peer pressure, surveillance, and other voluntary mechanisms.

The emphasis on voluntary mechanisms was also apparent when the G20 leaders at their November 2011 summit agreed to "intensify our monitoring of financial regulatory reforms" by endorsing a new FSB "coordination framework for implementation monitoring" that would build on the monitoring activities of other bodies.[68] Special emphasis was given in this framework to public reporting on implementation progress vis-à-vis key post-crisis reforms discussed in Chapter 4 such as the Basel capital and liquidity frameworks, over-the-counter (OTC) derivatives reforms, compensation practices, policy for systemically important financial institutions (SIFI), resolution frameworks, and shadow banking. As part of this new initiative, the FSB Secretariat began to produce an annual "status report" on the progress of implementation involving four grades (or "traffic lights").[69] When the FSB's charter was amended in June 2012, members also agreed to take on the additional commitment to "take part in implementation monitoring of agreed commitments, standards and policy recommendations."[70]

To encourage implementation of the new standards, the G20 leaders also committed at the same summit to change the composition of the FSB's influential Steering Committee in order to give more weight to finance ministry officials who had a critical role to play in steering national legislative initiatives as well as to jurisdictions that have been less well represented in the past. Here is how they explained the reform: "as we move into a phase of policy development and implementation that in many cases will require significant legislative changes, we agree that the upcoming changes to the FSB steering committee should include the executive branch of governments of the G20 Chair and the larger financial systems as well as the geographic regions and financial centers not currently represented, in a balanced manner consistent with the FSB Charter."[71]

Alongside these initiatives to encourage implementation among FSB members, more extensive efforts were also made vis-à-vis nonmembers. Building on the outreach activities of the FSF, the FSB invited seventy nonmember jurisdictions to join six new formal regional consultative groups covering the Americas, Asia, the Commonwealth of Independent States, Europe, the Middle East and North Africa, and sub-Saharan Africa. The groups involve both FSB members and nonmembers, and are meant to promote implementation as well as encourage a sharing of views and interaction between members and nonmembers. Their role in the FSB governance structure was formalized when the charter was amended in June 2012.

These initiatives intensified but did not move beyond the basic soft-law governance model of the pre-crisis period. The commitment to that model was very much in evidence even when FSB members decided in January 2013 to establish a formal legal personality for their organization for the first time as an association under Swiss law (and still hosted by the BIS). The initiative did not stem from any desire to "harden" the commitments of members to implement standards. Instead, it was driven by some very practical concerns about the need to hire permanent staff (instead of relying on secondments) and clarify more stable funding arrangements. The Articles of Association created under Swiss law continued to make very clear that the FSB's activities and decisions "shall not be binding or give rise to any legal rights or obligations under the present Articles. Members can recuse themselves at any time from these activities or decision-making where such activities or decision-making are not consistent with their legal or policy frameworks."[72]

The FSB thus remained a remarkably toothless organization, just as its FSF predecessor had been. As Sheng put it, "the present FSB structure is essentially a talking shop with influence over some regulators and standard setters, but little implementation capacity."[73] Similarly, Blustein noted that FSB was constrained by "its lack of authority to bring them [member governments] to heel. In that crucial respect, it is no different from the FSF."[74] While international trade law had "hardened" since the mid-1990s with the creation of the WTO, the FSB and international financial standards regime still relied on largely soft law, with implementation and compliance remaining voluntary. Like the FSF, the FSB remained a network-based organization with limited staff and capacity and little formal power. Rather than innovating, the G20 leaders thus reproduced the status quo in this respect, despite the FSB's new features and the vaulted rhetoric about establishing a new "fourth pillar" of global economic governance.

A number of analysts had hoped for much more, arguing that compliance challenges could be addressed effectively only through a more powerful international institution. For example, Eichengreen called in 2008–09 for the creation of a "World Financial Organization" that would have the power to authorize sanctions against countries that did not comply with significant international standards. He suggested that judgments about compliance could be made by an "independent body of experts, not unlike the WTO's Dispute Settlement panels" and that evaluations could be triggered not just by member country complaints (as under the WTO) but also by the experts themselves in response to FSAP results.[75] In his proposal, sanctions would include the right of members to restrict access to their market to financial institutions chartered in the noncomplying country. Eichengreen noted that an advantage of this proposal was that private institutions seeking to operate abroad would have a clear incentive to lobby for tighter reforms at home.

The idea of a WTO-equivalent institution for financial regulation with a binding dispute resolution mechanism and sanctioning power was put forward by others as well, including the secretary general of IOSCO, David Wright. In late 2012 (and speaking in a personal capacity), he lamented the fact that the only tools available to encourage compliance with international standards were "soft" ones such as peer review, transparency, and monitoring with the consequence that "any jurisdiction can basically do what it wants and face no effective or deterrent repercussions." He called for:

> a global institutional framework, probably established by International Treaty, that has some enforcement authority, binding disputes settlement and sanctioning possibilities…This global Institutional framework should encompass at least the FSB and the main global sectoral standard setters. Its role would not be to try to enforce a one-size-fits-all harmonized set of rules—but rather to ensure and, if necessary legally require, that the basic globally agreed policy principles are properly implemented by all jurisdictions who are signatories to the Treaty arrangements.

Given the importance of US financial markets, Wright argued that the United States had a unique capacity to lead the creation of this framework. But he warned that it had "window" to do so that might last "5–10 years or so, but not more" after which "its relative share of global financial market is set to decline significantly."[76]

Others, such as Louis Pauly, lamented that policymakers did not do more strengthen the IMF's role in this sphere. He was skeptical of those who placed too much trust in loose "networked governance" instead of binding, treaty-based arrangements. As he put it, "in the wake of the recent financial crisis, the term begins to sound like "no government, except the national one."[77] Indeed, the weakness of the FSB reminded him of the ineffective informal financial arrangements of pre-IMF days of the League of Nations:

> the small, impermanent and very loosely mandated staff of the FSB suggests an historical reversion…. it is only too easy to imagine the equivalent of the FSB being created by and within the League, say around 1922, when Arthur Salter became director of the Economic, Financial, and Transit Section of the Secretariat. A plenary body agreeing on policies by consensus, a chair dealing with the politics associated with the quest for unanimity, a secretary general with very limited powers, a tiny and mainly analytical secretariat, and the expectation of the voluntary implementation of "best practices" by autonomous national authorities. This was the essence of the League's core economic and financial machinery.[78]

HEIGHTENED COMPLIANCE CHALLENGES AND THE
STATUS QUO CHOICE

The G20 policymakers were unwilling to embrace proposals to "harden" international financial standards in the ways these analysts suggest. The FSB itself also explicitly noted in a June 2012 report that it considered "a treaty-based inter-governmental organisation not to be an appropriate legal form at this juncture."[79] The G20's failure to depart from the soft-law nature of the pre-crisis governance of international financial standards in a significant way meant that the challenges in enforcing implementation and compliance remained. These challenges in fact intensified in the wake of the crisis, making the failure to innovate in a more substantial way even more significant.

Domestic political constraints facing regulators were intensified by the fact that the crisis generated unprecedented interest in financial regulatory issues among politicians and the general public in many jurisdictions. The heightened public salience of regulatory issues was particularly noticeable in the United States and Europe, where large public bailouts of financial institutions took place.[80] The expanded agenda of post-crisis international financial regulatory reforms also politicized regulatory issues in these and other jurisdictions. For example, discussions about how to regulate SIFIs—and even how to identity them—cut to the core of the distinctive styles of national capitalisms in ways that mobilized domestic societal interests well outside the financial sector.

Even when legislative approval was not required, this new political environment context diminished the ability of regulators to implement standards without controversy. But it was also significant that many of the new international standards endorsed by the G20 and FSB required legislative initiatives in order to be implemented at the national (or regional in the case of the European Union) level. In the pre-crisis period, scholars had noted that "regulators who initiate international negotiations over harmonization do not face a ratification requirement and therefore can conduct themselves in a relatively opaque and seemingly apolitical environment."[81] When legislative approval was required, the political context surrounding implementation was very different as many domestic societal groups found ready access points to influence implementation outcomes. Regulators often discovered that the ideas around which consensus had formed with the technocratic transgovernment networks associated with the G20, FSB, and SSBs were not necessarily shared by domestic politicians and interest groups whose support was needed to implement them into law.[82]

The effectiveness of "peer group pressures" within transgovernmental networks of financial officials as a mechanism for encouraging compliance with international standards may also have diminished.[83] In a context of domestic politicization, the reputational risks of noncompliance eroded because financial officials could more easily blame domestic pressures for outcomes. The normative commitment of those officials to the international standards they were being asked to implement may also have declined as the content of those standards was no longer determined through the transgovernmental technocratic channels of which they were a member. The expansion of the membership of bodies such as the FSB and SSBs may also have lessened the intensity of the peer pressure.

Some more traditional barriers to effective implementation also resurfaced. Competitive pressures discouraged compliance vis-à-vis some of the new international financial standards, particularly when it appeared as though implementation was being delayed or watered down abroad.[84] As distance from the crisis grew, private financial interests also became increasingly bold in their efforts to lobby against reforms.

In the face of these various developments, it was hardly surprising that implementation of many of the new international financial standards was slow. Even when reforms were being put in place, they were often implemented inconsistently across jurisdictions, thereby generating the result that the FSB was supposed to prevent: an uneven international playing field. At each G20 summit, the leaders ritualistically committed to "timely, full and consistent implementation" of the agreed standards.[85] But their actions often worked in a different direction, uninhibited by any international legal constraint. As one senior executive in charge of regulation at one of the world's top banks put it in describing the problems of implementation in April 2012, "it's a bloody nightmare. The regulators have no respect for one another at all. Each country is looking after itself."[86]

In the face of these challenges, why have policymakers not been willing to innovate more in the governance of international financial standards? Why have national authorities refused in the post-crisis period to accept more serious international constraints on their regulatory behavior? A number of explanations have been put forward in past literature for the prevalence of the network-based, soft-law quality of the governance of international financial standards since the 1970s. Some scholars have argued that it has appealed to policymakers for functional reasons: its flexibility allowed them to create and amend standards quickly in the face of financial innovation and fast-moving technological and financial market trends.[87] Others have argued that this loose governance model is preferred by certain interests, such as regulators seeking to preserve their autonomy and discretion as well as powerful financial industry actors who anticipate that it will generate fewer constraints on their behavior.[88] Great powers are also said to "prefer fragmented and informal international governance over strong collective institutions where they can less easily wield their influence."[89] Analysts have also suggested that there is a certain path dependency involved in this model of governance that was set by its earlier evolution.[90]

All of these explanations may help to explain the weak nature of the FSB. Perhaps the most important point, however, is that many national policymakers remained very wary of accepting infringements of national sovereignty in this sector of economic policymaking.[91] Financial regulation was widely seen to play an important strategic role in domestic political economies, a role whose importance was brought out well by the crisis experience. The crisis also highlighted the link between fiscal issues and financial regulation more clearly than ever, a link that only reinforced resistance to the delegation of authority. As Brummer put it in 2012, "nation-states are unlikely to cede power to a global financial regulator as long as they retain the responsibility for guaranteeing liquidity, serving as the capital providers of last resort, and protecting the public treasury."[92] Many officials were also deeply committed to the idea that regulatory practices must be adapted to distinct national circumstances; as Sheng puts it, "we must accept that there can be no 'one size fits all' approach for financial regulation, reform, crisis prevention or resolution."[93] As financial regulatory issues were politicized domestically during the crisis, any willingness of policymakers to delegate power to an international authority or accept binding constraints on their behavior only diminished further.

Not all policymakers were wary of a strong global institution. French government officials were supportive of the creation of a treaty-based FSB that enforced legally binding standards with a WTO-style dispute settlement mechanism.[94] British Prime Minister Gordon Brown—who hosted the London G20 summit at which the FSB was created—had long been a champion of a stronger global institution in the regulatory sphere. When he was British Chancellor of the Exchequer at the time of the FSF's creation, he had outlined some ambitious ideas along these lines.[95] In mid-October 2008, in advance of the first G20 summit, he returned to these ideas and advocated "very large and very radical changes" in the governance of global financial markets that would be nothing less than a "new Bretton Woods." As he put it, "we now have global financial markets, global corporations, global financial flows. But what we do not have is anything other than national and regional regulation and supervision." He argued: "we need a global way of supervising our financial system."[96]

US officials were wary of Brown's ambitious ideas during the late 1990s and again in the wake of the 2008 crisis. In the late 1990s, US officials were particularly concerned about constraints on their country's sovereignty, concerns that only intensified after the election of the Bush administration. As Blustein notes, "the Bush administration was not eager to empower the FSF — partly because the forum was a Clinton-era creation, but more importantly because Bush officials wanted to avoid any semblance of giving influence over US financial policy to an international group."[97] This concern for US sovereignty was also apparent in the way that the Bush administration refused even to participate in a FSAP assessment.[98] As one US representative to FSF meetings during the Bush years later noted, the US sought to prevent the FSF from taking "steps that might limit our freedom of action, where we might have to say to some constituency in the United States, 'Well, we promised the Indonesians'— or worse, the French. It would be counterproductive if Congress thought there was somebody out there who had obtained commitments or claims on the US government."[99]

It was not until the outbreak of the crisis in late 2007 that the Bush administration became more supportive of the FSF as a body that could help coordinate the development of an international regulatory reform agenda. As noted in Chapter 4, however, that coordination role was viewed largely in instrumental terms as a means to prevent foreign jurisdictions from taking competitive advantage of US regulatory tightening. In other words, rather than reflecting a new willingness to pool US sovereignty, the FSF was viewed a tool to enhance US capacity to achieve domestic goals without external constraint. In advance of the first G20 summit, Bush administration officials cautioned against ambitious reforms. In early November 2008, for example, one unnamed White House official told the press that "this meeting is not about discarding market principles or about moving to a single global market regulator. There is very little support for that."[100]

The Obama administration was more multilateral in its outlook. Indeed, its top financial official, Tim Geithner, had been a member a decade earlier of a G22 group that had recommended in late 1998 the creation of a body similar to the FSF (called the Financial Sector Policy Forum). That group had been co-chaired by Mario Draghi (representing Italy), who ten years later, as head of the FSF, would work together closely with Geithner to design the FSB. In 1998, that G22 group had rejected the idea of setting up "a new large international financial institution," favoring instead "small-scale institutional innovations" such as the proposed Forum.[101] Despite his rhetoric about a "fourth pillar", he displayed a similar preference for incremental change when initiating the idea of transforming the FSF into the FSB.[102] Indeed, just days before the London summit, Geithner made clear his commitment to maintaining US regulatory sovereignty: "We are not going to give anyone else the responsibility for deciding what balance between stability and efficiency is right for our markets."[103]

Skepticism of the ambitious French and British ideas was also apparent among other US officials. For example, Edwin Truman—who was influential in the US preparations for the London summit—did not see the FSF as anything more than "primarily a coordinating body" and he explicitly opposed any proposals to transform the FSF into a "global financial regulator."[104] Another Obama administration official influential in international regulatory politics was Daniel Tarullo who had been appointed the Fed's Board of Governor by Obama in January 2009. In a book published just before his appointment on the future of international financial regulation, he had argued strongly against a global regulator because of concerns about "the loss of regulatory flexibility to respond to local conditions (including macroeconomic conditions), the suppression of possibly healthy regulatory experimentation or competition, and the removal of regulatory authority further away from points of democratic accountability."[105]

DISTRUST AND FRAGMENTATION: TOWARD PLAN B?

US wariness of the idea of delegating regulatory authority to an international body was shared by officials from many other countries, particularly large emerging market countries such as China where regulatory sovereignty was also highly prized.[106] These sentiments were subsequently reinforced by the failure of G20 and FSB efforts to reach meaningful agreements for international burden-sharing arrangements to fund future bailouts or cross-border resolution of failing firms. The former was discussed briefly in the lead-up to the June 2010 G20 summit, but went nowhere, particularly because many governments at the time were intent on declaring their opposition to engage in future bailouts altogether. Indeed, the US Dodd–Frank bill passed one month after the summit prohibited future bailouts and required instead forced liquidation of troubled firms.

The cross-border resolution issue was the subject of much more discussion in the G20 and FSB (as it had been within the FSF). At their September 2009 summit, the G20 leaders declared that SIFIs "should develop internationally-consistent firm-specific contingency and resolution plans" that would enable failing firms to be wound down without bailouts or risk of financial instability. [107] They initially focused on G-SIFIs, requiring them to develop "recovery and resolution planning" which included drafting "living wills" explaining how they will be wound down in the event of trouble. The G20 leaders also committed to subject these firms to institution-specific cooperation agreements between home and host countries.[108] At the same time, they explored extending these initiatives to other SIFIs, including non-banks, and backed the creation of a new international standard for national resolution regimes.

But the results of these efforts to develop international agreements on the cross-border dimensions were disappointing. Differences in countries' bankruptcy and insolvency laws have long made this a very difficult issue to negotiate.[109] National authorities were also very wary of undermining their freedom to act in this sphere. As Brummer notes:

> many countries have shied away from cross-border resolution and bankruptcy cooperation since new rules could make it more difficult for local institutions, including local regulators, to determine when financial institutions are insolvent, as well as how the institutions are restructured or liquidated. The financial consequences could be very substantial, too, if a distressed bank is a systemically important institution that serves as the primary source of capital in a country. International rules could prevent courts from tailoring the disposition of assets to protect local creditors and achieve the most benefit for local economic interests.[110]

While the IMF and some global banks favored a legally binding international treaty, the US and British governments opposed the idea.[111] Instead, the Bank of England began to push for bilateral memoranda of understanding with US and Asian regulators that set the terms of resolution, including provisions for host governments to step aside if the home country authorities could resolve the whole group more effectively. But

Paul Tucker at the Bank of England acknowledged that "these memoranda are not legally binding agreements. A regulator has to make a judgement over whether it can trust its opposite number in another country." This approach has left many skeptical. As one unnamed European regulator put it, "you can't run the vital process of bank resolution on a gentleman's agreement that isn't legally binding. It just won't work."[112]

In the absence of significant international agreements in this area, it remained very unclear whether cooperation would be forthcoming in a future crisis. Indeed, in January 2013, US authorities told banks preparing living wills that they could no longer assume that countries would work together to prevent their collapse (as many of them had assumed when preparing the first version of the wills the previous year). Some *Financial Times* journalists described the reaction of some of the banks:

> Several executives said that the guidance—which one called 'shocking'— left them believing regulators were losing confidence in their ability to improve on 2008 when countries either failed to co-operate, or fought over assets, in banks from Lehman to Landsbanki in Iceland. 'Part of the difficulties we saw in 2008 was in Lehman, when push came to shove, the regulators stopped talking to each other,' said another executive. 'Everything that you hear, including "Do your resolution refresh assuming the authorities aren't speaking to each other," shows we've made no progress in one of the key areas.'[113]

There were also increasing signs that policymakers' distrust of international cooperation was generating support for initiatives that would lead to greater regulatory and market fragmentation as a way of empowering national authorities to act effectively in the event of a crisis. This trend could be seen in the growing interest being expressed by policymakers in "host country" regulation. Analysts have long debated whether banks should be regulated and supervised on a "home" or "host" country basis. The core principle that emerged from the Basel standards over time was one of "home country control" in which core supervisory and regulatory responsibilities for an international bank lay with the authorities in the country where the bank is headquartered.[114] This principle was usually favored by large international banks because it allowed them to manage their global operations in an integrated manner.

But it attracted a growing number of critics in the wake of the 2008 crisis because the costs of the failures of financial institutions and their bailouts usually fell on the host country in the absence of meaningful international cooperation. Indeed, the poor nature of international cooperation in the handling of failing financial institutions was a striking feature of the management of the crisis. Even in the European Union, national authorities often responded unilaterally and prioritized the interests of domestic depositors, creditors, and taxpayers. As Bank of England Governor Mervyn King remarked in early 2009, it quickly became clear in the crisis that "global banks are global in life, but national in death."[115]

If host countries were going to bear the costs of failing financial institutions, it was understandable that they would insist on greater host country control.[116] The failure of efforts to coordinate international burden-sharing or cross-border resolution only strengthened the case for officials to insist that banks be "subsidiarized"; that is, that international banks be forced to establish separately capitalized local subsidiaries that could be regulated by the host authority.[117] As one reporter put it in May 2013, "there is a push towards subsidiaries over branches because there is no global system in place for bank resolution. Countries fear being left with the bill if an event like the Lehman collapse happened again, leaving the taxpayer unprotected."[118]

There were a number of signs of the growing interest in host country regulation to protect regulatory autonomy, depositors, and taxpayers. After Britain's experience of guaranteeing British deposits in failed Icelandic banks in 2008, the country's Financial Services Authority began pressuring foreign institutions in London to establish locally regulated subsidiaries with their own capital and liquidity.[119] Asian regulators also became much more interested in host country regulation after the crisis.[120] With European banks repatriating the profits of their Latin American operations in order to recapitalize European operations in the context of the Eurozone crisis, prominent Latin American figures such as Guillermo Ortiz, former Governor of the Bank of Mexico, urged local regulators in his region to "enforce a regulatory framework that ringfences subsidiaries from parent banks' weaknesses."[121] And finally, US authorities in late 2012 proposed forcing foreign banks to hold more local capital and liquidity, with Tarullo paraphrasing King's comments: "our regulatory system must recognise that while internationally active banks live globally, they may well die locally."[122] Reporters speculated that the US initiative was aimed particularly at weakly capitalized foreign institutions such as Deutsche Bank that had drawn heavily on the Fed's emergency lending during the crisis and that could be vulnerable again to the Eurozone crisis.[123] If German and French authorities were going to resist stronger international bank regulation in the Basel III negotiations. US officials were now signaling their willingness to unilaterally force European banks operating in the United States to meet US preferences for tough standards.

Because greater use of host country control risked creating more fragmented global financial markets, international banks often opposed it.[124] As one industry figure noted in late 2012, "if that is the new strategy among regulators, it really throws into question this whole globalisation of these [large financial] firms. It also means each country for themselves."[125] Anticipating that "national subsidiarisation" was "gathering pace quickly," a report from Morgan Stanley and Oliver Wyman in April 2013 similarly concluded that: "with diverging national regulatory agendas, it poses a major risk to the global banking model."[126] In this sense, these unilateral initiatives—if they became more widespread—could ultimately have a more "anti-market" impact than the various G20-led reforms of international financial standards discussed in Chapter 4. That result could be reinforced by the fact that host country regulation would allow national regulators more room to regulate banks in nationally distinctive ways, including tighter ways. Indeed, analysts noted nationally distinctive host country regulations would greatly simplify the implementation of the new macroprudential counter-cyclical buffers that the G20 and FSB have endorsed, and enable developing countries to better tackle distinctive risks associated with currency mismatches or pro-cyclical capital flows.[127]

In the wake of the crisis, policymakers also turned to greater host country control in other areas as a way of reducing their dependence on, and vulnerability to, regulatory practices abroad. One of the most strik-ing was with respect to the clearing of OTC derivatives. When the G20 backed mandatory clearing for standardized OTC derivatives, many ana-lysts assumed initially that these products would be cleared through a few globally oriented central counterparties (CCPs). One benefit of that outcome would be that regulators would gain a better and more global view of market risks if one single CCP existed for each product, regardless of location. It rapidly became clear, however, that a different outcome was emerging. Authorities in Europe and elsewhere encouraged the creation of local CCPs whose purpose was to clear transactions involving parties in their jurisdiction.

One motivation was to capture some of the rapidly growing clearing business for local firms, but another was distrust of foreign regulators. As CCPs cleared more and more OTC derivatives trades, these institu-tions concentrated risk and rapidly became very significant SIFIs. If these institutions were located in foreign jurisdictions, authorities would be forced to place their trust in foreign authorities to regulate and supervise them well. In the event of a CCP crisis, it was also unclear whether finan-cial support received from host authorities would extend to foreigners or whether foreign interests would be protected in the event of their wind-ing down. In this context, some national authorities concluded that it was safer to encourage OTC trades to be cleared through local CCPs. As one European official put it, "can we afford the luxury of having a CCP clear-ing the whole world, over which we have no regulatory and supervisory powers or guaranteed access to information? And what if it goes belly up?"[128]

The proliferation of national CCPs risked contributing to the fragmen-tation of OTC derivatives markets and their regulation. A single global CCP would allow internationally oriented market actors to net their exposures on a worldwide basis. By contrast, a world of many national CCPs, particularly when backed by location policies, would require multiple postings of collateral and thus create multiple pools of liquid-ity. Questions have also been asked about complications relating to interoperability and cross-border bankruptcy, as well as the fact the rules governing CCPs often vary across jurisdictions.[129] Similar "territorialization" pressures have also emerged with respect to trade repositories—to which OTC trades must be reported—because of the uncertainties of cross-border sharing of information between regulators.[130]

To curtail these fragmentation pressures and encourage greater international use of CCPs, the FSB developed in January 2012 four safeguards for CPPs. Regulators were asked to ensure that CCPs had the following: open access, cooperative oversight where appropriate, resolution and recovery regimes that consider the interests of all jurisdictions where the CCP is systemically important, and appropriate liquidity arrangements for CCPs in the currencies in which they clear.[131] Whether these safeguards succeed in stemming the proliferation of national CCPs remains an open question.

The growing interest in host country control revealed the distrust of many national regulators in the prospects for international regulatory cooperation in the wake of the crisis. In the face of uncertainty, and with the memory of the crisis still fresh in their minds, regulators sought to protect their countries' interests unilaterally rather than delegate power to foreigners or any kind of global regulator. The slow and uneven implementation of many of the new international financial standards only reinforced the case for these attempts to insulate a country's financial system from potentially poor regulatory practices and financial instability abroad. In these instances, policymakers identified nation-states (or the region in the case of the European Union) as the key pillar of global economic governance in the financial regulatory realm rather than the FSB.[132] These kinds of initiatives also risked creating a more decentralized and fragmented international regulatory order rather than the kind of globally integrated, international level playing field envisioned in the FSB's charter.[133]

Indeed, this result was anticipated early on by analysts such as Dani Rodrik. In a widely discussed March 2009 article in *The Economist*, Rodrik argued against the ambitious post-crisis efforts of the G20 to strengthen international financial standards. In his view, the drive to create one-size-fits-all global standards overlooked the fact that "desirable forms of financial regulation differ across countries depending on their preferences and levels of development." It was also imprudent because policymakers could easily "end up converging on the wrong set of regulations," a possibility that the crisis appeared to have revealed very starkly. Moreover, he questioned whether it was really politically realistic to expect that leading countries, such as the United States, would agree to "surrender significant sovereignty to international agencies."[134]

In place of strong harmonized international standards, Rodrik advocated a "Plan B for global finance" that would place the choice and responsibility for financial regulation and supervision much more squarely at the national level (or perhaps regional level, in a case such as Europe) with global financial firms supervised and regulated by host country authorities. His plan still saw a role for international regulatory cooperation, but of a less ambitious kind. To prevent "adverse spillovers," he suggested that countries would still need to agree to "an international financial charter" that was "focused on financial transparency, consultation among national regulators, and limits on jurisdictions (such as offshore centres) that export financial instability." Regulatory arbitrage, in particular, would be dealt with by giving governments the "right to intervene in cross-border financial transactions—but only in so far as the intent is to prevent competition from less-strict jurisdictions from undermining domestic regulations."[135]

Rodrik acknowledged that his plan would result in a more fragmented international financial order, but he argued the following: "The world economy will be far more stable and prosperous with a thin veneer of international co-operation superimposed on strong national regulations than with attempts to construct a bold global regulatory and supervisory framework. The risk we run is that pursuing an ambitious goal will detract us from something that is more desirable and more easily attained."[136] This vision of a kind of "cooperative decentralization" in international regulatory affairs was very different than the initial ambitions for the FSB.[137] By 2013, however, it was one that looked increasingly like a possible legacy of the crisis for the governance of international financial standards over the medium term.

CONCLUSION

The FSB was the only new international financial institution to be created in the wake of the 2008 global financial crisis. Its establishment was initially heralded by some as a development of major importance in helping to enforce the new international financial standards being developed by the G20. But the FSB's ability to enforce the implementation of international financial standards remained extremely limited, just as was that of its predecessor, the FSF.

To be sure, unlike the FSF, FSB members committed to implement standards and undergo peer reviews under the institution's charter. But these commitments had no legal standing; indeed, FSB members were subject to no formal legal obligations of any kind. The effectiveness of the new peer review process was also undermined by the small size of the FSB's staff, the infrequency for each country's peer review, and the limited consequences for noncompliance with recommendations. Building on the FSF's initiative vis-à-vis OFCs, FSB members threatened to use sanctions as a means of promoting compliance, but the initiative was focused only on some very basic pre-crisis principles rather than the post-crisis international regulatory reforms. The threat was also not credible against member countries because of the FSB's consensus decision-making rule. The FSB's post-2011 "coordination framework for implementation monitoring" also did not move beyond voluntary measures.

The FSB's limitations were particularly evident because of the political challenges associated with implementing post-crisis international financial reforms. Some of these challenges stemmed from similar factors that complicated the implementation of international standards before the crisis such as private sector lobbying and competitive pressures. But new challenges also emerged after the crisis because of the politicization of financial regulatory issues in the United States and Europe, and new questions about the effectiveness of peer group pressures among transgovernmental networks. In the face of these challenges and the failure of the G20 to create a stronger organization, the implementation of post-crisis international financial standards was often slow and uneven.

The refusal of the G20 to endorse a more significant departure from the pre-crisis soft-law, network-based governance of international financial standards reflected the enduring reluctance of the United States and other countries to accept serious international constraints on their regulatory policies. It also reflected a distrust of delegating regulatory responsibilities to an international body. That distrust was only reinforced by the failures of international cooperation vis-à-vis burden-sharing and cross-border resolution issues during and after the crisis period as well as vis-à-vis the uneven implementation of international standards. Indeed, because of that distrust, there were growing signs of support among policymakers in the United States and elsewhere for initiatives that would reduce their vulnerability to poor regulation abroad, such as host country regulation for banks and the encouragement of local clearing of OTC derivatives.

In this context, the FSB's creation looked even less significant. Geithner and others hoped the FSB would take on a major role fostering compliance with new common international financial standards for globally integrated markets. Increasingly, however, the FSB appeared to be presiding over an international financial order characterized by pressures for greater financial market and regulatory fragmentation along national lines. In this capacity, the FSB played a more minor role of protecting what Rodrik called the "thin veneer of international cooperation" than rather serving as a major fourth pillar of the global economic governance. It was nation-states that remained the key pillars of global economic governance in the financial regulatory realm.

What Next?

This book has analyzed the impact of the 2008 financial crisis on global financial governance. It has argued that the consequences of the crisis across a number of issue areas—crisis management, the dollar's global role, the content and governance of international financial regulation—have been much less dramatic than was initially anticipated. Viewed from the perspective of five years on, the crisis of 2008 has been more of a status quo event in these areas than a transformative one.

But even if the transformative impacts of the crisis on global financial governance look limited now, could they become more substantial over the longer term? As historical institutionalists remind us, change in global financial governance often comes slowly. Even the famous 1944 Bretton Woods conference built on many years of negotiations, proposals, and incremental political developments drawn out over the previous decade.[1] Is it possible that the 2008 financial upheaval has generated developments that—although limited in their impact now—will encourage more significant change over the longer term? If so, what kind of change will that be?

While the previous chapters look backwards to analyze what has happened since 2008, this concluding chapter explores these more forward-looking questions. The discussion is necessarily speculative. Instead of drawing any firm conclusions, the chapter outlines three scenarios of change for the future evolution of global financial governance. Each scenario highlights how developments already described in the book could have more significant impacts on global financial governance over the longer term than they have had so far. The chapter concludes by noting a fourth scenario: the status quo endures.

STRENGTHENED LIBERAL MULTILATERALISM?

The first scenario is one in which the longer term legacy of the crisis is a strengthening of the liberal multilateral features of global financial governance across the issue areas examined in this book. As we have seen, the crisis has already generated several international institutional innovations that point in this direction. Although the limitations of these innovations have been highlighted in this book, it is certainly possible that they could be overcome in the coming years.

Many analysts believe that the key institutional innovation to emerge from the crisis has been the new G20 leaders' forum and that its effectiveness was demonstrated particularly well by its management of the crisis. This book has questioned that argument, but the G20 leaders forum could well emerge as a more influential global crisis manager in the coming years. For example, the G20 has begun to position itself more effectively to foster macroeconomic coordination through the creation of a new non-binding "Framework for Strong, Sustainable and Balanced Growth" in September 2009 involving mutual assessment of each other's medium-term economic policy frameworks. This mutual assessment process has been criticized for its failure to achieve much progress in resolving global imbalances, but it could play a more immediate and meaningful role in fostering coordinated macroeconomic policy responses in the event of a future global crisis.

The G20 leaders could also take up the suggestion advanced by the South Korean government and others in 2010 to create a more institutionalized multilateral swap regime that could supply emergency lending in a future crisis. Such an initiative would draw on the successful experience of the Fed's swaps during the crisis to create a more permanent and reliable international financial "safety net" that was inclusive of more countries. At the time of the South Korean proposal, the Fed and European Central Bank (ECB) had concerns about both moral hazard issues and the risks of assuming permanent commitments in this area. But we have seen how the Fed and ECB did eventually agree to establishment permanent swap lines in October 2013 with monetary authorities in Canada, England, Japan, and Switzerland, and how countries have taken up the idea of a multilateral swap regime in contexts such as the regional Chiang Mai Initiative Multilateralization (CMIM) and the BRICS (Brazil, Russia, India, China, and South Africa) recent initiative. A G20-led initiative could build on these experiences in ways that strengthened the multilateral nature of global financial governance.

More ambitiously, the G20 countries could give the International Monetary Fund (IMF) a more significant international lender-of-last-resort role of that kind that Edwin Truman suggested at the height of the crisis. Under Truman's proposal, the IMF would be empowered to swap Special Drawing Rights (SDRs) with leading central banks in return for unlimited amounts of their national currencies, thereby enabling it to take on the kind of international role that the Fed played during the crisis. In the context of growing domestic constraints, US officials might see this reform as one that helpfully reduced the burdens and responsibilities of its leadership in this area.

To be effective, however, this initiative would require that the stigma associated with IMF borrowing in many emerging market governments was overcome. The latter could be achieved only through the implementation of more serious governance reforms to cultivate the trust and confidence of these governments in the institution. The crisis already acted as a catalyst for some limited IMF governance reforms. More dramatic reforms require the support of the United States and Europe, support that could well emerge as their fiscal constraints encourage them to become more welcoming of the financial contributions that emerging markets can make to the Fund.

The IMF's centrality in global financial governance would also be boosted if the SDR assumed a larger role in international monetary system. We have seen how the crisis generated the first new allocation of SDRs in almost three decades as well as renewed interest in SDR's longer term prospects as a more significant reserve currency. For the SDR to assume a larger international monetary role, a number of issues would need to be addressed, such as the need for more regular SDR allocations, the encouragement of a private market for SDRs, and perhaps the creation of a substitution account. As we have seen, a number of countries signaled their support for these kinds of initiatives in the wake of the crisis, including France, China, and other BRICS countries. The United States blocked reform, but groups of like-minded states favoring reserve reform could follow the advice of the Stiglitz Commission in creating regional reserve currencies with the longer term objective of building an alternative global reserve system "bottom-up."

US views could also change if the costs of the dollar's international role that are highlighted by critics such as Stiglitz, Bergsten, and others became more politicized domestically. US officials backed the SDR's initial creation and subsequent strengthening at moments—such as the late 1960s and late 1970s—when the costs of the dollar's international role were apparent.[2] Those costs are likely to rise as the US dominance in the world economy erodes.[3] At least that was the British experience in the second half of the 20th century as the sterling's international role was increasingly criticized for constraining national macroeconomic policy and imposing political and economic burdens associated with the maintenance of foreign official support for the currency. By the 1960s and 1970s, British officials were actively seeking to de-internationalize sterling in order to shed these costs of currency leadership, including by backing the creation and strengthening of the SDR as an alternative reserve asset.[4]

One final legacy of the crisis that may have greater longer term significance for a scenario of strengthened liberal multilateralism is the creation of the Financial Stability Board (FSB). Chapter 5 highlighted the limitations of the FSB, particularly in the face of growing challenges relating to the compliance with international financial standards. But the FSB could emerge as a more significant "fourth pillar" of global economic architecture in the coming years if it was transformed into a more universal organization with greater power to enforce compliance with international financial standards.

Under this scenario, the FSB would preside over a globally integrated financial order, in a similar manner as the World Trade Organization (WTO) does vis-à-vis the international trading system. Drawing on the WTO model, its enforcement power could stem from a dispute settlement procedure backed by the power to authorize sanctions against member countries that did not comply with international standards. Those standards could include stronger treaty-based international rules covering a full range of financial markets and institutions in a cohesive manner. The content of these rules could either retain the market-friendly character described in Chapter 4, or they might shift in a more anti-market direction. The FSB could also be empowered to address decisively the kinds of cross-border recovery and resolution issues discussed in Chapter 5.

As we have seen, some policymakers in Britain and France, already favored this kind of scenario at the time of the FSB's creation. More supporters may emerge in the face of growing costs—in terms of spillovers from poor regulation abroad and competitive pressures—generated by uneven national regulations in the context of increasingly integrated global financial markets. Powerful internationally oriented private sector firms might also lobby for this outcome as a way of minimizing transaction costs and constraining some of the regulatory trends noted in Chapter 5 that threaten to undermine an open and integrated global financial system and complicate their cross-border operations.

In these ways, it is possible to see how the 2008 crisis could be seen in future years as laying the ground for a strengthening of the liberal multilateral features of global financial governance. Even if some of the institutional innovations of the crisis—such as the creation of G20 leaders forum and FSB, the SDR issue, IMF governance reforms—were not enormously significant initially, they could become much more so over time. This scenario could unfold only with the backing of the dominant states in the global financial system, but there are reasons to believe this support could be forthcoming over time. Another major international financial crisis could perhaps serve as the catalyst for significant reform of this kind..

FRAGMENTATION AND CONFLICT?

A second scenario involves a very different future in which liberal multilateralism in global financial governance was increasingly undermined. Instead of being characterized by strengthening cooperation, the global financial system would witness growing fragmentation and conflict between the major powers. The 2008 crisis encouraged some trends in this direction across the issues examined in this book. Under this scenario, those trends would intensify in the coming years.

Instead of becoming more important, the G20's role in global financial governance would weaken over time. Even among the G20's staunchest supporters, there are already growing questions about the body's effectiveness. After the three initial headline-grabbing G20 summits of 2008–09, subsequent summit meetings were much less impressive, with consensus being more difficult to reach among the leading powers.[5] Once the crisis passed, many political leaders appeared less invested in the G20 process and they were unwilling to strengthen its institutional foundations. In the coming years, the commitment of leading powers to the G20 could erode further, particularly if policymakers everywhere devoted more attention to regional, bilateral, and unilateral financial initiatives.

In many parts of the world, this trend could be associated with efforts to reduce dependence on the US-centered global financial order and broader US structural power.[6] Particularly significant for global financial governance would be a transformation in China's foreign economic policy in this respect. The crisis of 2008 already provoked much greater Chinese discussion on this topic, including the need to reorient the country's development model in a more inward-oriented direction.[7] Those discussions could well encourage a gradual realignment of domestic coalitions and policy frameworks over the longer term in ways that undermined the country's support for financial cooperation with the United States in the G20 and other international institutions.

During and after the crisis, there was a strong complementarity between powerful domestic interests and state priorities in both the United States and China favoring the status quo. This kind of realignment in China could provoke political reactions in the United States that generated a quite different foreign economic policy stance. Over the longer term, the United States may also independently experience domestic coalitional realignments that prompt American policymakers to question the costs associated with their country's central role in the global economy. As we have seen, the 2008 crisis already provoked some questioning of this kind among prominent US analysts. If the concerns gained influence in the coming years, they could provoke a US backlash against commitments made to support for the G20 and other international financial institutions such as the IMF and FSB.

That kind of a US backlash could, in turn, trigger further reactions abroad. For example, if the United States lost interest in IMF governance reforms, distrust of that institution among potential borrowers could well intensify in ways that encouraged greater resort to "self-insurance." Governments in East Asia and elsewhere might also be prompted to strengthen regional financial arrangements as well as their independence from the IMF. In addition, the BRICS' post-crisis efforts to pool reserves might accelerate. Initiatives to create more bilateral swaps—such as those of China after 2008—might also intensify, particularly as part of wider efforts to cultivate alliances in an increasingly conflictual world. An early sign of this latter phenomenon was witnessed already in late 2008 when South Korea received competing offers from the United States, China, and Japan for bilateral support within the space of a few months.

Some of these bilateral financing mechanisms might also be linked to efforts to encourage closer monetary cooperation. As noted in Chapter 3, the new Chinese bilateral swap arrangements are closely tied to post-crisis Chinese efforts to encourage greater use of the renminbi (RMB) abroad and reduce dependence on the dollar. To date, Chinese policymakers have pursued this goal in a cautious manner and the RMB's international role has remained insignificant in comparison to that of the dollar (and euro). But the Chinese authorities could begin promoting RMB internationalization more aggressively through full capital account liberalization and other ambitious initiatives. Under this scenario, the RMB would challenge the dollar more seriously in the East Asian region and even globally. Indeed, with the appropriate reforms, some anticipate that the RMB could easily overtake the dollar as the world's leading reserve currency by the early 2020s.[8]

As noted in Chapter 3, Chinese authorities are not the only ones seeking to reduce their dependence on the dollar's international role in the wake of the 2008 crisis. The widespread foreign criticism of the US currency's global dominance could generate more serious efforts to minimize exposure to the greenback elsewhere in the coming years. If European authorities can strengthen the euro's governance, they may emerge from the euro crisis with more serious ambitions for the euro's international role. The combination of new frustration with dollar dependence and fear of the RMB's growing influence may also prompt Japanese policymakers to promote the yen's internationalization more aggressively. Governments in regions such as Latin America could also expand their efforts to minimize exposure to the dollar through bilateral and regional payments arrangements.

The proliferation of more serious challenges to the dollar's international role could well trigger competitive reactions from US authorities seeking to maintain some of the benefits associated with the dollar's influence. Indeed, Cohen predicts the emergence of a wider growing currency rivalry in the coming years between leading powers such as the United States, China, Japan, and Europe, with each seeking to maximize the international use of their respective currencies in order to secure benefits such as seigniorage, macroeconomic flexibility, power, and prestige. If policymakers in leading powers resorted to direct inducements to foreign governments, the fight for currency dominance could become particularly intense in what Cohen calls regional "currency battlegrounds" where the economic and geopolitical stakes are high such as the Middle East (the euro vs. the dollar) and East Asia (the RMB vs. the yen vs. the dollar).[9] Under this scenario, the longer term legacy of the 2008 crisis would be an increasingly "leaderless currency system" characterized by friction and instability in international monetary relations.[10]

One more legacy could be a breakdown of global multilateral cooperation in the financial regulatory realm. As noted in Chapter 4, the

2008 crisis generated widespread criticism of the market-friendly nature of international regulatory standards that had been promoted by the Anglo-American powers before the crisis. That criticism has encouraged various international regulatory reforms, but their limitations may trigger growing frustrations among policymakers seeking more significant regulatory initiatives. These officials may increasingly be tempted to pursue tighter regulation unilaterally at the domestic or regional level without regard to the FSB's efforts to maintain a level playing field internationally.

Those initiatives might be accompanied by greater resort to host country regulation, forced local clearing of derivatives, and restrictions on cross-border financial activity in order to boost national autonomy to pursue more ambitious regulatory initiatives. These policies might also be seen as mechanisms to insulate countries from competitive pressures arising from looser regulation abroad and the instability of foreign markets, particularly in the wake of another major international financial crisis in the coming years. The desire for greater regulatory autonomy could be reinforced by the distrust of foreign regulators that was generated by crisis experience, as noted in Chapter 5. Under this scenario, the legacy of the crisis would be a more fragmented global financial system along national (or regional) lines instead of one characterized by strengthened multilateral cooperation. Already in 2009, historian Harold James was writing of "the recently ended era of financial globalisation."[11] These trends would strengthen the force of that observation.

International regulatory cooperation could also be undermined in future years by two other legacies of the crisis. The first is the politicization of financial regulatory issues within the United States and Europe, which has generated new resistance to delegation of sovereignty to international bodies and new domestic constraints on technocrats working with the FSB and other international bodies. Second, the task of reaching consensus on international regulatory issues has been complicated further by the undermining of the legitimacy of Anglo-American regulatory models (which had acted as a focal point for coordination in the pre-crisis years) and by the new post-crisis prominence within international regulatory bodies of emerging market countries which often bring quite distinct perspectives to the issue.

In this context, global regulatory cooperation—and its lead institutional champion, the FSB—would become increasingly ineffectual. In some parts of the world, regional financial standards might become more consequential than global ones. Those regional standards might be created by powerful regional authorities (as in the European Union) or looser FSB-style regional bodies (the 2008 crisis already generated proposals in East Asia for such a body[12]). Elsewhere, the domestic standards of powerful states might become the de facto norm for economic partners to follow. As rival national and regional standards proliferated, leading powers might also seek to encourage the spread of their own practices abroad, generating a world of growing conflict between rival standards instead of the kind of cooperative harmonization envisaged in the FSB's charter.

COOPERATIVE DECENTRALIZATION?

If the first and second scenarios represent polar opposites, there is a third possibility that exists somewhere in between them. Under this scenario, the multilateral features of global financial governance would endure but their content would be transformed to be supportive of a more decentralized global financial order. In this way, divergent legacies of the crisis noted in the two previous scenarios would be reconciled in innovative ways. We might call this scenario one of "cooperative decentralization."[13]

In the realm of crisis management, the provision of emergency finance would increasingly be handled by regional, bilateral, and national arrangements, as under the second scenario. But rather than being marginalized, global institutions could still supplement these arrangements and play a supportive role of either coordination or collaboration. For example, international bodies could develop certain standards for bilateral swap arrangements or national policies of reserve accumulation to meet, or IMF funding could be used to supplement that of alternative arrangements. Already, the Fund was working in this latter way in the context of its relationship to the CMIM and particularly through its involvement in the European sovereign debt crisis after early 2010.

Similarly, the IMF could make greater efforts to cultivate relationships with regional financial arrangements in ways that encouraged complementarity between its activities and theirs, and left it "positioned at the apex of a network of regional reserve funds and swap arrangements."[14] Once again, there were also already signs of this in the wake of the 2008 crisis. At their late 2010 summit, the G20 leaders formally encouraged improved collaboration between the Fund and RFAs. One year later, they even agreed on some rather vague non-binding principles for cooperation between the IMF and RFAs.[15] These initiatives came on the heels of the very first high-level meeting ever in October 2010 between the IMF and representatives associated with regional financing arrangements in Europe, East Asia, Latin America, and the Middle East. As one set of analysts put it at the time, the meeting showed "what a long way the Fund has come from being the institution that vehemently opposed the idea of creating an Asian Monetary Fund, as proposed by the Japanese government after the outbreak of the Asian financial crisis."[16]

In the international monetary arena, this cooperative decentralization scenario could involve the emergence of a more multipolar currency order but through a process characterized more by cooperation than conflict and rivalry. For example, instead of resisting the de-internationalization of the dollar, US policymakers could welcome the shedding of the costs of currency leadership and work closely with foreign authorities to foster the process. International institutions could also assist this process, just as the IMF and Bank for International Settlements (BIS) helped to reduce sterling's international role in a cooperative manner during the 1960s and 1970s.[17] The IMF and the G20's mutual assessment process could also help mediate relations and encourage cooperation between currency zones that increasingly emerged around the world's dominant currencies such as the euro, dollar, the yen, or the RMB. The SDR's international role could also be strengthened in modest ways that help to reinforce the cooperative dimensions of this more decentralized monetary order.

In the international regulatory realm, the diverse legacies of the crisis could also be reconciled in creative ways. For the reasons noted in the previous section, financial markets might become increasingly segmented along national and regional lines through mechanisms such as greater host country regulation and use of capital account restrictions. But this process could take place within a cooperative framework established by the FSB (and IMF in the case of capital account restrictions). For example, the FSB could foster international agreements that facilitated interactions between distinct regulatory regimes as well as broad principles for the use of host country rules that prevented their use for protectionist purposes. The FSB could also provide assistance to boost the capacity of poorer countries that may lack sufficient capacity to implement effective host country regulation. Equally important would be the task of strengthening the capacity of all countries to regulate at the national level through cooperative research, early warning systems for global risks, and extensive information gathering (relating to market developments, activities of large firms, regulatory initiatives abroad).

In addition, governments could continue to develop certain minimum international standards through the FSB to address systemic risks as well as minimize competitive problems and negative externalities arising from poor regulatory practices abroad. Rather than detailed one-size-fits-all rules, those standards could be based around broad principles that allowed significant national or regional policy space. The FSB could then even take on a role of endorsing members' restrictions against firms and transactions from jurisdictions that were known to be flaunting these basic standards.

This regulatory scenario is one that already has prominent advocates after the 2008 crisis. It is, for example, very similar to the "Plan B" that Dani Rodrik put forward in early 2009, as noted at the end of Chapter 5. The report of the Warwick Commission on International Financial Reform later that same year also advanced detailed arguments for regulatory reform along these lines, and argued that the FSB might be particularly well suited to support it. If these ideas gain wider traction in the coming years, the crisis might come to be seen as a turning point in the construction of an international regulatory order organized around cooperative decentralization principles.

Across these various issue areas, this scenario outlines perhaps the most plausible way in which global financial governance might be transformed in significant ways in the coming years. Unlike the first scenario of strengthened liberal multilateralism, it takes seriously the centrifugal pressures for decentralization that have been encouraged by the crisis and post-crisis experience. Unlike the second scenario of conflict and fragmentation, it also recognizes that the leading powers have continued during and after the crisis to profess their commitment to strengthen multilateral cooperation (even if the significance of those commitments is easily overstated, as this book has suggested). A world of cooperative decentralization suggests a way in which these seemingly conflicting legacies of the crisis might be reconciled.

ENDURING STATUS QUO?

Each of the three scenarios described in this chapter assumes that the 2008 crisis will leave an imprint over the longer term that encourages substantial change. From these perspectives, the status quo outcomes in the first half decade after the crisis hide deeper transformative legacies. There is, however, a final scenario in which the patterns of the first half decade after the 2008 crisis endure. In other words, the legacy of the crisis could be a status quo outcome in both the short *and* longer term, particularly if there are no major shifts in the power and interests of dominant states in the coming years.

Under this scenario, international financial crisis management would continue to rely heavily on *ad hoc* US international lender-of-last–resort activities, as efforts to strengthen alternative multilateral and regional arrangements failed. The world monetary system would remain dollar-dominated in a context where the SDR was not reformed, the Eurozone was plagued by further instability, and barriers to the internationalization of the RMB and yen were not overcome. The content of international financial standards would continue to evolve but only in incremental market-friendly ways. And the FSB would continue to be a weak institution that attempted, with very inconsistent results, to secure countries' compliance with international standards.

Under this scenario, it is a virtual certainty that the global financial system would experience further global financial crises, with all their tremendous economic social costs for millions of people across the globe. It might seem implausible that the status quo in global financial governance could persist over the longer term in the face of repeated crises. But it seemed just as unlikely at the height of the 2008 financial crisis that so little would change in global financial governance as a result of that momentous upheaval. In the end, the existing order proved much more durable than many expected. If that massive shock to the system did not generate major transformative change, what will?

CHAPTER 1

1. Eichengreen and O'Rourke (2010).
2. The writing of this manuscript was finished in January 2014.
3. Reinhart and Rogoff (2009).
4. Joe Stiglitz quoted in Bases (2008).
5. Quoted in Jabko (2012: 97).
6. Quoted in Kirkup and Waterfield (2008).
7. See, for example, Kahler (2013a: 30).
8. Brown (2010: 128–129).
9. *The Economist* (2007: 15).
10. For "structural power" in global finance and money, see Strange (1987, 1988, 1990), Kirshner (1995), and Helleiner (2006).
11. See also Germain (2009, 2010), Schwartz (2009), Panitch and Gindin (2012), Suominen (2012), and Oatley et al. (2013).
12. Kahler (2013a).
13. See, for example, Cammack (2010), Soederberg (2010), and Overbeek and Apeldorn (2012),
14. For analyses that highlight the enduring dominance of neoliberalism, see, for example, Blyth (2013a, b), Crouch (2011), Wilson and Grant (2012), and Mirowski (2013).
15. These structures can of course be interconnected in complicated ways; see, for example, Panitch and Gindin (2005, 2012), who argue that the US state serves as a kind of "superintendent" for the interests of global capital.
16. See, for example, Drezner (2012); Kahler (2013a: 41–44); and Kahler and Lake (2013: 21–22).
17. For analyses using historical institutionism to explain post-crisis global economic governance, see for example Fioretos (2012: 390–391); Moschella and Tsingou (2013). Historical institutionalist insights can even help to explain the "Bretton Woods moment" of the early 1940s (Helleiner forthcoming).

18. Helleiner and Pagliari (2011).

19. It is also worth noting that the book does not discuss a number of other aspects of global financial governance where the case for a "status quo crisis" is *stronger* because they remain entirely untouched by the post-crisis reforms. For example, some have lamented the absence of any renewed effort to build a global sovereign debt restructuring mechanism, particularly in light of the European debt crises.

CHAPTER 2

1. This shift was confirmed at the G20 leaders' third summit in September 2009 when they "designated the G-20 to be the premier forum for our international economic cooperation" (G20 2009b: 3). The G7 countries are Canada, France, Germany, Italy, Japan, the United Kingdom, and the United States. The G20 members also include Argentina, Australia, Brazil, China, India, Indonesia, South Korea, Mexico, Russia, Saudi Arabia, South Africa, Turkey, and the European Union. For overviews of the G20, see Cooper and Thakur (2013) and Kirton (2013).

2. G20 (2009b: 1).

3. See, for example, Jones (2010: 6), Bradford and Linn (2011), and Carin and Schorr (2013).

4. Sarkozy (2010b).

5. Quoted in Beattie and Oliver (2010). See also the quote from Gordon Brown in Chapter 1.

6. Carin and Schorr (2013: 9).

7. G20 (2009a: 6).

8. Drezner (2012: 2).

9. Pontassun and Raess (2012: 30); Baccini and Kim (2012); Drezner (2012); Kahler (2013a: 35).

10. See, for example, Bradford and Linn (2011: 10–11) and Kirton (2013: 252).

11. G20 Leaders (2008: 2).

12. G20 (2009a: 2).

13. G20 (2009b: 1).

14. See, for example, Bordo and James (2010) and Roubini and Mihm (2010).

15. See, for example, Bayne (2008), Paulson (2009: 339), and Irwin (2013: 161–162).

16. As much as half of the growth in government deficits in advanced economies in 2009 stemmed from automatic stabilizers (Callinicos 2012: 66).

17. Rajan (2010: 2078).

18. Darling (2011: chapter 8).

19. Wade (2011: 358).

20. Kahler (2013a: 44).

21. Schmalz and Ebenau (2012: 494).

22. Drezner (2012: 9).

23. Schirm (2011); Schelkle (2012); Vail (forthcoming).

24. Schirm (2011); Cameron (2012); Schelkle (2012).

25. Armingeon (2012: 544, 561).

26. G20 (2009a: 1).

27. Brown (2010: 113).

28. Wade (2009: 547). See also Reuters (2009), which argues that the commitment of $250 billion was not all new money. I have not been able to confirm how much new money was actually spent as a result of this initiative.
29. Moon and Rhyu (2010: 454).
30. Helleiner (2005).
31. Rajan (2010: 82). See also Wolf (2008c); Ocampo (2010a); and Obstfeld, Shambaugh, and Taylor (2009). As noted in Chapter 3, reserve accumulation was also driven by some other motivations than "self-insurance."
32. Wolf (2010)).
33. Quoted in Helleiner and Momani (2008).
34. Grabel (2011: 808).
35. G20 Leaders (2008: 2, 5).
36. IMF (2009).
37. IMF (2009).
38. IMF (2009).
39. The funds did, however, become useful when demand for IMF lending subsequently came from European governments caught up in the Eurozone crisis.
40. G20 Working Group 3 (2009: 16).
41. Grabel (2011: 821–824).
42. Quoted in Chey (2012b: 7).
43. Quoted in McKay and Volz (2010: 28).
44. G20 (2008: 3).
45. Woods (2010); Chin (2010).
46. IMF (2009).
47. Board of Governors of the Federal Reserve System (2012).
48. Allen and Moessner (2010).
49. Chey (2012b: 2fn2).
50. Grimes (2011: 295).
51. Allen and Moessner (2010: 66–68; 2011: 190).
52. McDowell (2012). With the outbreak of the Greek crisis, the Fed reestablished swaps in May 2010 with the central banks of Canada, England, Europe, Japan, and Switzerland.
53. McGuire and von Peter (2009); Allen and Moessner (2010); McDowell (2012).
54. Obstfeld, Shambaugh, and Taylor (2009); Obstfeld, Shambaugh, and Taylor (2009); Allen and Moessner (2010: 43).
55. Wessel (2009: 141).
56. Tett (2009: 186).
57. Allen and Moessner (2011).
58. Duke (2012). As noted previously, Brazil and Singapore also did not draw on their swaps.
59. Moessner and Allen (2011: 18).
60. Broz (2012), Harding, Simon, and Oliver (2010).
61. Financial Crisis Inquiry Report (2011: 377); Barofsky (2012: chapter 10).
62. Board of Governors of the Federal Reserve System (2012).
63. Latvia also received a small swap from the Danish and Swedish central banks in December 2008 as a bridge to its IMF loan. The central banks of Denmark,

Sweden, and Norway also extended a small swap to Iceland in May 2008 before that country received an IMF loan (Allen and Moessner 2010, 2011).

64. Grimes (2011: 295).

65. Allen and Moessner (2010).

66. Allen and Moessner (2010); Yang (2012).

67. Yang (2012).

68. Grimes (2009: 81, 91).

69. Sussangkam (2010: 6).

70. Moessner and Allen (2011: 18).

71. The countries were Belgium, Canada, France, Germany, Italy, Japan, Netherlands, Sweden, Switzerland, the United Kingdom, and the United States.

72. The swaps were largely retired in 1998, although swaps created with Canada and Mexico in the mid-1990s remained (Moessner and Allen 2010).

73. Aizenman and Pasricha (2009); Broz (2012); McDowell (2012).

74. McDowell (2012). See also Allen and Moessner (2011). Chey (2012b) notes that US officials may also have been worried that if countries such as Korea sold more reserves to defend their currency, this behaviour might adversely affect the US Treasury market. From a more political perspective, Chey also argues that the choice of emerging market countries to receive a swap may have been linked to the US desire to mobilize support in advance of the discussions on international financial reform to be held at the first G20 summit; Mexico, Brazil, and Korea were all members of the G20, and Singapore was a member of the Financial Stability Forum that was helping to draft reform recommendations at the time. To support this case, he highlights how the Fed initially opposed Korea's request for a swap in mid-October, but then became very supportive a few days after President Bush's October 22 announcement of the upcoming G20 summit.

75. Pauly (2009: 359).

76. G20 (2008: 2).

77. Brown (2010: chapter 1).

78. Kim and Chey (2012).

79. Oliver (2010); Allen and Moessner (2010: 78).

80. Kim and Chey (2012: 7).

81. Allen and Moessner (2010: 78).

82. Central Banking Newsdesk (2103d).

83. Chey (2012b); Agrawal and Goyal (2012); Suominen (2012: 117).

84. Hill and Menon (2012: 1). See also Henning (2011). For a skeptical view of the usefulness of the CMIM in crisis management, see also Grimes (2011).

85. Kim and Chey (2012).

86. Quotes from BRICS (2013a: 1).

87. BRICS (2013b).

88. Quotes from Truman (2008: 27).

89. Truman (2010b).

90. Broz (2012). This was certainly true for countries such as Japan and Norway, both of which had enormous dollar reserves, but it was not the case for countries such as the United Kingdom, Switzerland, and Australia, whose reserves were smaller than the domestic shortage of dollars (Allen and Moessner 2011).

91. Quoted in Harding (2010).
92. Broz (2012).
93. IMF (2010b: 31).
94. IMF (2010b: 26).
95. IMF (2010c: 4).
96. IMF (2010c: 14).
97. IMF (2010c); Elson (2012); Suominen (2012: 117–118).
98. Suominen (2012: 118).
99. IMF (2011c: 6).
100. Perhaps recognizing the weaknesses of the actual commitments, some of the key participants in that summit highlight this point. As British Chancellor of the Exchequer Alistair Darling (2011: 215) puts it in his memoirs: "Looking back, the significance of the summit was perhaps not so much what it agreed as the signal it sent, that countries were ready to act together."
101. As noted footnote 39, those funds did begin to be used when IMF lending to the Eurozone grew after the spring of 2010.

CHAPTER 3

1. BIS (2010).
2. Bertuch-Smuels and Ramlogan (2007); ECB (2008); Cohen (2009a: 146).
3. Cohen and Benney (2012: 26–27).
4. Quotes from *The Economist* (2006: 28).
5. Bertuch-Samuels and Ramlogan (2007). For example, the share of the euro in non-industrial countries reserves had risen from 19% to 30% since the euro's creation, while that the dollar's share had fallen from 70% to 60% (Kester 2007), although some of this change in the value of dollar reserves reflected exchange rate effects rather than lower actual holdings.
6. Eichengreen (2006); Dieter (2007); Kirshner (2008); Helleiner (2009a). Concerns about this dependence were also widespread in the media, for example, *The Economist* (2006).
7. Wolf (2008c).
8. Cohen (2008: 462).
9. Eichengreen (2006).
10. See, for example, Dieter (2007), Kirshner (2008: 428), and Helleiner (2009).
11. Johnson (2008).
12. Momani (2008).
13. Quoted in Helleiner (2009a).
14. Blustein (2012a).
15. Quote from Kirshner (2008); see also Murphy (2006: 62) and Dieter (2007).
16. See, for example, *The Economist* (2007: 15), quoted in Chapter 1 of this book.
17. Paulson (2009); Sorkin (2009: 222).
18. Soros (2009a).
19. Chin and Helleiner (2008); Wade (2009).
20. James (2009: 224). See also p. 227.
21. Sheng (2009: 3). See also Rajan (2010); Stigliz (2010: 221–222); Mahathir (2012); Otero-Iglesias and Steinberg (2013a).

22. Quoted in Johnson and Kwak (2010: 174).
23. McCauley and McGuire (2009: 85); see also Kohler (2010).
24. McCauley and McGuire (2009).
25. See also Kohler (2010).
26. For the link between key currency status and the power of the issuing state, see, for example, James (2009) and Chey (2012a).
27. Reinhart and Rogoff (2009: 222).
28. Cooper (2009: 1–2).
29. See, for example, Oakley and Tett (2008).
30. McCauley and McGuire (2009).
31. Gallagher and Shrestha (2012). In aggregate terms, Wolf (2010) notes that the size of the world's official reserves (not just dollars) decreased by about 6% (or $472 billion) between July 2008 and February 2009, but then began to rise rapidly again.
32. Paulson (2009: 242).
33. Gallaher and Shrestha (2012). The share of China's reserves held in dollars is not public information, but a leak in September 2010 revealed that 65% (or almost $1.6 trillion) of its $2.45 billion reserves at the time was in dollars (Zhou and Rabinovitch 2010). As its total reserves were not quite that size at the time the crisis broke out, it is quite certain that China's holdings of dollar rose during the crisis (even if the share of reserves in dollars may have declined). By late 2013, Chinese reserves had risen further to $3.66 trillion (Strauss 2014).
34. Schwartz (2009: 211).
35. Drezner (2008: 116).
36. For a review, see, for example, Helleiner (2011a).
37. See, for example, Chin (2010: 700). For the general theme of risk aversion, see Kahler (2013b). It is worth noting that before World War 1, many emerging powers also accumulated reserves because of concerns about the increasingly uncertain international political environment (De Cecco 2009).
38. See, for example, Otero-Iglesias and Steinberg (2013b).
39. Spiro (1999); Murphy (2006); Momani (2008); Otero-Iglesias and Steinberg (2013a).
40. Dooley, Folkerts, and Garber (2003).
41. Steinberg and Shih (2012).
42. Vermeiren (2013).
43. Hung (2009: 24).
44. Schwartz (2009).
45. Quoted in Sender (2009). See also Otero-Iglesias and Steinberg (2013b).
46. Schwartz (2009: 172).
47. Quoted in Otero-Iglesiasis and Steinberg (2013a: 323). For domestic interest group pressure from export industries at this time, see also He (2011: 28–29).
48. James (2009).
49. Yang (2011); Sang-Jin and Peng (2012: 155–156); Vermeiren (2013).
50. Setser (2008: 22).
51. Paulson (2009: 161). See also Sorkin (2009: 222) for his fears about Chinese and Russian selling of agency bonds.

52. Setser (2008: 28); Paulson (2009: 161); Thompson (2009, 2012).
53. Quote in Hamlin (2008).
54. Drezner (2009).
55. Statistic from Cohen (2008: 462).
56. Quoted in Bradsher (2009).
57. Otero-Iglesias and Steinberg (2013a).
58. For foreign official interest in these decisions, see Paulson (2009: 233, 318); Sorkin (2009); Tett (2009: 211).
59. Blustein (2012a).
60. Paulson (2009: 161, 242, 318); Sorkin (2009: 269–274, 444–453, 469–470, 482, 509, 518).
61. Setser (2008: 29). See more generally Kahler (2013a: 44–45).
62. Strange (1988).
63. Hausmann (2008).
64. Zhou (2009a).
65. Zhou (2009a: 1–2).
66. Zhou (2009a: 2).
67. IMF (2011b); Ly (2012).
68. Zhou (2009a: 2–3).
69. Zhou (2009a: 3).
70. Gowa (1984); Boughton (2001: 936–943).
71. Quoted in Otero-Iglesias and Steinberg (2013: 326). See also Mallaby (2009) and Eichengreen (2011: 142).
72. Chin (2014).
73. Zhou (2009b). See also Chin (2014) for earlier China's emphasis on this point.
74. Otero-Iglesias and Zhang (2013a).
75. Somerville (2009).
76. IMF (2011b).
77. Eichengreen (2009).
78. Commission of Experts (2009a).
79. Quote from Commission of Experts (2009b: 116).
80. Reuters (2008b).
81. BRIC (2009a).
82. Johnson (2013).
83. Otero-Iglesias and Steinberg (2013a); Chin (2014).
84. BRIC (2009b).
85. Xinhua (2009)
86. See, for example, Sarkozy (2010a).
87. Carmichael (2010).
88. Otero-Iglesias and Zhang (2013a); Chin (2014).
89. The substitution account also received a brief mention, although the staff wondered whether the risks of disorderly dollar selling were high enough to warrant the effort that would be required to create a substitution account (Mateos y Lago, Duttagupta, and Goyal 2009: 19).
90. IMF (2011a).

91. Carney (2010: 5, 5fn9). Because governments could exchange their dollar reserves for SDRs in the IMF-run substitution account, they might be tempted to accumulate more such reserves in order to take advantage of the possibility of this exchange.

92. See, for example, Moon and Rhyu (2010); Chin (2014).

93. Truman (2008: 26); Brown (2010: 117).

94. Kirton (2013: 274–275).

95. Chin (2014).

96. Bergsten (2009a: 21). See also Bergsten (2009b).

97. Helleiner (2010a).

98. Setser (2008: 26); Helleiner and Malkin (2012).

99. Quotes from Evans-Pritchard (2009).

100. G20 (2011: 3).

101. BRICS (2011).

102. BRICS (2012).

103. Johnson (2013: 5). In March 2013, it came back on agenda of BRICS (2013a): "We support the reform and improvement of the international monetary system, with a broad-based international reserve currency system providing stability and certainty. We welcome the discussion about the role of the SDR in the existing international monetary system including the composition of SDR's basket of currencies."

104. Eichengreen (2011: 140).

105. IMF (2011b: 14).

106. Ocampo (2010a: 6).

107. Eichengreen (2011: 143).

108. See also Chey (2012a).

109. See, for example, Henning (1998: 563–565).

110. Quoted in Otero-Iglesias and Steinberg (2013a: 320). Just before the first G20 summit, he had made a similar comment: "I am leaving tomorrow for Washington to explain that the dollar cannot claim to be the only currency in the world…that was what true in 1945 can no longer be true today" (Global Research 2008).

111. Kester (2007); Harding (2013). For growing official skepticism in emerging market countries, see Otero-Iglesias and Steinberg (2013a, b).

112. BIS (2013: 3).

113. See for example ECB (2013: 8) which noted the following in discussing barriers to the euro's internationalization: "further efforts are needed both at the euro area and the national level to tackle the fundamental causes of the financial fragmentation in the euro area, and a strengthening of the institutional framework of Economic and Monetary Union will also make a positive contribution to this end."

114. See especially Chin (2014).

115. Tang Jiaxuan quoted in Otero-Iglesias (2013: 5).

116. Otero-Iglesias (2013); Otero-Iglesias and Steinberg (2013b); Chin (2014).

117. Chin (2014), Bowles and Wang (2013).

118. For these various benefits, see He (2012); Helleiner and Malkin (2012); Yu (2012); Chin (2014), Chey (2013).
119. He (2012).
120. See for example Chey (2013).
121. Yang (2014); Chey (2013).
122. Zhang (2012), In the first nine months of 2012, approximately 11% of China's trade was settled in RMB (Bowles and Wang 2013: 1370).
123. Zhang (2012); Yu (2012); Chey (2013).
124. BIS (2013: 5).
125. SWIFT (2013).
126. Chey (2013), Bowles and Wang (2013). The one area where RMB use began to challenge the euro is the share of international trade finance. The RMB's share grew from 1.89% in January 2012 to 8.66% in October 2013, a figure larger than the euro's 6.64% but much lower than the US dollar's 81.08% share (SWIFT 2013). Some of this RMB trade finance data may include disguised capital flows.
127. Eichengreen (2011: 7).
128. Schwartz (2009: 172); Eichengreen (2011: 146); Helleiner and Malkin (2012).
129. BRIC (2010).
130. BRICS (2012b).
131. Johnson (2013).
132. Maziad et al. (2011); Johnson (2013).
133. Quoted in Otero-Iglesias and Steinberg (2013b: 22).
134. Chin (2014).
135. Eichengreen (2011: 144); Otero-Iglesias and Steinberg (2013a); Trucco (2012: 114).
136. Baumgarten de Bolle (2013: 13).
137. Trucco (2012: 114).
138. Baumgarten de Bolle (2013: 13–14).
139. Maziad et al. (2011: 15).
140. See, for example, Katada (2008) and Grimes (2009).
141. Cohen (2010: 157).
142. Murphy (2008).
143. Quote from Bergsten (2009a: 25–6). See also Austin (2011) and Pettis (2011).
144. See for example Austin (2011) in the US Treasury, who also stressed that his views and analysis were his own and did not reflect those of the Treasury Department or the US Government.
145. It also urged the US to "live within its means" by making substantial cuts to its "gigantic military expenditure and bloated social welfare costs (quoted in Hook 2011).
146. Schenk (2010).
147. Schenk (2010).
148. Cohen (2010).
149. Eichengreen (2011: 7).
150. Allen and Moessner (2011: 194).

151. Ross and Jones (2013).
152. BIS (2013: 3).
153. Cohen and Benney (2012: 26–27).
154. Kahler (2013a: 40–41).

CHAPTER 4
1. Stiglitz (2010: 219).
2. Cohen (2009: 437).
3. Soros (2009a: 99). For other similar arguments, see the examples cited in Mirowski (2013: 31–33).
4. Wolf (2008b).
5. Wolf (2008a).
6. It was initially called the Basel Committee on Banking Regulations and Supervisory Practices.
7. Walter (2008).
8. Quote from Walter (2008: 8).
9. For an overview, see Pagliari (2013a).
10. Bair (2012: 32).
11. Perry and Nölke (2006).
12. Pagliari (2013a).
13. Blyth (2003); Best (2005); Mackenzie (2006).
14. Quoted in Wolf (2008a).
15. Quoted in Helleiner (2010b: 628).
16. Quoted in Benoit and Wilson (2008).
17. Quoted in Barber, Benoit and Williamson (2008).
18. Quoted in Mangasarian (2008). See also Benoit (2008). When Gordon Brown endorsed tighter European financial regulation in March 2009 in the lead up to the second G20 leaders summit, German officials also spoke of their sense of vindication: "We all remember the British and Americans opposing this kind of thing whenever we suggested it in the past. There was an arrogance about it—they were always boasting about how their economies had faster growth rates" (unnamed German official quoted in Parker 2009).
19. Quoted in Quaglia (2012: 529). See also Jabko (2012).
20. For European's growing market power in international financial regulatory policymaking, see Posner (2009, 2010) and Quaglia (2013).
21. See, for example, Katada (2011).
22. Liao Min, director-general and acting head of the general office of the China Banking Regulatory Commission, quoted in Anderlini (2008).
23. Agence France Press (2008).
24. Quoted in Burleigh (2008).
25. For the US leadership, see Blustein (2012b: 18).
26. FSF (2008); Giles and Guha (2008); Blustein (2012b: 19).
27. Quotes from Giles and Guha (2008).
28. Palan and Nesvetailova (2010).

29. The focus of the analysis in this chapter is also entirely on the content of international financial standards rather than their implementation (and the divergences from these standards in national legislation).

30. G20 (2010: 11).

31. G20 (2009a: 4).

32. Baker (2013).

33. G20 Working Group 1 (2009: 2).

34. G20 (2009b: 9).

35. Even before Basel III was negotiated, the G20 leaders backed in April 2009 a new set of international principles developed by the FSF for promoting "sound compensation practices " particularly at "large, systemically important firms" (FSF 2009a: 1). The rationale was that bonus payments linked to short-term profits at such firms had contributed to the crisis by encouraging "excessive risk-taking" and leaving firms with fewer resources to absorb losses (FSF 2009a: 1). Given their vague content, it was not surprising that the new standards proved a disappointment. As the FSF put it, the standards were "*not* intended to prescribe particular designs or levels of individual compensation" (FSF 2009a: 1). Instead, they focused on quite general provisions relating to issues such as oversight of compensation schemes by boards of directors, aligning compensation with risk taking, and enhanced disclosure to stakeholders.

36. Masters and Jenkins (2013); Verdier (2013: 1464).

37. Central Banking Newsdesk (2013b).

38. Boone and Johnson (2011). See also Central Banking Newsdesk (2013c).

39. Quoted in Vestergaard and Wade (2012: 484).

40. Turner (2011: 5); Lall (2012: 630).

41. Quotes respectively from Bair (2012: 265, who would prefer an 8% leverage ratio—see p. 326) and FDIC chair Martin Gruenberg in 2013 (quoted in Alloway and Jenkins 2013 at the time that US regulators proposed a higher 5% ratio).

42. Quoted in Central Banking Newsdesk (2013a).

43. Daniel Davies quoted in Fleming and Chon (2014). Other quote from same source.

44. Lall (2012); Vestergaard and Wade (2012).

45. See, for example, Warwick Commission (2009).

46. Paul Sharma quoted in Masters (2011).

47. Masters (2011).

48. Lall (2012).

49. Young (2012, 2013).

50. Bair (2012: chapter 22). Other resisting countries included Italy and Japan. See also Quaglia (2012, 2013).

51. For the German and French positions, see Jabko (2012: 100–101, 116–117), Quaglia (2012), Howard and Quaglia (2013).

52. G20 (2008: 6).

53. Botzem (forthcoming).

54. IASB Trustees (2008).

55. IFRS Foundation Monitoring Board (2012: 4–5).

56. Nölke (2010: 47).
57. IFRS Foundation Monitoring Board (2012: 1).
58. G20 Leaders (2008: 2); FSF (2009b: 5); G20 (2009c: 5).
59. G20 (2009c: 5).
60. Sanderson (2009); Tait and Sanderson (2009). For British defense of FVA, see Campbell-Verduyn (forthcoming).
61. Hughes and Tait (2009). US banks had also argued against the introduction of FVA in the 1990s (Lagneau-Ymonet and Quack 2012: 219).
62. Sanderson (2010); Jones (2011).
63. Campbell-Verduyn (forthcoming). For another analysis that highlights the enduring strength of fair value accounting, see Botzem (forthcoming).
64. G20 (2008: 2).
65. G20 (2009a: 3).
66. G20 (2008: 2–3).
67. Pagliari (2012, 2013a).
68. Edward Shugrue quoted in Popper (2013).
69. G20 (2009a: 4).
70. G20 Working Group 1 (2009: xiii, 15); IOSCO (2009: 7).
71. G20 (2009c: 3).
72. IOSCO (2009).
73. Pagliari (2012: 59).
74. G20 Working Group 1 (2009: 16); IOSCO (2009: 12); Fioretos (2010); Quaglia (2011); Pagliari (2013a).
75. Quaglia (2011: 667).
76. Fioretos (2010: 717); Quaglia (2011: 671); Pagliari (2013a); Buller and Lindstrom (2013).
77. The material in this section draws on Helleiner (2011b, 2014).
78. At the November 2011 Cannes summit, the G20 leaders also declared that non-cleared derivatives transactions would be subject to internationally harmonized margins in order to help counterparties cover losses from defaults and to minimize pro-cyclical margining practices (i.e., margins were lowered in booms and raised in crises).
79. Brian Daly quoted in Grant (2010).
80. The addition of internationally harmonized margins for non-cleared contracts to the G20 regulatory agenda at the 2011 Cannes summit also followed a very public expression of concern by US officials a few months earlier about how foreign banks might undercut their US counterparts by not following US policy on this issue (Helleiner 2014).
81. Pagliari and Young (forthcoming).
82. See, for example, BIS (2009).
83. Quoted in Gapper (2009).
84. See, for example, Bair (2012: 333–335).
85. Soros (2009b). Even Myron Scholes, the Nobel Prize–winning economist who had helped pioneer the Black-Scholes formula that contributed to the growth of derivatives products, was quoted as saying "[The] *solution is really to blow up or burn the OTC market, the CDSs and swaps and structured products, and…start over…*" (quoted in Das 2009).

86. Pagliari (2013a).
87. G20 (2011: 7).
88. See, for example, European Commission (2010: 68) and FSB (2010a: 32).
89. Bank of England (2010: 10).
90. Tucker (2014: 10). See also Tucker's comments in Central Banking Newsdesk (2013e).
91. Backed by the G20, the CPSS and IOSCO released in April 2012 international standards for "financial market infrastructures," including CCPs that covered a wide range of issues, including governance ones. With respect to the latter, they highlighted need for CCPs to have objectives that "explicitly support financial stability and other relevant public interest considerations," but they fell short of recommending a nonprofit (or public ownership) governance model, despite acknowledging that "excessive competition between FMIs may lead to a competitive lowering of risk standards" (CPSS-IOSCO 2012: 26, 11). The report makes similar kinds of recommendations about the governance of trade repositories.
92. IOSCO (2011: 40, 41, 43). For Cannes endorsement, G20 (2011: 7).
93. G20 (2011: 7).
94. Clapp and Helleiner (2012).
95. It is worth noting that efforts to implement the Dodd-Frank provisions relating to the strengthening of US position limits have been very slow in the face of legal and political challenges from private financial lobbies.
96. Pagliari (2012: 61).
97. Rodrik and Subramanian (2008).
98. Rodrik (2009a).
99. Global Unions (2008: 9).
100. Quoted in Godov (2008).
101. G20 Leaders (2008: 3). My emphasis.
102. G20 Working Group 2 (2009: 8).
103. See, for example, G20 Leaders (2008: 4).
104. See, for example, Cohen (2002).
105. See, for example, Helleiner (1994), Kirshner (2003), and Doyran (2011).
106. G20 (2009b: 10); Kirton (2013: 308).
107. IMF (2010a).
108. Quoted in *Prospect Magazine* (2009).
109. Darling (2011: 261); Kirton (2013: 308, 328–329).
110. Beattie (2010).
111. McCarty (2012: 222).
112. See, for example, Beattie (2010); Giles (2010); Darling (2011: 261–262), Bair (2012: 335); Kirton (2013: 329, 335, 336, 340), Milner (2010).
113. G20 (2010: 13).
114. G20 (2010: 3).
115. Bair (2012: 263); Davis (2012); Baker (2013).
116. Caruna (2012: 3).
117. Gallagher (forthcoming).
118. Subramanian and Williamson (2009).
119. Guha (2009b).

120. Grabel (2011: 814).
121. G20 Finance Minister and Central Bank Governors (2011a: 2, 3). See also Gallagher (forthcoming).
122. G20 Finance Minister and Central Bank Governors (2011b).
123. IMF (2012: 35, 13).
124. Paulo Nogueira Batista (Brazil's representative on the IMF's executive board) quoted in Beattie (2012).
125. Grabel (2011: 813).
126. Chwieroth (forthcoming).
127. Horsefield (1969: 13); emphasis in the original.
128. Ostry, Ghosh, and Korinek (2012: 20). See also Blanchard and Ostry (2012).
129. IMF (2012: 36).
130. China also resisted French initiatives at the April 2009 G20 summit to tighten regulations over tax havens because of concerns about Hong Kong and Macau (e.g., Rawnsley 2010: 628, 631).
131. Jabko (2012) also highlights the conservativism of the French bureaucratic elite.
132. See also Moschella and Tsingou (2013).
133. For the idea of "first-mover" advantages and "regulatory templates," see Quaglia (2013). See also McCormick (2009: 112).
134. Paulson (2009: 91).
135. See, for example, Johnson and Kwak (2010), Bair (2012), Barofsky (2012), Barth, Caprio, and Levine (2012); Ferguson (2012), and McCarty (2012).
136. Barofsky (2012: 160).
137. For the links between the financial sector and the Democratic Party, see McCarty (2012).
138. For example, the resistance to tougher regulatory reforms of leading US policymakers such as Treasury Secretary Tim Geithner has been attributed to their close relationships to the financial sector (Bair 2012: 142, 199, 229, 267). Bair notes: "I couldn't think of one Dodd-Frank reform that Tim strongly supported. Resolution authority, derivatives reform, the Volcker and Collins amendments—he had worked to weaken or oppose them all" (p. 229).
139. Barofsky (2012: 160, 217, 229, 255fn17).
140. See, for example, Konings (2009), Panitch and Konings (2009), and van Apeldoorn, de Graaff, and Overbeek (2012: 477).
141. Sheng (2009: 391). For discussions of regulatory capture, see Underhill and Zhang (2008), Johnson (2009), and Baker (2010).
142. For the former, see Bair (2012: 344). See also Helleiner and Porter (2009).
143. Barth, Caprio, and Levine (2012: 10).
144. See more generally Young (2012, 2013).
145. See, for example, Wade (2009: 559).
146. Baker (2013).
147. Unnamed official quoted in Baker (forthcoming). See also Persaud (2010).
148. In the few instances when distributional arguments have surfaced as rationales for reform in technocratic circles, they have usually focused on distributional issues *within* the financial sector such as the need to protect investor interests

vis-à-vis hedge funds or against "market abuse" in opaque OTC derivatives markets (G20 2009b: 9).
149. Tietmeyer (1999: 2, 3).
150. See also Cooper (2011) for an interesting analysis of the links between neoliberalism and important aspects of macroprudential thinking.

CHAPTER 5
1. Brummer (2012).
2. See, for example, Walter (2008).
3. US Treasury (2009).
4. The FSB was given some other mandates (see the second section of this chapter) that are not evaluated here.
5. To be sure, there was some very limited discussion of the need for international lending to meet certain international standards, but these proposals did not find their way into the final Bretton Woods agreements. See, for example, J.E.M. "International Investment," Sept. 9, 1943 in The National Archives (UK), Treasury Papers, T247/76; John Parke Young, "Draft of Proposed International Investment Agency, Sept. 4, 1943" in US National Archives, Record Group 82, International Subject Files, Box 55, "Bretton Woods Institutions, IBRD, Plans, State Department."
6. See, for example, Kapstein (1992) and Chey (2007). Under the 1983 revision of the Concordat, bank supervisors were permitted to prevent their banks from operating in jurisdictions that were improperly supervised. If they had undertaken this move, it would have been devastating for countries whose financial systems were heavily dependent on banks from BCBS countries (e.g., offshore financial centres). Seventy-five non-G10 countries endorsed the Concordat the next year.
7. Kapstein (1994: 121); Brummer (2012: 147).
8. G7 (1999).
9. Blustein (2012b: 10).
10. Porter (2007:124).
11. Blustein (2012b: 22).
12. See, for example, G22 (1998).
13. Thirkell-White (2007).
14. Porter and Wood (2002).
15. Blustein (2012b: 12).
16. Walter (2008). See also Mosley (2010).
17. Quotes from FSF (2000: 29). The working group included representatives from some nonmember countries such as Singapore and Thailand.
18. FSF (2000: 31–32).
19. Quote from FSF (2005: 1). See also Sharman (2006: 35) and Palan, Murphy, and Chavagneux (2009: 210, 219).
20. Davies and Green (2008: 223, 116).
21. G20 (2008: 3).
22. Quoted in Blustein (2012b: 23). See also Draghi's (2008) *Financial Times* article on November 14 which argued: "There is now a strong case for enlarging the FSF's membership and this must be translated into action soon."

23. The FSF had in fact agreed to broaden its membership at its plenary meeting in March 11-12 to include all G20 members, Spain and the European Commission.

24. To make plenary discussions manageable with the enlarged membership, the initial charter of the FSB included the following provision: "Delegations with more than one seat have one representative seated at the back. Representatives sitting at the back have the rights of the table. Representation at the table can be changed according to the topic discussed" (FSB 2009: 4). The revised charter of June 2012 removed this wording.

25. G20 (2008: 3).

26. It expanded the membership of the board from 14 to 16 and then required that four members were from Asia/Oceania, four from Europe, four from North America, one from Africa, one from South America, and two others. The IASB's trustees who oversee its operations are also selected with guaranteed regional representation. As noted in the last chapter, the IASB was also given a new monitoring board, on which a representative of IOSCO's Emerging Markets Committee sits (along with a representative from IOSCO's Technical Committee, the US SEC, Japan's Financial Services Agency, and the European Commission). Under governance reforms announced in February 2012, the IASB committed to expand the monitoring board's membership to include up to eleven members, including up to four authorities from "major emerging markets" (IFRS Foundation Monitoring Board 2012).

27. Helleiner and Pagliari (2010).

28. FSB (2009: 2, 3).

29. The only standard created by the FSF was an international standard to govern the compensation practices of significant financial institutions announced as one of its very last formal acts in April 2009. When the FSB Charter was amended in June 2012, some new wording was added to the section on its mandate and tasks that clarified its standard-setting role: "The FSB should, as needed to address regulatory gaps that pose risk to financial stability, develop or coordinate development of standards and principles, in collaboration with the SSBs and others, as warranted, in areas which do not fall within the functional domain of another international standard setting body, or on issues that have cross-sectoral implications" (FSB 2012a: 3).

30. FSB (2009: 1).

31. FSB (2012a: 2).

32. FSB (2009: 3).

33. FSF (2009c: 1).

34. FSB (2009: 7).

35. FSB (2009: 2).

36. The FSF had been governed via a Chairperson, Secretary-General, a Plenary (that worked by consensus), and various working groups. The FSB retained these features but added a permanent Steering Committee and three Standing Committees (for Vulnerabilities Assessment, Supervisory and Regulatory Cooperation, and Standards Implementation).

37. FSB (2009: 3).

38. G20 (2008: 2).
39. These commitments were not in the FSB charter. They were contained in the January 2010 "FSB Framework for Strengthening Adherence to International Standards" (FSB 2010b). In September 2010, IMF members also agreed that countries with systemically important financial sectors must undergo FSAPs every five years as a mandatory part of surveillance (Brummer 2012: 243–244).
40. Blustein (2012b: 12, 24).
41. The FSAPs had some elements of "peer review" in that they involved some outside experts from central banks and supervisory agencies (as well as SSBs) in the process (Gola and Spadafora 2009: 37). For discussions of peer reviews at the time of the FSF's creation, see G22 (1998: 48) and Tietmeyer (1999:1).
42. FSB (2011b: 1).
43. FSB (2010b: 2).
44. FSB (2011b: 12).
45. Verdier (2013: 1469).
46. Blustein (2012b: 25).
47. Pagani (2002); Porter and Webb (2008).
48. FSB (2011b: 6).
49. Verdier (2013: 1469).
50. FSB (2011b: 13).
51. G20 (2009c: 5).
52. G20 Finance Ministers and Central Bank Governors (2009: 1).
53. FSB (2010c: 10).
54. FSB (2010c: 20).
55. FSB (2010c: 11).
56. For the link to the FSF's work, see FSB (2010c: 15).
57. G20 (2011: 8).
58. FSB (2011a: 5).
59. FSB (2012c).
60. FSB (2011a: 3, 4).
61. FSB (2011a: 4).
62. FSB (2013b).
63. FSB (2010c: 10).
64. See, for example, IMF (2013: 7fn8), which notes: "As such measures are viewed to be inconsistent with the voluntary, cooperative approach underlying the ROSC program, the Fund has refrained from direct involvement in the decision-making on, or any resulting publication of, 'noncooperative jursidictions'."
65. The IMF (2013:5) reports the following about the term "consensus" in the FSB: "While this term has not been formally defined, the FSB has developed practices for reaching consensus under which 'the Chair makes clear on what issue a decision is being sought, and then asks for the views of members. If there is no immediate convergence of views, the different points of view are discussed and attempts are made to reconcile competing or conflicting views. In practice, a consensus, in the sense of general agreement, is reached when there is no sustained opposition to the Chair's proposal for decision'." It is unclear whether strong

objection to sanctions by a member would constitute "sustained opposition." As the IMF makes clear, this interpretation of the meaning of "consensus" is also not a formal one.

66. Verdier (2013: 1470).
67. For the initial suggestion in early 2010, see FSB (2010b: 3).
68. G20 (2011: 6).
69. FSB (2011c).
70. FSB (2012a: 4).
71. G20 (2011: 9).
72. FSB (2013a: 3).
73. Sheng (2010: 199).
74. Blustein (2012b: 26).
75. Quote from Eichengreen (2008: 26). See also Eichengreen (2009).
76. Wright (2012: 4, 8–10). See also Price (2013) and Reinhart and Rogoff (2008). See also Blustein's (2012b) proposal under which a country could be subject to sanctions only after repeatedly being found to have regulatory failures and the sanctions would be less severe (e.g., naming and shaming, higher capital requirements for the noncomplying country's banks). He also notes that the assessment of panels could be overruled by a supermajority of FSB members. For earlier proposals of this kind, see Eatwell and Taylor (2001). As far back as the early 1970s, scholars have anticipated the creation of the international financial regulatory authority; for an early discussion, see, for example, Strange (1971: 255–257).
77. Pauly (2010: 17–18).
78. Pauly (2010: 15).
79. FSB (2012d: 3).
80. Pagliari (2013a).
81. Singer (2007: 119).
82. Helleiner and Pagliari (2011).
83. Quote from Borio and Toniolo (2008: 65).
84. For the impact of competitive pressures, see, for example, Rixen (2013).
85. G20 (2012: 6).
86. Masters (2012a).
87. Simmons (2001: 591–592); Slaughter (2004); Brummer (2012: 62).
88. For the former, see, for example, Kapstein (1994: 50), Bach (2010), Verdier (2013). For the latter, see, for example, Verdier (2013) and also Eichengreen (2009: 9fn50), who argues that one reason the WTO model does not exist in finance because "in certain countries, such as my own, finance is more powerful than industry as a source of political funding." In advance of the first G20 summit, it is notable that some regulators voiced strong opposition to proposals to strengthen the IMF's supervisory role and called for the independence of international standard setting to be protected (Central Banking 2008a). At this time, the international private bank lobby group, the Institute for International Finance, also backed an enhanced role for the FSF rather than the Fund (Central Banking 2008b).
89. Verdier (2013: 1408).

90. See, for example, Brummer (2012), and Verdier (2012).
91. See also Pauly (2010: 16) and Brummer (2012: 269).
92. Brummer (2012: 269).
93. Sheng (2010: 197). For other skepticism of the goal of one-size-fits-all global standards, see Bryant (2003), Walter (2008: 81–83), Rodrik (2009a, b), Levinson (2010), and Persaud (2010).
94. Prabhakar (2013). See also Kirton (2013: 244, 270) for Sarkozy's support for a global regulator.
95. Paterson (1998); Blustein (2012b: 9).
96. Quoted in Kirkup and Waterfield (2008). He also explicitly invoked his ideas of ten years ago (Reuters 2008a). He had also given speech at Harvard in April 2008 that urged the United States to accept strengthened global governance and where he called for a "new international financial architecture and economic institutions that end the mismatch between global capital flows and only the national supervision of them" (quoted in MaximsNews Network 2008). One of Brown's ideas was that the IMF take on a greater role in coordinating oversight of the world's largest international banks, but the Bank of England and Financial Services Authority preferred to focus on the FSF/FSB (Prabhakar 2013).
97. Blustein (2012b: 12).
98. Truman (2008: 22fn41).
99. Randal Quarles quoted in Blustein (2012b: 13). See also Davies and Green (2008: 116).
100. Quoted in Winnett (2008). See also Kirton (2013: 244) and the press briefing on November 12 by Dan Price, Assistant to the President for International Economic affairs, who noted the effort to reform the world's financial markets "is not about moving to s single global regulator" (Price and McCormick 2008: 1).
101. G22 (1998: 48, 49).
102. For Geithner's lead role, see Prabhakar (2013).
103. Quoted in Guha (2009a).
104. Truman (2008: 30, 31). Truman worked for Tim Geithner as a temporary advisory in early 2009 developing policy for the London summit.
105. Tarullo (2008: 252). Further evidence of US opposition to a treaty-based FSB is cited in Prabhakar (2013).
106. See, for example, Sheng (2010) and Kirton (2013: 245).
107. G20 (2009b: 9).
108. G20 (2011: 6).
109. Blustein (2012b: 17).
110. Brummer (2012: 259–260). See also Verdier (2013).
111. Prabhakar (2013).
112. Quotes from Watts (2013).
113. Braithwaite, Jenkins, and Nasiripour (2013). See also Braithwaite, Nasiripour, and Masters (2013).
114. Kapstein (1994).
115. Quoted in Persaud (2010: 642).
116. See, for example, Wolf (2009).

117. Some banks already used this kind of business model such as HSBC and Santander (Bair 2012: 330).
118. Chitkara (2013).
119. Masters (2012b); Nasiripour, Shahien, and Masters (2012). In an effort to attract Chinese financial business, however, British officials announced in October that they may offer an exception to Chinese banks who may be allowed to run their wholesale operations in London through branches (Parker, Fleming, and Jenkins 2013).
120. Sheng (2010: 196).
121. Ortiz (2012).
122. Quoted in Nasiripour, Shahien, and Masters (2012). For other US support, see Bair (2012: 330).
123. Barker and Braithwaite (2013); Plender (2013).
124. For foreign bank lobbying against US proposals in 2013, see Braithwaite (2013).
125. Larry Fink (chief executive of BlackRock) quoted in Nasiripour and Masters (2012).
126. Morgan Stanley and Oliver Wyman (2013: 3).
127. Brunnermeier et al. (2009); Warwick Commission (2009); Persaud (2010). Interestingly, the mutual recognition provision of Basel III that relates to the implementation of counter-cyclical buffers also "empowers host country authorities" (Caruna 2012: 3).
128. Unnamed Brussels official quoted in Grant and Tait (2009); see also Norman (2012: 286-288) and Pagliari (2013b).
129. See, for example, FSB (2012b: 4).
130. Helleiner (2013).
131. CPSS-IOSCO (2012c: 1fn3).
132. For this theme about the resurgent importance of nation-states as key pillars of global financial governance, see also Germain (2010).
133. For advocacy of an un-level international playing field, see especially Persaud (2010) and Warwick Commission (2009).
134. Rodrik (2009b).
135. Rodrik (2009b). See also Warwick Commission (2009).
136. Rodrik (2009b).
137. For "cooperative decentralization," see Helleiner and Pagliari (2011).

CHAPTER 6
1. Helleiner (2010b, forthcoming).
2. Odell (1982); Gowa (1984).
3. Cohen (2012).
4. Schenk (2010).
5. See, for example, Knaak and Katada (2013).
6. See especially Kirshner (2014).
7. Helleiner and Kirshner (2014).
8. Subramanian (2011).
9. Cohen (2010: 165).

10. Cohen (2009).
11. James (2010).
12. Helleiner (2009b: 19); Katada (2010: 144).
13. Helleiner and Pagliari (2011).
14. Ocampo (2010b: 27). See also Volz and Caliari (2010); McKay, Volz, and Wölfinger (2011); and Rana (2013).
15. G20 (2011).
16. Caliari and Voltz (2010::2)
17. Schenk (2010).

REFERENCES

Agence France Press. 2008. India, Brazil, South Africa slam rich nations over credit crisis. *Agence France Press.* October 16. Retrieved from http://archive.thedailystar.net/newDesign/news-details.php?nid=58844 (Accessed August 30, 2013).

Agrawal, Anoop and Kartik Goyal. 2012. U.S. hesitant on India's currency swap proposal, Subbarao says. *Bloomberg.* November 20. Retrieved from http://www.bloomberg.com/news/2012-11-20/u-s-hesitant-on-india-s-currency-swap-proposal-subbarao-says.html (Accessed August 30, 2013)

Aizenman, Joshau and Gurnain Kaur Pasricha. 2009. *Selective Swap Arrangements and the Global Fnancial Crisis.* NBER Working Paper 14821.

Allen, William and Richhild Moessner. 2010. *Central Bank Co-operation and International Liquidity in the Financial Crisis of 2008–9.* BIS Working Papers, No. 310. May.

Allen, William and Richhild Moessner. 2011. The international liquidity crisis of 2008–2009. *World Economics* 12(2): 183–198.

Alloway, Tracy and Patrick Jenkins. 2013. US banks face strict leverage proposals. *Financial Times.* July 10.

Anderlini, Jamil. 2008. China says West's lack of market oversight led to subprime crisis. *Financial Times.* 28 May.

Armingeon, Klaus. 2012. The politics of fiscal responses to the crisis of 2008–2009. *Governance* 25(4): 543–565.

Austin, Kenneth. 2011. Communist China's capitalism: The highest stage of capital imperialism. *World Economics* 12(1): 79–95.

Baccini, L. and S. Kim. 2012. Preventing protectionism: International institutions and trade policy. *The Review of International Organizations* 7(4): 369–398.

Bach, David. 2010. Varieties of cooperation: The domestic institutional roots of global governance. *Review of International Studies* 36: 561–589.

Bair, Sheila. 2012. *Bull by the Horns.* New York: Free Press.

Baker, Andrew. 2010. Restraining regulatory capture? Anglo-America, crisis politics and trajectories of change in global financial governance. *International Affairs* 86(3): 647–663.

Baker, Andrew. 2013. The new political economy of the macroprudential ideational shift. *New Political Economy* 18(1): 112–139.

Baker, Andrew. Forthcoming. The European Union, global financial governance and the macroprudential ideational shift. In D. Mugge, ed., *Europe's Place in Global Financial Governance*. Oxford: Oxford University Press.

Bank of England. 2010. *Financial Stability Report*. No. 28. December. Retrieved from http://www.bankofengland.co.uk/publications/Pages/fsr/2010/fsr28.aspx. (Accessed August 30, 2013).

Bank for International Settlements (BIS). 2007. *Triennial Central Bank Survey Foreign exchange, Derivatives Market Activity*, 2007. Basel: BIS.

Bank for International Settlements (BIS). 2009. *79th Annual Report*. Basel: BIS.

Bank for International Settlements (BIS). 2010. *Triennial Central Bank Survey: Report on Global Foreign Exchange Market Activity in 2010*. December. Basel: BIS.

Bank for International Settlements (BIS). 2013. *Triennial Central Bank Survey: Foreign exchange turnover in April 2013: preliminary global results*. September. Basel: BIS.

Barber, Lionel, Bertrand Benoit and Hugh Williamson. 2008. March to the middle. *Financial Times*, June 11.

Barker, Alex and Tom Braithwaite, EU and Fed clash over US bank move. *Financial Times*. April 23.

Barofsky. Neil. 2012. *Bailout*. New York: Free Press.

Barth, James, Geragrd Caprio, and Ross Levine. 2012. *Guardians of Finance*. Cambridge, MA: MIT Press.

Bases, Daniel. 2008. World faces New Bretton Woods moment: Stiglitz. Reuters UK. November 6. Retrieved from http://uk.reuters.com/article/idUK-TRE4A58BI20081106 (Accessed August 30, 2013).

Baumgarten de Bolle, Monica. 2013. *Brazil: Policy Responses to the Global Crisis and the Challenges Ahead*. BRICS and Asia, Currency Internationalization and International Monetary Reform, Paper No. 2. February. Waterloo: Centre for International Governance Innovation.

Bayne, N. 2008. Financial diplomacy and the credit crunch. *Journal of International Affairs* 62(1): 1–6.

Beattie, Alan. 2010. G20 unity frays as states go own way. *Financial Times*. June 23.

Beattie, Alan. 2012. IMF yields to curbs on capital. *Financial Times*. December 4.

Beattie, Alan and Christian Oliver. 2010. US hits at Greenspan comments on dollar. *Financial Times*. November 12.

Benoit, Bertrand. US 'will lose financial superpower status'. *Financial Times*. September 25.

Benoit, Bertrand and James Wilson. 2008. German president lashes out at 'monster' and its bankers. *Financial Times*. May 15.

Bergsten, Fred. 2009a. The dollar and the deficits. *Foreign Affairs* 88(6): 20–38.

Bergsten, Fred. 2009b. We should listen to Beijing's currency idea. *Financial Times*. 9 April.

Bertuch-Samuels, Axel and Parmeshar Ramlogan. 2007. The euro: Ever more global. *Finance and Development* 44(1): 46–49.

Best, Jacqueline. 2005. *The Limits of Transparency*. Ithaca, NY: Cornell University Press.

Blanchard, Olivier and Jonathan Ostry. 2012. The multilateral approach to capital controls. *Vox-EU*. December 11. Retrieved from http://www.voxeu.org/article/multilateral-approach-capital-controls (Accessed August 30, 2013).

Blustein, Paul. 2012a. *A Flop and a Debacle: Inside the IMF's Global Rebalancing Efforts.* CIGI Papers No. 4. Waterloo: Centre for International Governance Innovation.

Blustein, Paul. 2012b. *How Global Watchdogs Missed a World of Trouble.* CIGI Papers No. 5. Waterloo: Centre for International Governance Innovation.

Blyth Mark. 2003. The political power of financial ideas. In J. Kirshner, ed., *Monetary Orders*. Ithaca, NY Cornell University Press.

Blyth, Mark. 2013a. Paradigms and paradox: The politics of economic ideas in two moments of crisis. *Governance* 26(2): 197–215.

Blyth, Mark. 2013b. *Austerity*. Oxford: Oxford University Press.

Board of Governors of the Federal Reserve System. 2012. Central bank liquidity swap lines. Last updated December 13, 2012. Retrieved from http://www.federalreserve.gov/newsevents/reform_swaplines.htm (Accessed January 18, 2013).

Boone, Peter and Simon Johnson. 2011. The future of banking: Is more regulation needed? *Financial Times*. April 1.

Bordo, Michael and James, Harold. 2010. The Great Depression analogy. *Financial History Review* 17(2): 127–140.

Borio, Claudio and Gianni Toniolo. 2008. One hundred and thirty years of central bank cooperation. In C. Borio, G. Toniolo, and Piet Clement, eds., *Past and Future of Central Bank Cooperation*. Cambridge, UK: Cambridge University Press.

Botzem, Sebastian. Forthcoming. Continuity of expert rule: Global accountancy regulation after the crisis. In M. Moschella and E. Tsingou, eds., *Great Expectations, Slow Transformations: Incremental Change in Financial Governance*. Colchester, UK: ECPR Press.

Boughton, James. 2001. *Silent Revolution: The International Monetary Fund, 1979–89.* Washington: International Monetary Fund.

Bowles, Paul and Baotai Wang. 2013. Remnimbi internationalization: A journey to where? *Development and Change* 44(6): 1363–1385.

Bradford, Colin and Johannes Linn. 2011. A history of G20 summits: The evolving dynamic of global leadership. *Journal of Globalization and Development* 2(2): 1–21.

Bradsher, Keith. 2009. China slows purchases of US and other bonds. *New York Times*. April 12. Retrieved from http://www.nytimes.com/2009/04/13/business/global/13yuan.html?_r=0 (Accessed August 30, 2013).

Braithwaite, Tom. 2013. Foreign banks gain ally on Fed rules plan. *Financial Times*. May 2.

Braithwaite, Tom, Patrick Jenkins, and Shahien Nasiripour. 2013. Fed warns on lack of unity by regulators. *Financial Times*. January 28.

Braithwaite, Tom, Shahien Nasiripour, and Brooke Masters. 2013. Wrangling continues over how to deal with the next Lehman. *Financial Times*. January 28.

BRIC. 2009a. *BRICs Finance Communique*. Horsham, UK, March 14. Retrieved from http://www.brics.utoronto.ca/docs/090314-finance.html (Accessed August 30, 2013).

BRIC. 2009b. *Joint Statement of the BRIC Countries' Lead*ers. Yekaterinburg, Russia, June 16. Retrieved from http://www.brics.utoronto.ca/docs/090616-leaders.html (Accessed August 30, 2013).

BRIC 2010. *2nd BRIC Summit of Heads of State and Government: Joint Statement.* Brasilia, April 15. Retrieved from http://www.brics.utoronto.ca/docs/100415-leaders. html (Accessed August 30, 2013).

BRICS 2011. *Sanya Declaration.* Sanya, Hainan, China, April 14. Retrieved from http:// www.brics.utoronto.ca/docs/110414-leaders.html (Accessed August 30, 2013).

BRICS 2012a. *Delhi Declaration.* New Delhi, March 29. Retrieved from http://www. brics.utoronto.ca/docs/120329-delhi-declaration.html (Accessed August 30, 2013).

BRICS 2012b. *Agreements between BRICS Development Banks.* New Delhi, March 29. Retrieved from http://www.brics.utoronto.ca/docs/120329-devbank-agreement. html (Accessed August 30, 2013).

BRICS. 2013. *BRICS and Africa: Partnership for Development, Integration and Industrialisation, eThekwini Declaration.* Durban, South Africa, March 27, 2013. Retrieved from http://www.brics.utoronto.ca/docs/130327-statement.html (Accessed August 30, 2013).

BRICS 2013b. *Media Note on the Informal Meeting of BRICS Leaders Ahead of the G20 Summit in St. Petersburg.* September 5. Retreived from: http://www.brics.utoronto. ca/docs/130905-note.html (Accessed January 15, 2014).

Brown, Gordon. 2010. *Beyond the Crash.* New York: Free Press.

Broz, J. Lawence. 2012. The Federal Reserve as Global Lender of Last Resort, 2007–2010. November 14 draft. Mimeo.

Brummer, Chris. 2012. *Soft Law and the Global Financial System.* Cambridge, UK: Cambridge University Press.

Brunnermeier, Markus, Andrew Crockett, Charles Goodhart, Avinash Persaud, and Hyun Shin. 2009. *The Fundamental Principles of Financial Regulation.* Geneva, Switzerland: ICMB-CEPR.

Bryant, Ralph. 2003. *Turbulent Waters: Cross-Border Finance and International Governance.* Washington, DC: Brookings Institution Press.

Buller, Jim and Nicole Lindstrom. 2013. Hedging its bets: The UK and the politics of European financial services regulation. *New Political Economy* 18(3): 391–409.

Burleigh, Mark. 2008. Key emerging economies want financial system overhaul. *Agence France Press.* November 7.

Callinicos, A. 2012. Contradictions of austerity. *Cambridge Journal of Economics* 36(1): 65–77.

Cameron, David 2012. European fiscal responses to the Great Recession. In Nancy Bermeo and Jonas Pontusson, eds., *Coping with Crisis.* New York: Russell Sage Foundation, 91–129.

Cammack, Paul. 2010. The shape of capitalism to come. *Antipode* 41(S1): 262–280.

Campbell-Verduyn, Malcolm. Forthcoming. Conflicting trends and tensions in post-crisis reforms of transnational accounting standards. In Tony Porter, ed., *The Fate of Transnational Financial Regulation.* London: Routledge, 177–200.

Carin, Barry and David Schorr. 2013. *The G20 as a Lever for Progress.* CIGI G20 Paper No. 7. Waterloo: Centre for International Governance Innovation.

Carmichael, Kevin 2010. Sarkozy sets stage for open season on the dollar. *Globe and Mail*, November 15.

Carney, Mark. 2010. Restoring faith in the international monetary system. Remarks by Mr. Mark Carney, Governor of the Bank of Canada, at the Spruce Meadows Changing Fortunes Round Table, Calgary, Alberta, 10 September 2010.

Caruna, Jaime. 2012. Policymaking in an interconnected world. Speech to the Federal Reserve Bank of Kansas City's 36th Economic Policy Symposium on "The changing policy landscape," Jackson Hole, August 31, 2012.

Central Banking. 2008a. Regulator slams calls for IMF supervisory role. *Central Banking.com*. November 10.

Central Banking. 2008b. Global banks want greater role for FSF. *Central Banking.com*. November 10.

Central Banking Newsdesk. 2013a. Basel Committee reveals leverage ratio formula, *Central Banking.com*. June 26.

Central Banking Newsdesk. 2013b. FDIC's Hoenig blasts Basel III risk weights as insufficient. *Central Banking.com*. May 1.

Central Banking Newsdesk. 2013c. FDIC vice-chair says Basel III capital requirements provide illusion of safety. *Central Banking.com*. April 10.

Central Banking Newsdesk. 2013d. Leading central banks make emergency swap lines permanent. *Central Banking*. October 31.

Central Banking Newsdesk. 2013e. BofE's Tucker wants more robust CCP governance. *Central Banking*. October 8.

Chey, Hyoung-Kyu. 2007. Do markets enhance convergence on international standards? The case of financial regulation. *Regulation and Governance* 1: 295–311.

Chey, Hyoung-Kyu. 2012a. Theories of international currency and the future of the world monetary order. *International Studies Review* 14(1): 51–77.

Chey, Hyoung-kyu. 2012b. Why did the US Federal Reserve unprecedentedly offer swap lines to emerging market economies during the global financial crisis? Can We Expect Them Again in the Future? GRIPS Discussion Paper 11–18, January. Tokyo: National Graduate Institute for Policy Studies.

Chey, Hyoung-kyu. 2013. Can the renminbi rise as a global currency? The political economy of currency internationalization. *Asian Survey* 53(2): 348–368.

Chin, Gregory. 2010. Remaking the architecture: The emerging powers, self-insuring and regional insulation. *International Affairs* 86(3): 693–715.

Chin, Gregory. 2014. Conceptualizing China's rising international monetary power. In Eric Helleiner and Jonathan Kirshner, eds., *The Great Wall of Money: Power and Politics in China's International Monetary Relations*. Ithaca, NY: Cornell University Press.

Chin, Gregory and Eric Helleiner. 2008. China as a creditor: A rising financial power? *Journal of International Affairs* 61(2): 87–102.

Chitkara, Garima. 2013. Lack of co-ordination of bank resolution regimes behind subsidiarisation push. *Central Banking.com*. May 14.

Chwieroth, Jeff. Forthcoming. Controlling capital. *New Political Economy*.

Clapp, Jennifer and Helleiner, Eric. 2012. Troubled futures? The global food crisis and the politics of agricultural derivatives regulation. *Review of International Political Economy* 19(2): 181–207.

Cohen, Benjamin. 2002. Capital controls: Why do governments hesitate? In Leslie Elliott Armijo, ed., *Debating the Global Financial Architecture*. Albany: SUNY Press.

Cohen, Benjamin. 2008. The international monetary system. *International Affairs* 84(3): 455–470.

Cohen, Benjamin. 2009a. Toward a leaderless currency system. In E. Helleiner and J. Kirshner, eds., *The Future of the Dollar*. Ithaca, NY: Cornell University Press, 142–163.

Cohen, Benjamin. 2009b. A grave case of myopia. *International Interactions* 35(4): 36–44.

Cohen, Benjamin. 2010. *The Future of Global Currency*. London: Routledge.

Cohen, Benjamin. 2012. The benefits and costs of an international currency: Getting the calculus right. *Open Economies Review* 23: 13–31.

Cohen, Benjamin and Tabitha Benney. 2012. What does the international currency system really look like. August 22. Mimeo.

Commission of Experts of the President of the United Nations General Assembly on Reforms of the International Monetary and Financial System. 2009a. *Recommendations*. March 19, 2009. New York: United Nations.

Commission of Experts of the President of the United Nations General Assembly on Reforms of the International Monetary and Financial System. 2009b. *Report of the Commission of Experts of the President of the United Nations General Assembly on Reforms of the International Monetary and Financial System*, September 21, 2009. New York: United Nations.

Cooper, Andrew and Ramesh Thakur. 2013. *The Group of Twenty*. London: Routledge.

Cooper, Melinda. 2011. Complexity theory after the crisis: The death of neoliberalism or the triumph of Hayek? *Journal of Cultural Economy* 4(4): 371–385.

Cooper, Richard. 2009. *The Future of the Dollar*. Peterson Institute of International Economics, Policy Brief 9-21, September.

CPSS-IOSCO. 2012. *Principles for Financial Market Infrastructures*. April, BIS and IOSCO: Basel and Madrid.

Crouch, Colin. 2011. *The Strange Non-Death of Neo-Liberalism*. Cambridge, UK: Polity Press.

Darling, Alasidair. 2011. *Back from the Brink*. London: Atlantic Books.

Das, Satyajit. 2009. CDS market: Through the looking glass. *RGE Monitor*. March 23.

Davies, Howard, and David Green. 2008. *Global Financial Regulation: The Essential Guide*. Cambridge, MA: Polity Press.

Davis, Phil. 2012. Asian rules provide tough blueprint for Europe. *Financial Times*, January 16.

De Cecco, Marcello. 2009. From monopoly to oligopoly: Lessons from the pre-1914 experience. In E. Helleiner and J. Kirshner, eds., *The Future of the Dollar*. Ithaca, NY: Cornell University Press, 116–141.

Dieter, H. 2007. The US economy and the sustainability of Bretton Woods 11. *Journal of Australian Political Economy* 55: 48–76.

Dooley, M., D. Folkerts-Landau, and P. Garber. 2003. *An Essay on the Revived Bretton Woods System*. NBER Working Paper 9971. Cambridge, MA: National Bureau of Economic Research.

Doyran, Mine Aysen. 2011. *Financial Crisis Management and the Pursuit of Power: American Pre-eminence and the Credit Crunch*. Farnham: Ashgate.

Draghi, Mario. 2008. A vision of a more resilient global economy. *Financial Times*. November 14.

Draghi, Mario. 2011. *The Progress of Financial Regulatory Reforms*. October 31.

Drezner, Dan. 2008. Sovereign wealth funds and the (in)security of global finance. *Journal of International Affairs* 61(1): 115–130.

Drezner, Dan. 2009. Bad debts: Assessing China's financial influence in Great Power politics. *International Security* 34(2): 7–45.

Drezner, Dan. 2012. *The Irony of Global Governance: The System Worked*. Council on Foreign Relations, Working Paper. Retrieved from http://www.cfr.org/international-organizations/irony-global-economic-governance-system-worked/p29101 (Accessed August 30, 2013).

Drezner, Dan and Kate McNamara. 2013. International political economy, global financial orders, and the financial crisis of 2008. *Perspectives on Politics* 11(1): 155–166.

Duke, Elizabeth. 2012. Central Bank cooperation in times of crisis. Speech at the Center for Latin American Monetary Studies 60th Anniversary Conference, Mexico City, Mexico, July 20. Retrieved from http://www.federalreserve.gov/news-events/speech/duke20120720a.htm (Accessed August 30, 2013).

Eatwell, John and Lance Taylor. 2001. *Global Finance at Risk*. New York: New Press.

The Economist. 2006. A topsy-turvy world. *The Economist*, September 16, p. 28.

The Economist. 2007. The panic about the dollar. *The Economist*, December 1, p. 15.

Eichengreen Barry. 2006. *Global Imbalances and the Lessons of Bretton Woods*. Cambridge, MA: MIT Press.

Eichengreen, Barry. 2008. Not a new Bretton Woods but a new Bretton Woods process. In B. Eichengreen and R. Baldwin, eds., *What G20 Leaders Must Do to Stabilize Our Economy and Fix the Financial System*. London: Centre for Economic Policy Research, 25–27.

Eichengreen, Barry. 2009. *Out of the Box Thoughts about the International Financial Architecture*. IMF Working Paper. No. 09/116. Washington, DC: International Monetary Fund.

Eichengreen, Barry. 2010. Regional funds: Paper tigers or tigers with teeth? In Ulrich Volz and Aldo Caliari, eds., *Regional and Global Liquidity Arrangements*. Bonn: German Development Institute, 39–40.

Eichengreen, Barry. 2011. *Exorbitant Privilege*. Oxford: Oxford University Press.

Eichengreen, Barry and Kevin O'Rourke. 2010. What do the new data tell us? Vox. March 8. Retrieved from http://www.voxeu.org/article/tale-two-depressions-what-do-new-data-tell-us-february-2010-update (Accessed August 30, 2013).

Elson, Antony. 2012. Global financial reform—where do things stand? *World Economics* 13(2): 155–170.

European Central Bank (ECB). 2008. *Review of the International Role of the Euro*. Frankfurt: European Central Bank.

European Central Bank. 2013. *The International Role of the Euro*, July. Frankfurt: ECB.

European Commission. 2010. *Impact Assessment: Accompanying Document to the Proposal for a Regulation of the European Parliament and of the Council on OTC*

Derivatives, Central Counterparties and Trade Repositories. SEC(2010) 1058/2. Brussels: European Commission. September.

Evans-Pritchard, Ambrose. 2009. US backing for world currency stuns markets. *The Telegraph.* March 25. Retrieved from http://www.telegraph.co.uk/finance/economics/5050407/US-backing-for-world-currency-stuns-markets.html (Accessed July 15, 2013).

Ferguson, Charles. 2012. *Inside Job: The Financiers Who Pulled Off the Heist of the Century.* Oxford: Oneworld.

Financial Crisis Inquiry Report. 2011. *Final Report of the National Commission on the Causes of the Financial and Economic Crisis in the United States.* New York: PublicAffairs.

Financial Stability Board (FSB). 2009. *Charter.* http://www.financialstabilityboard. org/publications/r_090925d.pdf (Accessed October 30, 2009).

Financial Stability Board (FSB). 2010a. *Implementing OTC Derivatives Market Reforms.* Basel: FSB. October 25. Basel: FSB.

Financial Stability Board (FSB). 2010b. *FSB Framework for Strengthening Adherence to International Standards.* January 9. Basel: FSB.

Financial Stability Board (FSB). 2010c. *Promoting Global Adherence to International Cooperation and Information Exchange Standards.* March 10. Basel: FSB.

Financial Stability Board (FSB). 2011a. Global Adherence to Regulatory and Supervisory Standards on International Cooperation and Information Exchange. November 2. Basel: FSB.

Financial Stability Board (FSB). 2011b. *Handbook for FSB Peer Reviews.* December 19. Basel: FSB.

Financial Stability Board (FSB). 2011c. *Progress in Implementing the G20 Recommendations on Financial Regulatory Reform: Status Report by the FSB Secretariat.* November 4. Basel: FSB.

Financial Stability Board (FSB). 2012a. *Charter.* Retrieved from http://www.financial-stabilityboard.org/publications/r_120809.pdf (Accessed January 30, 2014).

Financial Stability Board (FSB). 2012b. *OTC Derivatives Market Reforms Fourth Progress Report on Implementation.* October 31. Basel: FSB.

Financial Stability Board (FSB). 2012c. *Global Adherence to Regulatory and Supervisory Standards on International Cooperation and Information Exchange: Status Update.* November 2. Basel: FSB.

Financial Stability Board (FSB). 2012d. *Report to the G20 Los Cabos Summit on Strengthening FSB Capacity, Resources and Governance,* June 12. Basel: FSB.

Financial Stability Board (FSB). 2013a. *Articles of Association.* Retrieved from http:// www.financialstabilityboard.org/publications/r_130128aoa.pdf (Accessed January 30, 2014).

Financial Stability Board. 2013b. *Global adherence to regulatory and supervisory standards on international cooperation and information exchange.* December 18. Retrieved from: http://www.financialstabilityboard.org/publications/r_131218.pdf (Accessed January 5, 2014)

Financial Stability Forum (FSF). 2000. *Report of the Working Group on Offshore Centres.* April 5.

Financial Stability Forum (FSF). 2005. *FSF announces a new process to promote further improvements in offshore financial centres.* March 11.

Financial Stability Forum (FSF). 2008. *Report of the Financial Stability Forum on Enhancing Market and Institutional Resilience*, April, Basel: Financial Stability Forum.

Financial Stability Forum (FSF). 2009a. *FSF Principles for Sound Compensation Practices.* Basel: FSF. April 2.

Financial Stability Forum (FSF). 2009b. *Report of the Financial Stability Forum on Addressing Procyclicality in the Financial System.* April 2.

Financial Stability Forum. 2009. *Press release: Financial Stability Forum re-established as the Financial Stability Board.* April 2.

Fioretos, Orfeo. 2010. Capitalist diversity and the international regulation of hedge funds. *Review of International Political Economy* 17(4): 696–723.

Fioretos, Orfeo. 2012. Historical institutionalism in international relations. *International Organization.* 65(2): 367–399.

Fleming, Sam and Gina Chon. 2013. Banks win concessions from Basel on leverage. *Financial Times.* January 13.

Gallagher, Kevin. Forthcoming. *Countervailing Monetary Power.* Ithaca: Cornell University Press.

Gallagher, Kevin and Elen Shrestha. 2012. The social cost of self-insurance: Financial crisis, reserve accumulation, and developing countries. *Global Policy* 3(4): 501–509.

Gapper, John. 2009. Volcker sets his sights on Goldman. *FT.Com/Gapperblog*, March 6. Retrieved from http://blogs.ft.com/gapperblog/2009/03/the-gl ass-steagall-act-revisited-by-paul-volcker/ (Accessed March 12, 2009).

Germain. Randall. 2009. Financial order and world politics: Crisis, change and continuity. *International Affairs* 85(4): 669–687.

Germain, Randall. 2010. *Global Politics and Financial Governance.* New York: Palgrave Macmillan.

Giles, Chris. 2010. An idea that was hot, but now is not. *Financial Times.* June 25.

Giles, Chris and Krishna Guha. 2008. Banks' self-regulation bid brushed aside. *Financial Times.* April 14.

Global Research. 2008. Sarkozy-US dollar no longer only currency in world. *Global Research.* November 13. Retrieved from www.globalresearch.ca/sarkozy-us-dollar-no-longer-only-currency-in-world/10942 (Accessed January 23, 2013).

Global Unions. 2008. Renew financial turbulence and global economic slowdown demand major policy shifts by the IFIs, Statement by Trade Unions to the spring meetings of the World Bank and International Monetary Fund, Washington, 12–13 April. Mimeo.

Godov, Julio. 2008. Finance: So, back to regulation, then. *SUNS newservice*, March 20.

Gola, Carlo and Franceso Spadafora. 2009. *Financial Sector Surveillance and the IMF.* IMF Working Paper, WP/09/247, November.

Gowa, Joanne. 1984. Hegemons, IOs, and Markets: The case of the substitution account. *International Organization* 38(4): 661–683.

Grabel, I. 2011. Not your grandfather's IMF: Global crisis, 'productive incoherence' and the developmental policy space. *Cambridge Journal of Economics* 35(5): 805–830.

Grant, Jeremy. 2010. Market structures face test of trust. *Financial Times*. November 3.

Grant, Jeremy and Nikki Tait. 2009. European CDS clearing hits hurdle. *Financial Times*. January 13.

Grimes, William. 2009. *Currency and Contest in East Asia: The Great Power Politics of Financial Regionalism*. Ithaca, NY: Cornell University Press.

Grimes, William. 2011. The future of regional liquidity arrangements in East Asia. *Pacific Review* 24(3): 291–310.

G7 1999. *Statement of G7 Finance Ministers and Central Bank Governors*, Washington, DC. October 19. Retrieved from http://www.g8.utoronto.ca/finance/fm071019.htm (Accessed August 30, 2013).

G20 2008. *Declaration: Summit on Financial Markets and the World Economy.* November 15.

G20 2009a. *London Summit: Leaders' Statement.* April 2.

G20 2009b. *Leaders' Statement: The Pittsburgh Summit.* September 24–25.

G20 2009c. *Declaration on Strengthening the Financial System.* London, 2 April.

G20 2010. *The G20 Seoul Summit: Leaders' Declaration.* November 11–12.

G20 2011. *Cannes Summit Final Declaration: Building Our Common Future: Renewed Collective Action for the Benefit of All.* November 4.

G20. 2012. *G20 Leaders Declaration.* June 18–19.

G20 Finance Ministers and Central Bank Governors. 2009. *Declaration on Further Steps to Strengthen the Financial System.* London, September 4–5.

G20 Finance Minister and Central Bank Governors. 2011a. *G20 Coherent Conclusions for the Management of Capital Flows Drawing on Country Experiences as endorsed by G20 Finance Ministers and Central Bank Governors.* October 15.

G20 Finance Minister and Central Bank Governors. 2011b. *G20 Action Plan to Support the Development of Local Currency Bond Markets as Endorsed by G20 Finance Ministers and Central Bank Governors.* October 15.

G20 Working Group 1. 2009. *Financial Report: Enhancing Sound Regulation and Strengthening Transparency.* March 2.

G20 Working Group 2. 2009. *G20 Working Group on Reinforcing International Cooperation and Promoting Integrity in Financial Markets, Final Report.* March 27.

G20 Working Group 3. 2009. *G20 Working Group 3: Reform of the IMF, Final Report.* March 4.

G22 Working Group on Strengthening Financial Systems. 1998. *Report of the Working Group on Strengthening Financial Systems.* October.

Guha, Krishna. 2009a. 'Robust and stable' system is goal of US. *Financial Times*. March 31.

Guha, Krishna. 2009b. IMF refuses to rule out use of capital controls. *Financial Times*. November 3.

Hamlin, Kevin. 2008. Fannie, Freddie failure could be world 'catastrophe', Yu says. *Bloomberg*, August 22. Retrieved from http://www.bloomberg.com/apps/news?pid =newsarchive&sid=aslo2E01QVFI (Accessed August 30, 2013).

Harding, Robib. 2010. Backlash over use of Fed crisis cash. *Financial Times*. December 28

Harding, Robin. 2013. Emerging nations dump euro reserves. *Financial Times*. April 1.

Harding, Robin, Bernard Simon and Christian Oliver. 2010. Fed fund profited overseas banks. *Financial Times*, December 28.

Hausmann, Ricardo. 2008. The crisis gives American new financial power. *Financial Times*. December 16.

He Dong. 2012. International use of the renminbi: Developments and prospects. Presented to conference, The BRICS and Asia, Currency Internationalization, and International Monetary Reform, Hong Kong Monetary Authority, December 10–11, 2012.

He Xingqiang. 2011. The RMB exchange rate: Interest groups in China's economic poliocymaking. *China Security* 19: 23–36.

Helleiner, Eric. 1994. *States and the Reemergence of Global Finance*. Ithaca: Cornell University Press.

Helleiner. Eric. 2005. The strange story of Bush and the Argentine debt crisis. *Third World Quarterly* 26(6): 951–969.

Helleiner, Eric. 2006. Below the state: Micro-level monetary power. In David Andrews, ed., *International Monetary Power*. Ithaca, NY: Cornell University Press, 72–90.

Helleiner, Eric. 2009a. Enduring top currency, fragile negotiated currency: Politics and the dollar's international role. In E. Helleiner and J. Kirshner, eds., *The Future of the Dollar*. Ithaca, NY: Cornell University Press, 69–87.

Helleiner, Eric. 2009b. Reregulation and fragmentation in global financial governance. *Global Governance* 15: 16–22.

Helleiner, Eric. 2010a. The new politics of global reserve reform. *Journal of Globalization and Development* 1(2): 1–12.

Helleiner, Eric. 2010b. A Bretton Woods moment? The 2007–08 crisis and the future of global finance. *International Affairs* 86(3): 619–636.

Helleiner, Eric. 2011a. Understanding the 2007–08 global financial crisis. *Annual Review of Political Science* 14: 67–87.

Helleiner, Eric. 2011b. Reining in the market: Global governance and the regulation of derivatives. In Dag Harald Claes and Carl Henrik Knutsen, eds., *Governing the Global Economy*. London: Routledge, 131–150.

Helleiner, Eric. 2014. Towards cooperative decentralization: The post-crisis governance of global OTC derivatives. In T. Porter, ed., *The Fate of Transnational Financial Regulation*. London: Routledge.

Helleiner, Eric. Forthcoming, International money and finance. In Orfeo Fioretos, Tulia Falleit, Adam Sheingate, eds., *The Oxford Handbook of Historical Institutionalism*. Oxford: Oxford University Press.

Helleiner, Eric and Jonathan Kirshner. eds. 2014. *The Great Wall of Money: Power and Politics in China's International Monetary Relations*. Ithaca: Cornell University Press.

Helleiner, Eric and Anton Malkin. 2012. Sectoral interests and global money: Renminbi, dollars and the domestic foundations of international currency policy. *Open Economies Review* 23(1): 33–55.

Helleiner, Eric and Bessma Momani. 2008. Slipping into obscurity? Crisis and reform at the IMF. In Alan Alexandroff, ed., *Can the World be Governed?* Waterloo: Wilfrid Laurier University Press.

Helleiner, Eric and Stefano Pagliari. 2010. Introduction. In Eric Helleiner, Stefano Pagliari, and Hubert Zimmermann, eds., *Global Finance in Crisis: The Politics of International Regulatory Change*. London: Routledge, 1–18.

Helleiner, Eric and Stefano Pagliari. 2011. The end of an era in international financial regulation? A post-crisis research agenda. *International Organization* 65: 169–200.

Helleiner, Eric and Tony Porter. 2009. Making transnational networks more accountable. In Sara Burke, ed., *Re-Defining the Global Economy*. New York: Friedrich Ebert Stiftung Occassional Paper #42.

Henning, C. Randall. 1998. Systemic conflict and regional monetary integration: The case of Europe. *International Organization* 52: 537–574.

Henning, C. Randall. 2011. *Coordinating Multilateral and Regional Financing Arrangements*, Peterson Institute for International Economics Working Paper 11-9, March. Washington: Peterson Institute for International economics.

Hill, Hal and Jayant Menon. 2012. Asia's new financial safety net: Is the Chiang Mai Initiative designed not to be used? *Vox.EU* July 25. Retrieved from http://www.voxeu. org/article/chiang-mai-initiative-designed-not-be-used (Accessed August 30, 2013).

Hook, Leslie. 2011. China tells US to 'live within means'. *Financial Times*, August 8.

Horsefield, J.K. 1969. *The International Monetary Fund 1945–1965: Twenty years of International Monetary Cooperation*, Vol. 1. Washington, DC: International Monetary Fund.

Howard, David and Lucia Quaglia. 2013. Banking on stability: The political economy of the new capital requirements in the European Union. *Journal of European Integration* 35(3): 333–346.

Hughes, Jennifer and Nikki Tait. 2009. Brussels yet to sign key accounting rules paper. Financial Times. *Financial Times*. April 7.

Hung, H. 2009. America's head servant: The PRC's dilemma in the global crisis. *New Left Review* 60: 5–25.

IASB Trustees 2008. *Trustee letter to G20 participants*, 11 November.

IFRS Foundation Monitoring Board. 2012. *Final Report on the Review of the IFRS Foundation's Governance*. February 9.

IMF. 2009. *Review of Recent Crisis Programs*. Washington, DC: International Monetary Fund. September 14.

IMF. 2010a. *A Fair and Substantial Contribution by the Financial Sector*. Final Report for the G20. June. Washington, DC: International Monetary Fund.

IMF 2010b. *The Fund's Mandate—Future Financing Role*. March 25. Washington, DC: International Monetary Fund.

IMF 2010c. The Fund's Mandate—The Future Financing Role: Reform Proposals. June 29. Washington, DC: International Monetary Fund.

IMF. 2011a. *IMF Executive Board Concludes the Meeting on Enhancing International Monetary Stability—A Role for the SDR?* Public Information Notice No.11/22. February 10, 2011.

IMF. 2011b. *Enhancing International Monetary Stability—a Role for the SDR?*. January 7. Retrieved from http://www.imf.org/external/np/pp/eng/2011/010711.pdf (Accessed August 30, 2013).

IMF 2011c. *Review of the Flexible Credit Line and Precautionary Credit Line.* November 1. Washington, DC: International Monetary Fund.

IMF. 2012. *The Liberalization and Management of Capital Flows: An Institutional View.* November 14. Washington, DC: International Monetary Fund.

IMF. 2013. IMF Membership in the Financial Stability Board. February 22. Washington, DC: International Monetary Fund. Retrieved from http://www.imf.org/external/np/pp/eng/2013/022213.pdf (Accessed August 6, 2013).

International Organization for Securities Commissions (IOSCO). 2009 *Hedge Fund Oversight: Final Report.* Madrid: IOSCO.

IOSCO. 2011. *Principles for the Regulation and Supervision of Commodity Derivatives Markets.* Final Report, September. Madrid: IOSCO.

Irwin, Neil. 2013. *The Alchemists.* New York: Penguin.

Jabko, Nicolas. 2012. International radicalism, domestic conformism: France's ambiguous stance on financial reforms. In Renate Mayntz, ed., *Crisis and Control: Institutional Change in Financial Market Regulation.* Frankfurt: Campus Verlag, 97–118.

James, Harold. 2009. *The Creation and Destruction of Value.* Cambridge, MA: Harvard University Press.

James, Harold. 2010. Unlearnt lessons of the Great Depression. *Financial Times.* January 4.

Johnson Juliet. 2008. Forbidden fruit: Russia's uneasy relationship with the dollar. *Review of International Political Economy* 15(3): 379–398.

Johnson, Juliet. 2013. *The Russian Federation: International Monetary Reform and Currency Internationalization.* The BRICS and Asia, Currency Internationalization, and International Monetary Reform, Paper No. 4, June. Waterloo: Centre for International Governance Innovation.

Johnson, Simon. 2009. The Quiet Coup. *The Atlantic Magazine.* May.

Johnson, Simon and James Kwak. 2010. *13 Bankers.* New York: Payntheon Books.

Jones, Adam. 2011. IASB optimistic on US rules timing. *Financial Times.* April 23.

Jones, Bruce. 2010. *Making Multilateralism Work: How the G-20 Can Help the United Nations.* Stanley Foundation, Policy Analysis Brief. April.

Jones, Claire. 2012. Power structures Emerging nations seek better balance. *Financial Times.* June 18.

Kahler, Miles. 2013a. Economic crisis and global governance: The stability of a globalized world. In Miles Kahler and David Lake. eds., *Politics in the New Hard Times.* Ithaca, NY: Cornell University Press, 27–51.

Kahler, Miles. 2013b. Rising powers and global governance: Negotiating change a resilient status quo. *International Affairs* 89(3): 711–729.

Kahler, Miles and David Lake. 2013. Introduction. In Miles Kahler and David Lake. eds., *Politics in the New Hard Times.* Ithaca: Cornell University Press, 1–26.

Kapstein, Ethan. 1992. Between power and purpose: Central bankers and the politics of regulatory convergence. *International Organization* 46(1): 265–287.

Kapstein, Ethan. 1994. *Governing the Global Economy: International Finance and the State.* Cambridge, MA: Harvard University Press.

Katada, Saori. 2008. From a supporter to a challenger? Japan's currency leadership in dollar-dominated East Asia. *Review of International Political Economy* 15(3): 399–417.

Katada, Saori. 2010. Mission accomplished, or Sisyphean task? Japan's regulatory responses to the global financial crisis. In Eric Helleiner, Stefano Pagliari, and Hubert Zimmermann, eds., *Global Finance in Crisis*. London: Routledge, 137–152.

Katada, Saori. 2011. Seeking a place for East Asian regionalism: Challenges and opportunities under the global financial crisis. *The Pacific Review* 24(3): 273–290.

Kester, Anne. 2007. Reserve dominance of the U.S. dollar declining. *IMF Survey*. September 12.

Kim, Kyung Soo and Hyoung-kyu Chey. 2012. *For a Better International Monetary System: An Emerging Economy Perspective*. National Graduate Institute for Policy Studies Paper 11-29. Tokyo: National Graduate Institute for Policy Studies. March.

Kirkup, James and Bruno Waterfield. 2008. Gordon Brown's Bretton Woods summit call risks spat with Nicholas Sarkozy. *The Telegraph*. 15 October. Retrieved from http://www.telegraph.co.uk/news/worldnews/europe/france/3205033/Gordon-Browns-Bretton-Woods-summit-call-risks-spat-with-Nicolas-Sarkozy.html (Accessed April 10, 2010).

Kirshner, Jonathan. 1995. *Currency and Coercion: The Political Economy of International Monetary Power*. Princeton, NJ: Princeton University Press.

Kirshner, Jonathan, ed. 2003. *Monetary Orders*. Ithaca, NY: Cornell University Press.

Kirshner, Jonathan. 2008. Dollar primacy and American power. *Review of International Political Economy* 15(3): 418–438.

Kirshner, Jonathan. 2014. *American Power After the Financial Crisis*. Ithaca: Cornell University Press.

Kirton, John. 2013. *G20 Governance for Globalized World*. Farnham, UK: Ashgate.

Knaak, Peter and Saori Katada. 2013. Fault lines and issue linkages at the G20: New challenges for global economic governance. *Global Policy* 4(3): 1–13.

Kohler, Marion. 2010. Exchange rates during financial crises. *BIS Quarterly Review* March: 39–50.

Konings, M. 2009. Rethinking neoliberalism and regulation: After the crisis. *Competition and Change* 13(2): 108–127.

Lagneau-Ymonet, Paul and Sigrid Quack. 2012. What's the problem? Competing diagnoses and shifting coalitions in the reform of international accounting standards. In Renate Mayntz, ed., *Crisis and Control: Institutional Change in Financial Market Regulation*. Frankfurt: Campus Verlag, 213–246.

Lall, R. 2012. From failure to failure: The politics of international banking regulation. *Review of International Political Economy* 19(4): 609–638.

Levinson, Marc. 2010. Faulty Basel. *Foreign Affairs* (May/June).

Ly, M. 2012. Special Drawing Rights, the dollar, and the institutionalist approach to reserve currency status. *Review of International Political Economy* 19(2): 341–362.

Mackenzie, Donald. 2006. *An Engine Not a Camera*. Cambridge, MA: MIT Press.

Mahathir Mohamad. 2012. The west needs to go back to the capitalist basics. *Financial Times*. January 12.

Mallaby, Sebastian. 2009 The world's new banker. *Washington Post*. May 30.

Mangasarian, Leon. 2008. US losing finance superpower status, says Germany. *Bloomberg News Service*. September 25.

Masters, Brooke. 2011. Onus on trust to take forth out of global bubbles. *Financial Times*. January 11.

Masters, Brooke. 2012a. Conflicting signals. *Financial Times*. April 2.

Masters, Brooke. 2012b. UK watchdog tightens grip on foreign banks. *Financial Times*. December 10.

Masters, Brooke and Patrick Jenkins. 2013. Risk models fuel fears for bank safety. *Financial Times*. February 1.

Mateos y Lago, Isabelle, Rupa Duttagupta, and Rishi Goyal, 2009. *The Debate on the International Monetary System*. IMF Staff Position Note, November 11, 2009. SPN/09/26.

MaximsNews Network. 2008. *UK Prime Minister Gordon Brown's Kennedy Memorial Lecture on Foreign Affairs: 19/04/2008*. Retrieved from http://www.maxims-news.com/news20080419gordonbrownkennedykeynotelecture10804191206.htm (Accessed August 30, 2013).

Maziad, Samar, Pacal Farahmand, Shengzu Wang, Stephanie Segal, and Faisel Ahmed, 2011. *Internationalization of Emerging Market Currencies*. IMF Staff Discussion Note, Oct. 19, SDN/11/17.

McCarty, Nolan. 2012. The politics of the pop: The US response to the financial crisis and the Great Recession. In N. Bermeo and Jonas Pontusson, eds., *Coping with Crisis*. New York: Russell Sage Foundation, 201–232.

McCauley, R.N. and McGuire, P. 2009. Dollar appreciation in 2008: Safe haven, carry trades, dollar Shortage and overhedging. *BIS Quarterly Review* (December): 85–93.

McCormick, David. 2009. Picking up the pieces. In R. Nicholas Burns and Jonathon Price, eds., *The Global Economic Crisis*. Washington, DC: The Aspen Institute, 105–120.

McDowell, Daniel. 2012. The US as sovereign international last-resort lender: The Fed's currency swap program during the great panic of 2007–09. *New Political Economy* 17(2): 157–178.

McGuire, Patrick and Goetz von Peter. 2009. The US dollar shortage in global banking. *BIS Quarterly Review* (March): 47–63.

McKay, Julie and Ulrich Volz. 2010. Rivals or allies? Regional financial arrangements and the IMF. In Ulrich Volz and Aldo Caliari, eds., 2010. *Regional and Global Liquidity Arrangements*. Bonn: German Development Institute, 28–31.

McKay, Julie, Ulrich Volz, and Regine Wölfinger. 2011. Regional financing arrangements and the stability of the international monetary system. *Journal of Globalization and Development* 2(1): 1–31.

Milner, Brian. 2010. Mexico sides with Canada on bank tax. *The Globe and Mail*. May 28.

Mirowski, Philip. 2013. *Never Let a Serious Crisis Go to Waste: How Neoliberalism Survived the Financial Meltdown*. London: Verso.

Moessner, Richhild and William Allen. 2010. Options for meeting the demand for international liquidity during financial crises. *BIS Quarterly Review* (September): 51–61.

Moessner, Richhild and William Allen. 2011. Banking crises and the international monetary system in the Great Depression and now. *Financial History Review* 18(1): 1–20.

Momani, Bessma. 2008. Gulf cooperation council oil exporters and the future of the dollar. *New Political Economy* 13(3): 293–314.

Moon, Chung-In and Sang-Young Rhyu. 2010. Rethinking alliance and the economy: American hegemony, path dependence, and the South Korean political economy. *International Relations of the Asia-Pacific* 10: 441–464.

Morgan Stanley and Oliver Wyman. 2013. *Wholesale and Investment Banking Outlook: Global Banking Fractures: The Implications.* April 11. Retrieved from: http://image.email.oliverwymangroup.com/lib/fef21d75726206/m/1/OW+MASTER+2013+VERSION_for+release+v2.pdf (Accessed January 15, 2014).

Moschella, Manuela and Eleni Tsingou. 2013. Explaining incremental change in the aftermath of the global financial crisis. In M. Moschella and E. Tsingou, eds., *Great Expectations, Slow Transformations: Incremental Change in Financial Governance.* Colchester, UK: ECPR Press.

Mosley, Layna. 2010. Regulating globally, implementing locally: The financial codes and standards effort. *Review of International Political Economy* 17(4): 724–761.

Murphy, R. Taggart. 2006. East Asia's dollars. *New Left Review* 40: 39–64.

Murphy, R. Taggart 2008. *Why Japan Clings to the Declining Dollar.* October 2. Retrieved from http://www.japanfocus.org/-S-Katada/2913 (Accessed August 30, 2013).

Nasiripour, Shahien and Brooke Masters. 2012. Regulators edge towards 'every country for itself.' *Financial Times.* December 10.

Nölke, Andreas. 2010. The politics of accounting regulation. In E. Helleiner, S. Pagliari, and H. Zimmermann, eds., *Global Finance in Crisis.* London: Routledge

Norman, Peter. 2012. *The Risk Controllers.* Chichester: John Wiley & Sons, 37–55.

Oakley, David and Gillian Tett. 2008. Credit markets point to strains in rich economies. *Financial Times.* October 8.

Oatley, Thomas, W. Kindred Winecoff, Andrew Pennock, and Sarah Bauerle Danzman. 2013. The political economy of global finance: A network approach. *Perspectives on Politics* 11(1): 133–153.

Obstfeld, M., J. C. Shambaugh, and A. Taylor. 2009. Financial instability, reserves, and Central Bank swap lines in the panic of 2008. *American Economic Review: Papers and Proceedings* 99(2): 480–486.

Ocampo, José Antonio. 2010a. *Why Should the Global Reserve System Be Reformed?* Friedrich Ebert Stiftung Briefing Paper 1. January.

Ocampo, José Antonio. 2010b. The case for and experiences of regional monetary co-operation. In Ulrich Volz and Aldo Caliari, eds., 2010. *Regional and Global Liquidity Arrangements.* Bonn: German Development Institute, 24–27.

Odell, John. 1982. *U.S. International Monetary Policy.* Princeton: Princeton University Press.

Oliver, Christian. 2010. South Korea pushes for global swaps regime. *Financial Times.* March 1. Retrieved from http://www.ft.com/cms/s/0/b0dc5784-24e6-11df-8be0-00144feab49a.html#ixzz2GvMIS1Lm (Accessed August 30, 2013).

Ortiz, Guillermo. 2012. It is time for emerging markets to lead reform of banking. *Financial Times.* March 5.

Ostry, Jonathan, Atish Ghosh, and Anton Korinek. 2012. *Multilateral Aspects of Regulating the Capital Account.* IMF Staff Discussion Note. September 7. SDN/12/10. Washington, DC: International Monetary Fund.

Otero-Iglesias, Miguel. 2013. *The Euro for China: Too Big to Fail*. Mimeo.

Otero-Iglesias, Miguel and Federico Steinberg, Federico. 2013a. Is the Dollar Becoming a Negotiated Currency? Evidence from the Emerging Markets. *New Political Economy* 18(3): 309–336

Otero-Iglesias, Miguel and Federico Steinberg. 2013b. Reframing the euro versus dollar debt. *Review of International Political Economy* 20(1): 180–214.

Otero-Iglesias and Ming Zhang. 2012. *EU-China Collaboration in the Reform of the International Monetary System: Much Ado About Nothing?* Research Center for International Finance, Working Paper No. 21012W07.

Overbeek, Henk and Bastiaan van Apeldorn, eds., *Neoliberalism in Crisis*. New York: Palgrave Macmillan.

Pagani, Fabrizio. 2002. *Peer Review: A Tool for Co-operation and Change*, SG/LEG(2002)1. Paris: Organisation for Economic Co-operation and Development.

Pagliari, S. 2012. Who governs finance? The shifting public-private divide in the regulation of derivatives, rating agencies and hedge funds. *European Law Journal* 18(1): 44–61.

Pagliari, Stefano. 2013a. *Public Salience and International Financial Regulation: Explaining the International Regulation of OTC Derivatives, Rating Agencies, and Hedge Funds*. PhD thesis, University of Waterloo.

Pagliari, Stefano. 2013b. A wall around Europe? The European regulatory response to the global financial crisis and the turn in transatlantic relations. *Journal of European Integration* 35(4): 391–408.

Pagliari, Stefano and Kevin Young. Forthcoming. The Wall Street-Main street complex? The role of financial and corporate coalitions in post-crisis financial regulatory change. In M. Moschella and E. Tsingou, eds., *Great Expectations, Slow Transformations: Incremental Change in Financial Governance*. Colchester, UK: ECPR Press.

Palan, Ronen, Richard Murphy, and Christian Chavagneux. 2009. *Tax Havens*. Ithaca, NY: Cornell University Press.

Palan, Ronen and Anastasia Nesvetailova. 2010. The end of liberal finance? The changing of global financial governance. *Millennium* 38(3): 797–825.

Panitch, Leo and Sam Gindin. 2005. Superintending global capital. *New Left Review* 35: 101–123.

Panitch, Leo and Sam Gindin. 2012. *The Making of Global Capitalism*. London: Verso.

Panitch, Leo and M. Konings. 2009. Myths of neoliberal deregulation. *New Left Review* 57: 67–83.

Parker, George. Prime minister gives ground over regulation. *Financial Times*. March 21.

Parker, George, Sam Fleming, and Patrick Jenkins. 2013. UK welcome for Chinese banks to boost London's renminbi role. *Financial Times*, October 15.

Paterson, Lea. 1998. Brown calls for a global regulator. *The Independent*. October 1.

Paulson Hank. 2009. *On the Brink*. New York: Business Press.

Pauly, Louis. 2009. Managing financial emergencies in an integrating world. *Globalizations* 6(3): 353–364.

Pauly, Louis. 2010. The Financial Stability Board in context. In. S. Griffith-Jones, E. Helleiner, and N. Woods, eds., *The Financial Stability Board*. Waterloo: Centre for International Governance Innovation, 13–18.

Perry, James, and Andreas Nölke. 2006. The political economy of international accounting standards. *Review of International Political Economy* 13(4): 559–586.

Persaud, Avinash. 2010. The locus of financial regulation: Home versus host. *International Affairs* 86(3): 637–646.

Pettis, Michael. 2011. An exorbitant burden. *Foreign Policy.* September 7. Retrieved from http://www.foreignpolicy.com/articles/2011/09/07/an_exorbitant_burden (Accessed December 12, 2012).

Plender, John. 2013. Global banking retreat risks cutting financial capacity. *Financial Times.* April 23.

Pontasson, Jonas and Damien Raess. 2012. How (and why) is this time different? *Annual Review of Political Science* 15: 13–33.

Popper, Nathaniel. 2013. Banks find S.&P. more favorable in ratings. *New York Times.* July 31.

Porter, Tony. 2007. Compromises of embedded knowledge. In S. Bernstein and L. Pauly, eds., *Global Liberalism and Political Order.* Albany: SUNY Press, 109–31.

Porter, Tony and Michael Webb. 2008. Role of the OECD in the orchestration of global knowledge networks. In R. Mahon and S. McBride, eds., *The OECD and Transnational Governance.* Vancouver: University of British Columbia Press, 43–59.

Porter, Tony and Duncan Wood. 2002. Reform without representation? The international and transnational dialogue on the global financial architecture. In Leslie Armijo, ed., *Debating the Global Financial Architecture.* Albany: SUNY Press, 236–256.

Posner, Elliot. 2009. Making rules for global finance: Transatlantic regulatory cooperation at the turn of the millennium. *International Organization* 63: 665–699.

Posner, Eliot. 2010. Is a European approach to financial regulation emerging from the crisis? In Eric Helleiner, Stefano Pagliari, and Hubert Zimmermann, eds., *Global Finance in Crisis.* London: Routledge, 108–120.

Prabhakar, Rahul. 2013. *Varieties of Regulation: How States Pursue and Set International Financial Standards.* PhD dissertation, University of Oxford.

Price, Daniel and David McCormick. 2008. Press briefing by Daniel Price and David McCormick on the Summit on Financial Markets and the World Economy, November 12. The White House, Office of the Press Secretary.

Price, Michelle. 2013. This is Iosco's chance. It must be seized. *Efinancial News.* March 11. Retrieved from http://www.efinancialnews.com/story/2013-03-11/this-is-ioscos-chance-it-must-be-seized (Accessed August 30, 2013).

Prospect Magazine. 2009. Roundtable: How to tame global finance. *Prospect Magazine* No. 162, 27 August.

Quaglia, Lucia. 2011. The 'old' and 'new' political economy of hedge fund regulation in the European Union. *West European Politics* 34(4): 665–682.

Quaglia, Lucia. 2012. The 'old' and 'new' politics of financial services regulation in the European Union. *New Political Economy* 17(4): 515–535.

Quaglia, Lucia. 2013. The European Union, the USA, and international standard setting in regulatory fora in finance. *New Political Economy.* DOI: 10.1080/13563467. 2013.796449.

Rajan, Rajhuram. 2010. *Fault Lines.* Princeton, NJ: Princeton University Press.

Rana, Pradumna. 2013. *From a Centralized to a Decentralized Global Economic Architecture: An Overview.* ADBI Working Paper No. 401. Tokyo: Asian Development Bank Institute Paper.

Rawnsley, Andrew. 2010. *The End of the Party: The Rise and Fall of New Labour.* London: Penguin.

Reinhart, Carmen and Kenneth Rogoff. 2008. We need an international regulator. *Financial Times.* November 19.

Reinhart, Carmen and Kenneth Rogoff. 2009. *This Time Is Different.* Princeton, NJ: Princeton University Press.

Reuters. 2008a. Brown calls for a new 'Bretton Woods' meeting. *Reuters.* October 13. Retrieved from http://uk.reuters.com/article/2008/10/13/uk-financial-brown-idUKTRE49C2HV20081013 (Accessed August 25, 2013).

Reuters. 2008b. FACTBOX: APEC, G20 meetings on global crisis. *Reuters News.* November 6.

Reuters. 2009. FACTBOX: G20 mobilizes funds for trade finance. Reuters. April 2. Retrieved from http://uk.reuters.com/article/2009/04/02/us-g20-trade-factbox-sb-idUKTRE5316AI20090402 (August 30, 2013).

Rixen, Thomas. 2013. Why reregulation after the crisis is feeble: Shadow banking, off-shore financial centers and jurisdictional competition. *Regulation and Governance* 7(4): 435–459.

Rodrik, Dani. 2009a. Let Developing Nations Rule. *Vox.EU.* January 28. Retrieved from http://www.voxeu.org/index.php?q=node/2885 (Accessed August 30, 2013).

Rodrik, Dani. 2009b. A Plan B for global finance. *The Economist* March 12.

Rodrik, Dani and Arvind Subramanian. 2008. Why we need to curb global flows of capital. *Financial Times.* February 26.

Ross, Alice and Claire Jones. 2013. High vaultage. *Financial Times.* March 12.

Roubini, Nouriel and Stephen Mihm. 2010. *Crisis Economics.* New York: Penguin.

Sanderson, Rachel. 2009. Time to speak out on Brussels' political delay to new rules. *Financial Times.* November 26.

Sanderson, Rachel. 2010. Don't waste chance of a wider debate on fair value. *Financial Times.* May 27.

Sang-Jin Han and Lü Peng. 2012. Chinese crisis management. In Ursula J. van Beek and Edmund Wnuk-Lipinski, eds., *Democracy Under Stress: The Global Crisis and Beyond.* Berlin: Barbara Burich, 151–171.

Sarkozy, Nicolas. 2010a. 50th Anniversary of the signature of the Convention of the Organization for Economic Cooperation and Development—Speech by Nicolas Sarkozy, President of the Republic. December 13. Retrieved from http://ambafrance-us.org/spip.php?article2050 (Accessed August 30, 2013).

Sarkozy, Nicolas. 2010b. Speech by the President of the Republic. 18th Ambassadors' Conference, Elysée Palace—Wednesday, August 25, 2010. Retrieved from http://www.ambafrance-ca.org/IMG/pdf/10-08-25-18th_Ambassadors_Conference.pdf (Accessed January 30, 2014).

Schelkle, Waltraud. 2012. Policymaking in hard times: French and German responses to the Eurozone crisis. In Nancy Bermeo and Jonas Pontasson, eds., *Coping with crisis.* New York: Russell Sage Foundation.

Schenk, Catherine. 2010. *The Decline of Sterling: Managing the Retreat of an International Currency*. Cambridge, UK: Cambridge University Press.

Schirm, Stefan. 2011. Varieties of strategies: Societal influences on British and German responses to the global economic crisis. *Journal of Contemporary European Studies* 19(1): 47–62.

Schmalz, S. and M. Ebenau. 2012. After neoliberalism? Brazil, India, and China in the global economic crisis. *Globalizations* 9(4): 487–501.

Schwartz, Herman. 2009. *Subprime Nation*. Ithaca, NY: Cornell University Press.

Sender, Henny. 2009. China to stick with US bonds. *Financial Times*. February 12.

Setser Brad. 2008. A neo-Westphalian international financial system? *Journal of International Affairs* 62(1): 17–34.

Sharman, Jason. 2006. *Havens in a Storm: The Struggle for Global Tax Regulation*. Ithaca, NY: Cornell University Press.

Sheng, Andrew. 2009. *From Asian to Global Financial Crisis: An Asian Regulator's View of Unfettered Finance in the 1990s and 2000s*. Cambridge, UK: Cambridge University Press.

Sheng, Andrew. 2010. The regulatory reform of the global financial markets: An Asian regulator's perspective. *Global Policy* 1(2): 191–200.

Simmons, Beth. 2001. The international politics of harmonization: The case of capital market regulation. *International Organization* 55(3): 589–620.

Singer, David. 2007. *Regulating Capital: Setting Standards for the International Financial System*. Ithaca, NY: Cornell University Press.

Slaughter, Anne-Marie. 2004. *A New World Order*. Princeton, NJ: Princeton University Press.

Soederberg, S. 2010. The politics of representation and financial fetishism: The case of the G20 summits. *Third World Quarterly* 31(4): 523–540.

Somerville, Glen. 2009. Geithner tells China its dollar assets are safe. *Reuters*. June 1. Retrieved from http://www.reuters.com/article/idUSPEK14475620090601 (Accessed August 30, 2013).

Sorkin, Andrew. 2009. *Too Big to Fail*. New York: Viking.

Soros, George. 2009a. *The New Paradigm for Financial Markets*. New York: PublicAffairs.

Soros, George. 2009b. The game changer. *Financial Times*. January 29.

Spiro, David. 1999. *The Hidden Hand of American Hegemony*. Ithaca, NY: Cornell University Press.

Steinberg, David and Victor Shih. 2012. Interest group influence in authoritarian states. The political determinants of Chinese exchange rate policy. *Comparative Political Studies* 45(1): 1405–1434.

Stiglitz, Joseph. 2010. *Freefall*. New York: W.W. Norton.

Strange, Susan. 1971. *Sterling and British Policy*. London: Oxford University Press.

Strange, Susan. 1982. Still an extraordinary power: America's role in a global monetary system. In R. Lombra and W. Witte, eds., *The Political Economy of Domestic and International Monetary Policy*. Ames: Iowa State University Press.

Strange, Susan. 1987. The persistent myth of lost hegemony. *International Organization* 41: 551–574.

Strange, Susan. 1988. *States and Markets*. New York: Basil Blackwell.

Strange, Susan. 1990. Finance, information and power. *Review of International Studies* 16: 259–274.

Strauss, Delphine. 2014. Central banks' influence set to wane despite reserves rise. *Financial Times*. January 8.

Subramanian, Arvind. 2011. *Eclipse: Living in the Shadow of China's Economic Dominance*. Washington, DC: Peterson Institute for International Economics.

Subramanian, Arvind and John Williamson. 2009. The Fund should help Brazil to tackle inflows. *Financial Times*. October 26.

Suominen, Kati. 2012. *Peerless and Periled: The Paradox of American Leadership in the World Economic Order*. Stanford, CA: Stanford University Press.

Sussangkam, Chalongphob. 2010. *The Chiang Mai Initiative Multilateralization: Origin, Development and Outlook*. ADBI Working Paper 230. July. Tokyo: Asian Development Bank Institute.

SWIFT 2013. RMB now 2nd most used currency in trade finance, overtaking the euro. December 3. Retrieved from: http://www.swift.com/about_swift/shownews?param_dcr=news.data/en/swift_com/2013/PR_RMB_nov.xml (Accessed January 5, 2014).

Tait, Nikki and Rachel Sanderson. 2009. EU delays adoption of accounting rule changes. *Financial Times*. November 13.

Tarullo, Daniel. 2008. *Banking on Basel: The Future of International Financial Regulation*. Washington, DC: Peterson Institute for International Economics.

Tett, Gillian. 2009. *Fool's Gold*. New York: Free Press.

Thirkell-White, Ben. 2007. International financial architecture and the limits of neo-liberal hegemony. *New Political Economy* 12(1): 19–41.

Thompson, Helen. 2009. The political origins of the financial crisis. *The Political Quarterly* 80(1): 17–24.

Thompson, Helen. 2012. The limits of blaming neo-liberalism: Fannie Mae and Freddie Mac, the American state and the financial crisis. *New Political Economy* 17(4): 399–419.

Tietmeyer, Hans. 1999. Report by the President of the Deutsche Bundesbank, Prof Hans Tietmeyer, on 11/02/99. *BIS Review* (21): 1–6.

Trucco, Pablo. 2012. The rise of monetary agreements in South America. In Pia Riggirozzi and Diana Tussie, eds., *The Rise of Post-Hegemonic Regionalism*. Tokyo: United Nations University Press.

Truman, Edwin. 2008. *On What Terms Is the IMF Worth Funding?* Working Paper 08–11. Washington, DC: Peterson Institute for International Economics.

Truman, Edwin. 2010a. The IMF as an international lender of last resort. October 12. Retrieved from http://blogs.piie.com/realtime/?p=1767 (Accessed August 30, 2013).

Truman, Edwin. 2010b. *The G20 and International Financial Institution Governance*. Working Paper 10–13. September. Washington, DC: Peterson Institute for International Economics.

Turner, Adair. 2011. Leverage, maturity transformation, and financial stability: Challenges beyond Basel III. Speech to Cass Business School, March 16. http://www.fsa.gov.uk/library/communication/speeches/2011/0316_at.shtml (Accessed August 30, 2013).

Tucker, Paul. 2014. *Regulatory Reform, Stability and Central Banking.* January 16. Washington: Brookings Institution.

Underhill, Geoffrey, and Xiaoke Zhang. 2008. Setting the rules: Private power, political underpinnings, and legitimacy in global monetary and financial governance. *International Affairs* 84(3): 535–554.

US Treasury. 2009. *Press Briefing by Treasury Secretary Tim Geithner on the G20 Meetings.* Pittsburgh Convention Center, Pittsburgh, Pennsylvania. September 24. Retrieved from http://www.whitehouse.gov/the-press-office/press-briefing-treasury-secretary-geithner-g20-meetings (Accessed February 19, 2012).

Vail, Mark. Forthcoming. Varieties of liberalism: Keynesian responses to the Great Recession in France and Germany. *Governance*

Van Apeldoorn, B, N. de Graaff, and H. Overbeek. 2012. The reconfiguration of the global state-capital nexus. *Globalizations* 9(4): 471–486.

Verdier, Pierre-Hugues. 2013. The political economy of international financial regulation. *Indiana Law Review* 88(4): 1405–1474.

Vermeiren, Mattias. 2013. Foreign exchange accumulation and the entrapment of Chinese monetary power: Towards a balanced growth regime? *New Political Economy* 18(5): 680–714.

Vestergaard, Jakob and Robert Wade. 2012. The governance response to the Great Recession: The 'success' of the G20. *Journal of Economic Issues* XLVI(2): 481–489.

Volz, Ulrich and Aldo Caliari, eds., 2010. *Regional and Global Liquidity Arrangements.* Bonn: German Development Institute.

Wade, Robert. 2009. From global imbalances to global reorganisations. *Cambridge Journal of Economics* 33(4): 539–562.

Wade, Robert. 2011. Emerging world order? From multipolarity to multilateralism in the G20, the World Bank, and the IMF. *Politics & Society* 39: 347–378.

Walter, Andrew. 2008. *Governing Finance: East Asia's Adoption of International Standards.* Ithaca, NY: Cornell University Press.

Warwick Commission, The. 2009. *The Warwick Commission on International Financial Reform: In Praise of Unlevel Playing Fields.* November. Coventry: University of Warwick.

Watts, Michael. 2013. Bank of England's Tucker weighs in on 'unco-ordinated' global regulation. *Central Banking.com.* May 15.

Wessel, David. 2009. *In Fed We Trust.* New York: Crown Business.

Wilson, Graham and Wyn Grant. 2012. Introduction. *Consequences of the Global Financial Crisis.* Oxford: Oxford University Press, 1–14.

Winnett, Robert. 2008. US Rejects Gordon Brown's Bretton Woods plan. *The Telegraph.* November 7. Retrieved from http://blogs.telegraph.co.uk/news/robert-winnett/5665177/US_rejects_Gordon_Browns_Bretton_Woods_plan/ (Accessed August 30, 2013).

Wolf, Martin. 2008a. The rescue of Bear Stearns marks liberalisation's limit. *Financial Times.* 26 March.

Wolf, Martin. 2008b. Why financial regulation is both difficult and essential. *Financial Times.* April 16.

Wolf, Martin. 2008c. *Fixing Global Finance*. Baltimore, MD: The John Hopkins University Press.

Wolf, Martin. 2009. New dynamics. *Financial Times*. November 6.

Wolf, Martin. 2010. Currency wars in an era of chronically weak demand. *Financial Times*. September 29.

Woods, Ngaire. 2010. Global Governance after the financial crisis: A new multilateralism or last gasp of the Great powers. *Global Policy* 1(1): 51–63.

Wright, David. 2012. Remarks by David Wright, Secretary General of IOSCO, The Atlantic Council, Washington, DC, 10 December 2012. Madrid: IOSCO. Retrieved from http://www.acus.org/files/wrightremarks.pdf (Accessed July 15, 2013).

Xinhua. 2013. Argentina supporteds China's proposal on new researve currency. *Xinhua*. March 31. Retreived from: http://news.xinhuanet.com/english/2009-03/31/content_11105749.htm (Accessed June 15, 2009).

Yang Jiang 2011. Rethinking the Beijing Consensus: How China responds to crises. *Pacific Review* 24(3): 337–356.

Yang Jiang 2014. The limits of China's monetary diplomacy. In Eric Helleiner and Jonathan Kirshner, eds., *The Great Wall of Money: Power and Politics in China's International Monetary Relations*. Ithaca: Cornell University Press.

Young, Kevin. 2012. Transnational regulatory capture? An empirical examination of the transnational lobbying of the Basel Committee on Banking Supervision. *Review of International Political Economy* 19(4): 663–688.

Young, Kevin. 2013. Financial industry groups' adaptation to the post-crisis regulatory environment: Changing approaches to the policy cycle. *Regulation and Governance* 7(4): 460–480.

Yu Yongding. 2012. *Revisiting the Internationalization of the Yuan*. Asian Development Bank Institute Working Paper 366. July. Tokyo: ADBI.

Zhang Ming. 2012. *The Development and Stagnation of RMB Internationalization*. October. Mimeo.

Zhou Xiaochuan. 2009a. Reform the International Monetary System. *BIS Review* 41: 1–3.

Zhou Xiaochuan. 2009b. *On Savings Ratio*. March 24, 2009.

Zhou Xin and Simon Rabinovitch. 2010. Heavy in dollars, China warns of depreciation. Reuters. September 3. Retrieved from http://www.reuters.com/article/2010/09/03/us-china-economy-reserves-idUSTRE6820G520100903 (Accessed August 30, 2013).